THE WORLD OF THE RANTERS

Other books by A. L. Morton

A PEOPLE'S HISTORY OF ENGLAND
LANGUAGE OF MEN
THE ENGLISH UTOPIA
THE EVERLASTING GOSPEL
THE LIFE AND IDEAS OF ROBERT OWEN
THE BRITISH LABOUR MOVEMENT, 1770–1920 (with George Tate)
SOCIALISM IN BRITAIN
THE MATTER OF BRITAIN

THE WORLD OF THE RANTERS

Religious Radicalism in the English Revolution

A. L. MORTON

1970
LAWRENCE & WISHART
LONDON

Printed in Great Britain by
The Camelot Press Ltd, London and Southampton

Contents

Foreword

This book is the result of many years' worming around the great Thomason Collection in the British Museum. Yet a general theme may perhaps be discovered. All its essays deal with aspects of the relationship between religious and political ideas and movements during the middle years of the seventeenth century. They all attempt to show how and why certain kinds of religion tend to coincide with certain kinds of politics.

The first essay sets out some of the problems in broad outline. Those which follow attempt to discuss them in greater detail: a certain amount of repetition and overlapping is therefore perhaps inevitable. The two last show how, with the Levellers, a new kind of secular politics emerges from its religious beginnings.

The essays on John Lanseter and Laurence Clarkson are reprinted, with some changes, from the *Proceedings of the Suffolk Institute of Archaeology;* "Religion and Politics in the English Revolution" from *Marxism Today.* "Leveller Democracy—Fact or Myth?" was No. 51 of *Our History.* The others have not previously been published.

I have to thank Christopher Hill, A. L. Merson and Lionel Munby for reading and commenting on some of these essays in manuscript. My mistakes are, of course, my own.

A. L. M.

I

Religion and Politics in the English Revolution

Few things have made it more difficult for us to understand fully the English Revolution of the seventeenth century than the religious forms in which political issues were often, though of course not inevitably, framed. This can lead us into all sorts of errors. Because the great religious controversies of the age may seem to us unreal and frequently grotesque, we may brush them aside altogether, may say, these people were hypocrites or self-deceivers who simply did not know what they were about. Or we may fall into the opposite error, like those nineteenth-century historians who coined the phrase "the Puritan Revolution": that is to say we may take the religious issues merely at their face value and fail to see the political and class implications which lay beneath them. Often we manage to combine both sorts of errors into an inextricable confusion, and, either way, we *degrade* the Revolution and fail to see the grandeur and seriousness of the men who made it.

To avoid such errors involves a double process. First, we have to put ourselves into the minds of the men of the seventeenth century—of Cromwell and Milton, of Lilburne, Walwyn and Winstanley, and even of Abiezer Coppe. We have to understand that to them religion was a reality and religious convictions were among the mainsprings of their lives. And then we have, as it were, to make the return journey, the journey from their world of religious conviction to our world of secular thought, and to see what were the objective political issues which their cultural and ideological circumstances led them to express in what may seem to us an indirect and perverse way.

We have to remember in the first place that religion and the Church occupied a much larger part of everybody's life than it does even of Christian believers today. The Catholic Church in the Middle Ages was an essential part of the structure of feudal society, reflecting its rigidly authoritarian and hierarchical character. It had a monopoly of the grace of God, which could only flow downward to man through the appointed channel of the priesthood, and it claimed the right to interfere in practically everything everyone did from the cradle to the grave. And, of course, the Church, with its vast holdings of land and with a huge income from tithes and other dues, was a central part of the feudal economic structure.

As the crisis of feudalism developed with the growth of bourgeois productive relations, the Church came increasingly under pressure: it became less and less able to carry out the services to society which alone justified its immense wealth. The Reformation may be regarded as a split within the ruling classes, through which strong forces from below, hitherto repressed, were able to make their way to the surface. The Reformation, in England especially, was complex, coming from above as well as below, but it is essential to remember the extent to which it began, and remained, a great popular movement.

At first, this movement was arrested. The Church of England, as it was established in the early years of Elizabeth I, was, like the State, feudal in content while national in form. At the top it was subordinated to the State, in the localities to the nobility and gentry. Puritanism began as an attempt to complete the work of the Reformation by giving the Church a bourgeois-democratic character. Hence, for example, the struggle of the burgesses in the towns to establish lecturers, paid by themselves and outside the established parochial structure—and the extent to which any such attempts were opposed by the hierarchy.

In this struggle, which reached a climax under Archbishop Laud in the 1630s, political battles were joined around what appear on the surface as entirely theological questions. Till we realise this, the controversies of the time appear to us almost senseless. Why, we are tempted to ask, should shrewd and intelligent men have been so deeply concerned over the siting of an altar or the colour and shape of a parson's clothes? What was the real point of the disputes over the sacraments?

Yet in fact men do not dispute over meaningless issues, nor did they do so in the seventeenth century. Take, for example, this question of the sacraments. Laud and the Government said that the altar should be placed at the east end of the church, raised above the nave, where the congregation sat, and fenced off with a railing. The priest stood, as it were, between God and the congregation, to whom his back was turned during a large part of the service. He wore special robes marking him off from the laity. The people were to come to the rail and kneel to receive the sacrament from the hands of the priest. The Puritans demanded that there should be a plain table in the body of the church, around which the people should sit while the minister, as they insisted on calling him, in a simple black gown such as was worn all the week, should serve it to them there. It is fairly easy to see that what was in dispute was not just a theological issue, but also a political issue, involving the question of Church democracy, and that the battle around it was one against feudal privilege. It was less a matter of the relationship of God and man than of man and man.

This becomes still plainer when we consider the beliefs of the more advanced sects. One, for example, declared:

> That Christians in receiving the Lord's Supper should receive with their hats on, with their heads covered, but the Ministers should administer it with their hats off, uncovered.[1]

Bearing in mind the great symbolic significance then attached to the wearing and removing of hats it is obvious that this was to claim that the people were not only on an equality with the clergy but were actually superior. Such a view appeared as wicked to the Presbyterian ministers as to the Anglican clergy.

Or take the question of the method by which the clergy were appointed. In the Anglican Church this had been done, as it still often is, by the principal landowners. The Puritans said they should be elected. And immediately a further dispute arose. The Presbyterians said the election should be by Elders, that is in practice, by the richer members of the congregation. The Independents, and more advanced sects, said, by the whole congregation. Each of these views represented definite stages of bourgeois democracy, but neither went beyond it, since in practice church membership was fairly rigorously restricted. In New England, where a new society was growing up at this time with very few feudal survivals, and in which political power tended to be restricted to church members, we can see very clearly the advance and the limitations which this involved.

Tithes, again, involved, and were felt to involve, deep class questions. The method of assessment for tithe meant that the great weight of the cost of supporting the Church fell on the poor and middle peasants, both the gentry and the town bourgeoisie escaping very lightly. Not only that, but the Reformation had transferred a large part of the tithe from the Church to the aristocracy—the lay impropriators. In the seventeenth century many of the nobility and gentry were both tithe receivers and tithe dodgers. The demand for the abolition of tithe

[1] Thomas Edwards, *Gangraena*, I, p. 29.

was therefore a demand for a redistribution of property for the benefit of the poorer classes, especially in the countryside. Such a demand was as unwelcome to the Puritan gentry and the Presbyterian ministers as it had been to their predecessors, and they were always successful in resisting it.

At a later stage not only tithe but the whole conception of the ministers as a special caste was challenged. The most advanced sects claimed that any man (or even woman) who felt the inner call should preach or fulfil any of the ministerial functions even if he was not, in Overton's words, "gifted with a black coat, an university dialect and the external advantages of Arts and Sciences".[1] Walwyn, another Leveller leader, is said to have called the professional ministers,

> a company of Mountebanks . . . and he knew no Scriptures for them to be Preachers more than other men, as he named Shoemakers, Cobblers, Weavers or Sopeboilers and the like . . . and that if their Tythes were taken from them, they would soon leave their trade; and said that the Apostles were tradesmen, and were not chargeable to the brethren.[2]

It was not by chance that men like Overton and Walwyn, who were to become leaders of the Levellers, the first fully democratic party in the Revolution, were also among the first and strongest advocates of the freedom of the pulpit, for in the seventeenth century the sermon was the main instrument for spreading not only religious, but also political and social ideas: there was no nonsense then about politics being out of place in the pulpit, and a free pulpit meant freedom for the propagation of democratic and revolutionary ideas. Walwyn himself, we are told, declared that the common man ought not only to be allowed to preach, but to fill any office in the State. If all things were in common, as they should be:

> There would be no need of standing Officers or a Committee, no need of Judges, &c, but if any difference fell out, or any criminal fact be committed, take a Cobbler from his seat, or Butcher from his shop, or any other Tradesman that is an honest and just man, and let him hear the case, and determine the same, and then betake himself to his work again.[3]

---

[1] *A Letter to Mr. Tho. Edwards*, p. 8.   [2] *Gangraena*, II, p. 27.
[3] *Walwins Wiles*, p. 14.

William Dell, a preacher with Leveller sympathies and a close associate of John Saltmarsh, said that just as the bishops used to say, "No Bishop, No King", so "their successors in the Kingdome of *Antichrist* [the Presbyterian Ministers] still cry *No Minister, No Magistrate*".[1]

If we can see plainly the political significance of such matters of Church organisation, it is not less plain in Puritan theology. The early Puritans were mostly Calvinists, stressing the doctrine of predestination which declares that a few people were chosen for salvation for no merit of their own, but solely because this was God's pleasure, while the majority, equally arbitrarily, were doomed before birth to eternal damnation. The elect were to be recognised by their piety, sobriety and, usually, by their material success, but these were the consequences, not the causes, of their election. It is easy to see the strength and assurance that could come to a bourgeoisie in an age of bourgeois revolution from this sense of being a chosen people. In the early stages this created no difficulties: while the Puritans were still in a minority the elect could be thought of as a virtuous bourgeoisie opposed both to a reprobate feudal aristocracy and to the rude and godless multitude. Of them Richard Baxter, who had a knack of blurting out what his more tactful colleagues left unsaid, wrote:

> Were not the multitude restrained, they would presently have the blood of the godly.... He knoweth not what prudence and piety are, or knoweth not England or mankind, that knoweth not that the major part of the vulgar are scarcely prudent and pious men.[2]

But you cannot have a revolution without this same multitude, and when the bourgeoisie needed to enlist the masses the more rigid, orthodox and prosperous Calvinists—the Presbyterians as a political party—began to find themselves at a disadvantage as compared with those who were prepared to open the door of salvation more widely. The Independents, like Cromwell, while not abandoning the general principles of Calvinist determinism, laid less stress on the idea that the majority were necessarily damned. They preferred to encourage them to think that they, too, might well be among the elect.

And to the left of them a host of democratic sects arose, declaring that Christ had died for all mankind, that all might be saved, that the desire to be saved was enough. Rationalist humanism and mysticism, a strange but powerfully effective unity of opposites, combined to

[1] William Haller, *Liberty and Reformation in the Puritan Revolution*, p. 202.
[2] From *The Good Old Cause*, ed. C. Hill and E. Dell, p. 462.

provide opposition to Calvinist orthodoxy. They argued, variously, that all men are God's children, that God exists in man and therefore to damn man would be to damn himself, that God is reason, and all men, by reason alone, can know God. "He that bade us try all things", wrote Walwyn, "and hold fast to that which is good, did suppose that men have faculties and abilities wherewithall to try all things, or else the counsell had been given in vain."[1] Therefore, he deduced, men should distrust the ministers and trust their own reason.

The political implications are clear. The Presbyterians thought that the saints, the elect, the minority of the godly bourgeoisie, should rule. Existing laws and institutions, as interpreted by themselves, were on the whole satisfactory as preserving a class structure guaranteeing the rights of property. It was a damnable error, declared the Rev. Thomas Edwards, that "instead of Legall Rights and the Laws and Customs of the nation, the Sectaries plead for naturall Rights and Liberties".[2]

But suppose that *all* men are saints? What then becomes of the claim of the elect to rule? The people have reason, they can understand the mysteries of the things of God, how much more the lesser mysteries of statecraft? So, by the end of the Civil War, the Levellers and others can be seen passing from Church democracy to political democracy, from claiming the brotherhood of the sons of God to claiming the birthright of freeborn Englishmen. The wheel has come round and we reach the concept of secular democracy. Yet the lessons learnt in the churches still help to determine the forms through which the political struggle makes its way. One example may be sufficient.

The most advanced sects had begun to form what they called "gathered churches". Setting aside the old parochial organisation, which by now was mostly in the hands of the Presbyterians, they declared that any group of believers in any place could constitute themselves as a church with full liberty to act and believe as they pleased. And when such a church was set up, all its members signed a covenant, an agreement binding themselves to unity and laying down the rights and duties of all.

And this is precisely what the Levellers proposed to do on a national scale. England was to become a gathered nation, with a covenant, *An Agreement of the People*, which was to be signed by all and was to guarantee the fundamental democratic rights and liberties of all. As a result of the war, they argued, "all legal Authority in England was broke", no body or person had any right to rule, and therefore the

[1] *The Compassionate Samaritaine*, p. 25.   [2] *Gangraena*, III, p. 16.

right had returned to its place of origin, the whole people of England. They alone could place themselves under a law, and this could only be done by a covenant or agreement, the idea of which was perfectly familiar to thousands of people, including most of the Leveller leaders, who had been at some time or another involved in the formation of a gathered church.

The idea was familiar, but the extension of the idea was revolutionary. The church covenant was exclusive and dividing, setting a group apart: *An Agreement of the People* was inclusive, uniting a whole nation. With incredible audacity it was even hoped that it might be extended to the Irish who, for most people at this time, were still outside the pale of common humanity. It marked the passing from the privilege of the saints to the right of the Englishman. Finally, it was to be the foundation of a new society by an act of will and reason. The fact that it was in practice not possible to carry out such a plan does not diminish the boldness of its conception.

In the face of all this, reactionary historians like W. Schenk still often argue that we are mistaken in regarding the Levellers as secular radicals, forerunners of Chartism and the modern working-class movement. They prefer to stress the extent to which Leveller thinking drew upon the past. Naturally, the Levellers, using what weapons came to hand, built upon the largely religious traditional forms of thought, but what is significant is not their debt to the past, but the extent of their departure from it. For the first time we can see emerging a secular, democratic, political theory, freeing itself from feudal survivals, including feudal religion.

This is more marked in Walwyn and Overton than in Lilburne. While Lilburne relies on his own interpretation of *Magna Carta* and the old laws of the realm, Overton writes:

> Whatever our forefathers were, or whatever they did or suffered, or were enforced to yeeld unto; we are the men of the present age, and ought to be absolutely free from all kinds of exorbitancies, molestations or *Arbitrary Power*.[1]

And Walwyn, though he can quote Scripture with telling effect when he chooses, seems happier with Montaigne, of whose essay on Cannibals he says:

> Go to this honest Papist, or these innocent Cannibals, ye Inde-

---

[1] "A Remonstrance", in *Leveller Manifestoes*, ed. D. Wolfe, p. 114.

pendent Churches, to learn civility, humanity, simplicity of heart;
yea, charity and Christianity.[1]

This is as far removed from the popular present-day conception of
Puritanism as is Overton's insistence that what counts in politics is the
policy and not the moral character of the individual:

> As I am myself in respect of my own personall sins and trans-
> gressions; so I am to myself and to God and so I must give an
> account; the just man must stand by his own faith; but as I am in
> relation to the Commonwealth, that all man have cognizance of,
> because it concerns their own particular lives. . . . So that the
> business is, not how great a sinner I am, but how faithfull and reall
> to the Commonwealth; that's the matter concerneth my neigh-
> bour, and whereof my neighbour is only in this publick con-
> troversie to take notice; and for my personal sins that are not of
> Civil cognizance or wrong unto him, to leave them to God, whose
> judgement is righteous and just.[2]

Throughout the period when the Revolution was developing we can
thus trace a steady secularisation of thought, of the transition from
Church democracy to civil democracy, from religious toleration to
civil liberties, from the demand for a free pulpit to the demand for a
free press. Yet it is essential to see that this is a process, that we cannot
understand the end without understanding that it was implicit in the
beginnings. After the defeat of the Levellers in 1649, which, if we do
not press the analogy too hard, might be called the Thermidor of the
English Revolution, we can notice a change, which is in a sense a
reversal of this process.

Instead of religious ideas developing into openly political ideas, we
find political ideas reclothing themselves in religious and even mystical
forms. In defeat, and the demoralisation and despair that defeat can
produce, what had seemed possible to human power and reason now
began to seem impossible. Yet, given the religious setting of the
Revolution, the conviction of the revolutionaries that they have been
fighting the Lord's battle, complete despair may be long in coming.
Surely the Lord will not desert the Old Cause "for which He has often
wonderfully declared Himself". He can, if He will, intervene even
more directly and bring victory out of defeat. It was in such an
atmosphere that the early Quakers appeared, or the Fifth Monarchy

[1] *Walwyns Just Defence*, p. 11.   [2] *The Picture of the Councell of State*, p. 44.

Men who rose in arms in the darkest hour of 1660, confident that God would give them victory as He had given it to Gideon when he led out a handful of heroes to free a nation. Yet at this stage hope often becomes a willingness to wait upon the Lord rather than a readiness for action.

Both Quakers and Fifth Monarchy Men have been the subject of considerable attention. A less known, but perhaps even more significant group, was the Ranters. A movement rather than a sect, they combined a variety of seemingly contradictory views from a mystical pantheism to a robust plebeian materialism. Nevertheless, the most common ground was a conviction that God existed in man and in material objects, "as much in the ivie leaf as in the most glorious Angel", a conviction that could lead in practice to materialist as well as mystical conclusions. This belief in an in-dwelling God was related to an extreme antinomianism—a conviction that "the moral law" was no longer binding upon true believers. And politically their conclusions were of an equalitarian nature—their common mode of address among themselves was "Fellow Creature", and Ranter writers have a marked tendency towards a naïve communism.

The Ranters came quite suddenly into prominence in 1649, soon after the final defeat of the Levellers at Burford, and for perhaps a year seem to have attracted a mass following, especially among the London poor, though there are reports of their activities from almost every part of England. They appealed especially to the lower strata of the population, the urban poor, and even the more or less criminal elements, people with whom no party in the Revolution had previously concerned itself. Often, as is perhaps not surprising, they combined extremely radical views with a rather negative pacifism. Thus Coppe, while saying that the executed Levellers were "hellishly murdered" and "died martyrs for God and their Country", declares himself opposed both to "sword levelling" and "digging levelling". The rich are unsparingly condemned and private property is "the cause of all the blood that ever has been shed, from the blood of the righteous Abell to the blood of the last Levellers that were shot to death".

The Revolution, which man has been unable to complete, must and will be completed by a miracle:

> Behold, I the eternal God the Lord of Hosts, who am that mighty Leveller am coming (yea even at the doores) to Level to some

B

purpose, to Levell with a witnesse, to Levell the Hills with the Valleys, and to lay the Mountains low.[1]

Hill and valley were well recognised class symbols in the seventeenth century, just as Abel, as opposed to Cain, was a symbol of the poor and exploited.

There is something moving in the writings of the Ranters, and it is easy to see what an appeal they had in a time of defeat, yet it is impossible not to find in them all the signs of a revolution in retreat, an abandonment of the rational hope that had inspired men like Overton and Walwyn, a realisation that they were calling upon their last resources when everything else had failed. The Ranters had a seed of life in them, but it was doomed never to germinate. However, the Ranter Movement was strong enough to alarm, if only for a moment, the Commonwealth Government and provoke a savage repression, which perhaps their own extravagances also invited.

Coppe's book was ordered to be publicly burnt, as containing "many horrid Blasphemies, and damnable and detestable opinions to be abhorred by all good and godly people". Coppe himself suffered a long imprisonment and was forced to recant, at least in part. Salmon and other Ranter leaders suffered in the same way. Ranter meetings were raided and broken up; many were imprisoned or flogged, they were slandered in a swam of scurrilous pamphlets. By 1651 Ranterism as an organised force was virtually stamped out, and every attempt was made to wipe it from the pages of history. As the Ranters declined the Quakers advanced, and the early Quakers were more akin to the Ranters than their present-day descendants would often care to admit. But what was lost was the aggressive radicalism, the underlying materialism and the hope of a new life for all: Quakerism marks a new stage in the retreat from the Revolution.

This is well illustrated in the title of a pamphlet George Fox issued in 1659, when the republic was about to fall:

> A Few Plain Words To be considered by those of the Army, Or others that would have a Parliament That is chosen by the voyces of the people, to govern the three Nations. Wherein is shewed unto them according to the Scripture of Truth, that a Parliament so chosen are not likely to govern for God and the good of his People.

[1] *A Fiery Flying Roll, passim.*

Fox in this pamphlet combines thoroughly anti-democratic sentiments with certain progressive demands, such as abolition of tithe, reform of the law and religious toleration.

The crux of the matter perhaps lies in the phrase "his People". If Lilburne or Rainborough had used such an expression it would have meant the people of England—the whole population with the exception of active Royalists, rich exploiters, monopolists and persecutors generally. For Fox it means no more than his own little church, the sanctified minority. So, as the Revolution passed its climax, revolutionary Puritanism began its long decline into apolitical nonconformity. The decline has been a long, complex and uneven process, which it is impossible to attempt to trace here. Nonconformist radicalism has its history, and has at various times made brave and fruitful stands for a variety of good causes. But the issues on which it has fought have been secondary and limited issues: never since the seventeenth century has it been able, or even wished, to take a central, leading position in the nation.

2

John Lanseter of Bury St. Edmunds

John Lanseter is an almost forgotten worthy of Bury St. Edmunds in Suffolk, whose name seems worth preserving, first because he was the principal founder of an Independent Church which has had more than 300 years of continuous life in the town, second as the central figure of a curious episode in Bury history—the Christmas riot of 1646—and finally as the author of *Lanseters Lance*, an extremely interesting contribution to the most celebrated pamphlet war of its time, that which centred around Thomas Edwards' *Gangraena*. Some account of Edwards and this controversy is necessary as a preliminary in order to place Lanseter in his true historical setting.

THE "GANGRAENA" CONTROVERSY

Thomas Edwards (1593–1647) was important to his generation as the most outspoken and persistent Presbyterian opponent of the Sects and of religious toleration. He is important to historians because his work is easily the most comprehensive contemporary account of the "Errours, Heresies, Blasphemies and pernicious Practices" which flourished in his time. The three parts of *Gangraena*, published at intervals during 1646, contain more than 270 such "errors", listed and numbered, in addition to a wide collection of anecdotes to the discredit of Independent and other opponents, named and unnamed.

Edwards was educated at Queens' College, Cambridge, where he became University Preacher. On April 6th, 1628, he was forced to recant some of the doctrines he had been teaching. In the next year he left Cambridge for St. Botolph's, Aldgate, and in 1640 he was again in trouble with the authorities, being brought before the Court of High Commission and deprived. This persecution he was the better able to bear as he had married a rich wife and so did not depend on the income from his benefice. With the meeting of the Long Parliament he was in a much stronger position and in August 1641 he published the first of his controversial works.[1] A second[2] appeared in 1644 and was so successful that, according to Baillie "all the ministers of London, at least more than a hundred of them", agreed to set up a weekly lecture for him at Christ Church in Newgate Street, "where he may handle these questions, and nothing else, before all that will come to hear".[3]

These books, though harsh and aggressive in tone, were still works of theological controversy on a theoretical level and have been long forgotten. With the publication of the First Part of *Gangraena*[4] in February 1646 the emphasis shifted to personal attacks and the deliberate collection of scandal against theological opponents. It is, indeed, its very abandonment of the decencies of controversy that makes it so useful to the historian. A Second Part of *Gangraena* appeared in May and a Third[5] in the last days of December. To some extent they may be considered as a single work, though the direction of Edward's attack changes considerably in the course of the year.

For Edwards the grand error and the source of all confusion was:

> The great opinion of an universall Toleration [which] tends to the laying all waste, and dissolution of all Religion and good manners.[6]

Thus, one of his charges against Walwyn was that

> he spake on behalf of *Paul Best* for his blasphemy;[7] saying, that if we could not convince his conscience, we ought not to punish his body.[8]

Scarcely less dangerous in the estimation of Presbyterians were the widely spread views which tended to place the congregation on an equality with, or even above, the Minister. Edwards regarded with horror the idea that "Shoemakers, Cobblers, Weavers, or Sope boylers

---

[1] *Reasons against Independent Government of particular Congregations.*

[2] *Antapologia: or a full answer to the Apologeticall Narration of Mr. Goodwin (and others), Members of the Assembly of Divines.*

[3] William Haller, *Liberty and Reformation in the Puritan Revolution*, p. 226.

[4] *Gangraena: or A Catalogue and Discovery of many of the Errours, Heresies, Blasphemies and pernicious Practices of the Sectaries of this time, vented and acted in England in these four last years.*

[5] *The Second Part of Gangraena: Or A fresh and Further Discovery* etc. *The Third Part of Gangraena; Or A new and higher Discovery* etc.

[6] *Gangraena*, Epistle Dedicatory.

[7] Best was an anti-trinitarian, then in prison for his views.

[8] *Gangraena*, II, p. 27.

and the like",[1] or even women,[2] had as good a right to preach, if they felt moved to do so, as regularly ordained and university trained Ministers, or that tithes were unlawful.[3] And, as usual, he is able to quote such fantastic but significant developments of the same ideas as the heresy

> That Christians in receiving the Lords Supper should receive with their hats on, with their heads covered, but the Ministers should administer it with their hats off, uncovered.[4]

A third group of "errors" undermined the doctrine of election, declaring

> That many shall be actually saved who are not elected; and they who preach none shall be saved but the elect and predestinate, are notable lyars.[5]

and that Christ died not only for all men[6] but for the devils in hell[7] and even "for kine and horses and all other creatures, as well as for men".[8]

These and many other theological matters occupy the bulk of all three parts of *Gangraena* and are, almost exclusively, the subject of the First Part. But as 1646 went on the situation changed. The last Royalist strongholds were reduced, the remains of their armies were beaten out of the field, quite early it was evident that the Civil War was virtually over. With its ending new problems arose—conflicts between the Army and Parliament, between the Parliamentarian parties over the next steps to be taken, between English and Scots. The question of sovereignty, of where did supreme power really rest, began to be raised, republican and democratic ideas spread rapidly. In March one of the first Leveller manifestos, *The Last Warning to all the Inhabitants of London*, appeared. As Walwyn, Overton and others came to the defence of the imprisoned Lilburne, the Levellers began to emerge as a clearly defined political party with their own press and programme. Edwards rightly saw a close connection between their ideas and those of the Sects, and, in Part II, and still more in Part III, we can see a shift in emphasis towards an attempt to counter the political consequences of the Independent and Sectarian doctrines.[9] Walwyn[10]

---

[1] *Gangraena*, II, p. 27   [2] *Ibid.*, I, p. 30.   [3] *Ibid.*   [4] *Ibid.*, I, p. 29.
[5] *Ibid.*, III, p. 9.   [6] *Ibid.*, I, p. 22.   [7] *Ibid.*, II, p. 2.   [8] *Ibid.*, III, p. 11.
[9] E.g. *Gangraena*, III, p. 23 for Army and Ireland, p. 74 hatred of the Scots.
[10] *Ibid.*, II, pp. 25–30.

and Lilburne,[1] who were barely mentioned in Part I, now receive special attention. Overton[2] and Rainborough[3] are also attacked.

A larger proportion of the "errors" are now political and social:

> That Kingly Government among Nations and Commonwealths is unlawful, and that for Kings it cannot be said to what use they serve, or that there is any use of them, except to debauch and vexe a people.[4]

> Instead of Legall Rights and the Laws and Customes of this Nation, the Sectaries talk of, and plead for naturall Rights and Liberties such as men have from *Adam* by birth, and in many of their Pamphlets they still speak of being governed by Right reason.[5]

or, finally,

> That Pigeons in Dove Houses are common to all men to take and eat them, as well as those who are owners of those Dove Houses, because Pigeons are fowls of the aire, and so common to the sons of men.[6]

Since Edwards attacked not only the ideas but the lives of individual opponents, his books created an immediate sensation and provoked many rejoinders. Some of those he attacked were obscure "tub preachers", but others were among the most experienced controversialists of the time, and these were not slow to reply. Among the better known of the answers to *Gangraena* were pamphlets by John Goodwin,[7] John Saltmarsh,[8] William Walwyn,[9] Jeremiah Bur-

---

[1] *Gangraena*, II, p. 104; and III, pp. 194–218.   [2] *Ibid.*, III, pp. 148–51.
[3] *Ibid.*, III, p. 132.   [4] *Ibid.*, II, p. 2.   [5] *Ibid.*, III, p. 20.
[6] *Ibid.*, p. 9. The right to keep a dovecote was a feudal privilege still generally excercised. Fuller, *The Worthies of England*, p. 424 in the edition of 1952, quotes Hartlib as estimating that there were in 1651 26,000 dove-houses in England and Wales with an average of 1,000 birds to the house.
[7] John Goodwin, *Cretensis: Or A Brief Answer to an ulcerous Treatise, lately published by Mr. Thomas Edwards* (March 1646).
[8] John Saltmarsh, *Groanes For Liberty . . . Also some Quaeres For the better understanding of Mr. Edwards last Book called Gangraena* (March). *Reasons For Unitie, Peace and Love. With an Answer . . . to Master Edwards his Second Part, called Gangraena, directed to me* (June).
[9] William Walwyn, *A Whisper in the Eare of Mr. Thomas Edwards Minister* (March). *An Antidote Against Master Edwards His Old And New Poyson* (June). *A Prediction of Master Edwards His Conversion and Recantation* (August). And others.

roughes,[1] John Lilburne,[2] and, possibly, Richard Overton.[3] Milton himself, whose doctrine of divorce is Error 154 in the First Part of *Gangraena*, retaliated with a passing reference in one of his occasional poems.[4] In the Second and Third Parts of *Gangraena* Edwards replied to those pamphlets that had appeared, and he was supported by other Presbyterian writers of whom John Vickars[5] is perhaps the best known.

The result of all this is a vast confusion of charges, rebuttals and counter-charges, from which it is impossible, in many cases, to establish the truth with any certainty. But since *Gangraena* and the *Gangraena* controversy are among our main sources of knowledge about the growth of the Sects and the battle of ideas in the seventeenth century, it is important to try to estimate the value of Edwards' work as evidence. Here it is possible to distinguish. In his lists of "Errours, Heresies and Blasphemies" a large proportion are taken from published works, and for these he gives precise and sufficiently accurate references. Others are from hearsay reports of sermons, or even of statements made in conversation, and here we are on less certain ground. Nevertheless it can be said that very few of them are out of key, and for the great majority parallels can be found in the pamphlet literature of the period. So many things were being said and written which seemed profoundly shocking to Edwards that he had little need to invent; I think it can be taken in general that what he tells us was said was really being said; how widespread and how typical these ideas were is another matter.

When we pass from ideas to personalities our difficulties increase. Obviously, Edwards was bitterly prejudiced. He was ready to believe the worst of his opponents and did not take much pains to check the correctness of tales to their discredit. Much of his information is second-

---

[1] Jeremiah Burroughes, *A Vindication of Mr. Burroughes Against Mr. Edwards . . . with a Brief Declaration What the Independents would have* (July). Burroughes was at one time preacher in Bury as assistant to Edmund Calamy.

[2] John Lilburne, *The oppressed Mans Oppression declared . . . As also there is thrown unto Tho. Edwards the Author of the 3 Ulcerous Gangraenes, a bone or two to pick* (Jan. 1647).

[3] It has never been suggested that Overton is the author of the anonymous *A Letter to Mr Tho Edwards* (Feb. 1647), but it is exactly in his style. For example, it is addressed to Edwards "At his dwelling in *Club Court*, between the *Pope* and the *Prelate*, a little on this side of the Fagot in Smithfield". Compare the fictitious address on Overton's earlier pamphlet *The Araignment of Mr. Persecution*, in which Edwards is also attacked: "Printed by Martin Clawclergie, Printer to the *Reverend Assembly of Divines* and are to be sold at his Shop in *Toleration Street*, at the *Signe* of the *Subjects Liberty*, right opposite to *Persecuting Court*".

[4] "shallow *Edwards*" in *On the new forcers of Conscience under the Long Parliament*.

[5] John Vickars, *The Schismatick Sifted. Or the picture of Independents freshly and fairly washt-over again* (June).

hand and most of it anonymous. When challenged, as by John Goodwin,[1] to name his witnesses and to bring specific rather than loose and
general charges he often failed to do so. A passage by Walwyn not
unfairly describes his controversial method:

> If you observe any man to be of a publique and active spirit,
> (though he be no Independent or Separatist) he can never be
> friend to you in your work, and therefore you are to give him out,
> to be strongly suspected of whoredom, or drunkennesse, pro-
> phanenesse, an irreligious person or an Atheist, and that by
> Godly and religious persons he was seen and heard blaspheming
> the holy Scriptures, and making a mock of the Ordinances of
> Christ, or say he is suspected to hold intelligences with Oxford,
> or anything no matter what, some what will be believed, you
> cannot be ignorant how much this hath prevailed against divers
> able persons.
>
> If you see any such man but once talking with a Papist, or
> (though not) you may give out that very honest men suspect him
> to be a Jesuit: if any one but demand of you or any other, how
> you know the Scriptures to be the word of God, give it out for
> certain he denieth them, or if any put questions concerning God
> or Christ or the *Trinity*, you have more than enough to lay accu-
> sations upon them, that shall stick by them as long as they live.[2]

At the same time, Edwards does sometimes seem to attempt to
estimate the value of his evidence, as when he writes that in Lincolnshire "there is a woman preacher who preaches (its certain) and 'tis
reported also she baptizeth, but that's not so certain".[3] Edwards
invariably puts the worst construction on the actions of his opponents
and is frequently careless and inaccurate about details, but I have not
found any case in which, where his version of events can be compared
with others, his charges seem absolutely without foundation. In this
respect Walwyn's estimate is extremely shrewd; Edwards' method is to
mix truth and falsehood in such a way that the true lends colour to the
false, yet I think this is more often the outcome of prejudice and care-
lessness than of deliberate fabrication. In an essay on Laurence Clarkson
I give some examples of his methods as applied to Hanserd Knollys and
others,[4] and we shall see that *Lanseters Lance* is of special interest for the
light it throws on Edwards' mind and methods. I will therefore give

---

[1] *Cretensis*, pp. 28–9.   [2] *Antidote*, p. 8.   [3] *Gangraena*, I, p. 84.
[4] See this volume, pp. 118–19.

only one further example, from the dispute between him and Goodwin.

Edwards alleged in very general terms that Goodwin and members of his congregation were addicted to playing cards and were "loose on the Sabbath day".[1] Goodwin replied that such vague accusations were meaningless, challenged Edwards to bring more specific charges and admitted that on one occasion—in company with members of Edwards' own congregation—he had played at bowls for a short time on the evening of the day appointed for thanksgiving for the victory at Naseby. He invited Edwards to produce "some law either of God or man" to prohibit such harmless recreation.[2] Edwards in replying made no attempt to meet the question of principle raised. Instead he insisted that Goodwin, after preaching on the morning of the Naseby thanksgiving day, attended no place of worship in the afternoon but played at bowls two whole hours in the evening. If Presbyterians also played, they were to blame, but this did not excuse Goodwin who, as a Minister, should have been setting them a good example instead of leading them into sin. He added that the Presbyterians might have been at church in the afternoon.[3] The very triviality of the issue makes it, I think, an instructive example of Edwards' method.

Gangraena, then, is a document of first-rate historical value, but it must be read with special care and, to extract its full value, should be taken not alone but with some at least of the many replies which it provoked. If, at the end, we are not always in a position to be able to be certain of the truth in detail we shall have vastly extended our understanding of the points of view which were contending for mastery at the time. For this reason an examination of *Lanseters Lance* can have a more than local importance.

"LANSETERS LANCE"

After the publication of the First Part of *Gangraena* Edwards began to receive letters from Presbyterian Ministers all over the country with accounts of the misdeeds of the Separatists. One such came from Clare in Suffolk, dated March 30th, 1646:

> The true copie of a Letter written to me from a worthy and godly Minister in *Suffolk*,[4] in the name, and by consent and agreement of other Ministers of the Country at a meeting of theirs and sent

---

[1] *Gangraena*, I, p. 73.   [2] *Cretensis*, pp. 28–33.   [3] *Gangraena*, II, pp. 76–8.
[4] The Presbyterian Minister at Clare was Roger Cooke.

up by the hands of a godly Minister in those parts, who delivered it to me.

This letter, among other matters, referred to one

Lancester, of *Bury*, a Pedler and of his opening the whole book of *Ezra* at a private meeting, instead of opening his pack, and of the prayer that followed his Exercise etc.[1]

On the same page Edwards continues,

One *Lancester* in a private meeting at *Bury*, condemned all the Ministers of *England* for *Sanballats* and *Tobiahs* of this time, and the sectaries to those who build the Temple, but it was withstood by Ministers who hindered it: At that meeting there was a plain godly man, a solid old Christian of Master *Faircloths* congregation[2] who opposed him, and God was so mightily with him that it turned to the reproach and shame of this *Lancester*, and those who adhered to him.

In September Lanseter replied after having tried without success, as we shall see, to obtain any kind of satisfaction or correction from Edwards, with

Lanseters Lance,
FOR
Edwards'es Gangrene:
or
A ripping up, and laying open some rotten, putrified, corrupt, stinking matter in Mr. *Thomas Edwards* his Gangren, or Book intituled, *The second part of Gangrena*.
Wherein, among others, he hath abused and belied Mr. *John Lanceter*, calling him Pedler, and saying, that he opened the whole book of *Ezra* at a privat meeting instead of opening his Pack, which is proved false, and other things also.

So that in consideration of the particulars, judicious men may

---

[1] *Gangraena*, II, p. 21.

[2] Samuel Faircloth (Fairclough) was Minister at Kedington. He published *The Troublers troubled . . . A Sermon preached before the House of Commons* (1641); and *The Prisoners Praises . . . In a Sermon preached at Rumford* (1648, after the surrender of Colchester). A biography of Fairclough is included in Samuel Clarke's *The Lives of Sundry Eminent Persons in this Later Age*, 1683. The same work has a life by Fairclough of his patron Sir Nathaniel Barnadiston.

well conceive the cause of his *Gangren* to be his blind ignorance of the truth, and his mad malice against the wel-
affected conscientious people.

NEHEM. 6. 8.

*Then I sent unto him, saying, There are not such things done as thou
sayest, but thou fainest them out of thine own heart.*

2 TIM. 2. 16. 17.

*Shun profane and vain bablings: for they will increase unto more un-
godlinesse, and their word will eate as doth a Canker. [or, Gangren].*

Published according to Order.

LONDON,
Printed in the Yeare, 1646.

In a foreword Lanseter went out of his way to pay a tribute to
Katharine Chidley, with whom, and her son Samuel, he had been
closely associated in Bury:

> When Mr *Thomas Edwards* his book against *Independencie* and
> *Toleration*, came forth, about foure years agoe, O what boasting
> there was then among the Prelaticall party, and Temporizers, as
> if the day had been their own! But when the woman[1] came and
> strook the naile of *Independency* into the head of his *Sisera*,[2] with
> the Hammer of Gods holy word; then their sport was spoyled
> and quasht, the effects whereof appeareth: for since that time he
> could never set forth anything but *Gangraena*, or such like stuff
> (as his *Antipologia* before it, which the same party answered and
> presented as a new-years gift, that he might break off his old sins,
> etc.[3] And what is *Gangrena* (or the *Gangren?*). It is a putrified,
> rotten, dead insensible soare, whose nature is to fret, to the
> mortifying of that member that hath it growing upon him.
> Therefore is that which he produceth, rightly called by him
> *Gangrena*: for the ripping up and opening of which, this *Lance*
> was made, whereby the Christian Reader may see that the bitter
> effects of persecution (or want of publick toleration of true
> religion) causeth nothing but corruption and putrefaction tend-
> ing to utter destruction. But happy is he that is forewarned by
> other mens harm.

[1] Katharine Chidley.
[2] In *The Justification of the Independent Churches of Christ*, 1641.
[3] *A New-Yeares-Gift, or a Brief Exhortation to Mr. Thomas Edwards* (Jan. 1645).

Having quoted the passages referring to himself in *Gangraena*
Lanseter continued:

This being so in *Mr Edwards*'es book, Mr *Lanseter* thought it
meet to cleare himselfe as publiquely as he had aspersed him, yet
determined first to go to Mr *Edwards* to speake unto him about this
in a peacable way, which Hee did accordingly, before he went out
of *London* upon *June* the 29, and tooke Mr *Edwards* his book with
him; who coming to Mr *Edwards* his house, and a friend or two
more with him to be as Testimonies, Hee asked him saying: Sir,
doe you know me? No, saith Mr *Edwards*, I doe not know you;
Sir (saith hee) my name is *Lanseter*, and I come from *Bury*, and
you have mentioned me in your book; I have so, saith *Edwards*:
Sir, saith *Lanseter*, do you know that those things are truths which
you have written here of me? They are none of mine saith*Edwards*
but the relation of others. *Lanseter*: that's all one, seeing you are the
divulger thereof, and this book is yours: Sir, saith *Lanseter*, what
if these things be proved false: how then? Saith *Edwards* it will not
lye upon me, but upon those from whom I had the relation: Sir,
saith *Lanseter* I pray you tell me their names. I will send,
saith *Edwards*, first to those from whom I had the relation, and I
believe that they are able to make it good. Well, saith Mr *Lanseter*,
I pray you tell me their names, or show me the letter; I know not
where to finde it, saith *Edwards*, but I will (when I have time) look
for it.

Sir, saith Mr *Lanseter*, I am able to prove that there was not such
things as you have related here.

It may be, saith *Edwards*, you are not the man; Then it was
testified that there was no other such name in Bury, beside him,
and therefore he was the man that they meant. Moreover (saith
one present) Mr. *Edwards*, if one should write false things of you,
and then say he did not mean you, he meant another, would that
excuse him and if he be not the man, who is?

Then, saith Mr. *Edwards* No, it may be you are not the man,
neither is your name so, but you come in his name; for I have been
served so by divers before now? Saith Mr. *Lanceter*: Sir it may be
you have: but my name is *Lanceter*, and I dwell in *Bury*, and I am
the man, and there is no other of that name;

How shall I know that? (saith *Edwards*:) another that stood by,
said, I know the man and his name is Lanseter and he dwells in

Bury, and moreover I know the man to be an honest man, and he tels you his name, but you have set no name to the relation, and I have ground to believe that which Mr. *Lanceter* saith is true; but therefore in the meane while your letter that hath no name, will go under the notion of a Libel.

You say here, I am a pedler. Its well known I am no pedler, but I served my Master a *Mercer* 11. years and a halfe, and do keep shop in *Bury*; but let that passe, saith *Lanceter*: you say that I opened the whole book of *Ezra* at a private meeting, in stead of opening my pack; Sir this is untrue also: as those that were present can justifie.

Saith one by, what a base abuse is this, that you should call him a pedler in such a disgraceful manner? [I know him to be a shop-keeper in Bury;] And to say he opened the whole book of *Ezra* at a private meeting instead of opening his pack, what should his pack do at the private meeting?

Then said *Lanseter*, you say that I condemned all the Ministers of the Church of *England* for Sanballats and Tobiases of this time. Sir, I did not, this is false also: but suppose (saith *Lanseter*) that I had; what evil had I done?

Then you had done very wickedly (saith *Edwards*) and deserved to be called in question for it, and its the Sectaries that hindered reformation and not the Ministers of the Church of *England*.

Said another that stood by: what was Sanballat and Tobias? Were they not hinderers of the blessed work? And what are the Ministers of the Church of *England*, are they not hinderers also of the blessed work of reformation? And had Sanballat and Tobias any calling? And what calling have these, any at all? Yea, saith *Edwards*, that they have, You must go to Roome for it then, saith the party. No, not so, saith Edwards: yea but you must, saith the party, or else you will have no calling at all; did you ever read Mr. *Samuel Rutherfords* book, there he fetcheth his Church and Ministry from Rome.[1] Then *Edwards* refused to reason with him about it. Neither have you speld my name right; for it should not be *Lansister* but *Lanseter*.[2]

Lanseter: If these things which you have here related, be false,

---

[1] Samuel Rutherford wrote a number of theological works. The one probably meant here is *The Due Right of Presbyteries* (1644).

[2] No one, including Lanseter himself, seems to have been very sure how to spell his name. At least six variants exist.

which I am able to prove to be so, I pray you vindicate me in your next fruits that you set forth. But Mr. *Edwards* would not assent unto that, then said one by to Mr. *Lanseter*: Mr. *Lanseter* seeing that Mr. *Edwards* will not vindicate you in his next fruits upon your proving the relations to him to be false, which is a very reasonable request of yours; Now you know what you have to do, even to publish your own vindication to the world, as publicly as he hath cast aspertions upon you.

After that Mr. *Lanseter* went to his own Country againe, and sent his vindication, and the observations that he raised from some parts of the first Chapter of *Ezra*, at a private meeting, that so reasonable men may judge whether these things therein are truth or no. Then some of his friends went again on the 27. of *July* to Mr. *Edwards* to know his resolution whether he would deliver up the names of the parties from whom he had the relation, and the name of the messenger that brought it? but in stead of doing it, he shewed himself agrieved, that the party demanding it came with 2. or 3. witnesses, and fell a rayling on them, saying, you bring here 2. or 3. witnesses, I know your way of lying. Then said the party, Tax us if you can with lying in the least, yea, in the least with any one lye, if you can: Then saith he, I desire to talk no more with you, nor to have any thing to do with you, you may be gone, I will not have anything to do with you, nor do I desire to meddle any more with you. But saith another to Mr. *Edwards*: we will have to do with you as a lyer and a slanderer.[1]

The next seven pages contain "the substance of what Mr. *Lanseter* spake from *Ezra* Chap. 1. verse 1. at the private meeting". On pages 14 and 15 he replied to what Edwards had said about the "solid old Christian" of Mr. Faircloth's congregation:

Note that whereas Mr. *Edwards* hath set down, in his second part of *Gangraena*, that at this meeting one of Mr. *Faircloths* congregation opposed Mr. *Lanseter*, and that God was so mightily with him that it turned out to the shame and reproach of this *Lanceter*, and those who adhered to him, This is very false; and Mr. *Lanseter* spoke since with the two men of Mr. *Faircloths* congregation, whose testimonies concerning the matter, are sufficient to disprove Mr. *Edwards* his relation in the sight of the Sun;

[1] *Lanseters Lance*, pp. 4–7.

The testimonies, then quoted, add little of interest, nor do the remaining eight pages which contain "Several observations gathered from some observable expressions in Mr. *Edwards* book called the Second Part of *Gangraena*."

It is the dialogue already quoted from the earlier part of the pamphlet which is indeed quite unique in the literature of the *Gangraena* controversy for its fresh and personal style and the light it throws upon Edwards' character and methods. It is clear that once he has made a statement nothing will persuade him to admit himself wrong, even when, as in this case, he was obviously so in important respects. In the Third Part of *Gangraena*, far from retracting, he repeated and amplified his charges, and would probably have done so in any case. There was, however, a special reason for his obstinacy here, namely, the friendship between Lanseter and Katharine and Samuel Chidley, of which I suspect he was unaware when he wrote the Second Part, but which he must have found out once he began to concern himself more closely with Lanseter.

The Chidleys were objects of his special dislike. He hated women preachers, and Katharine was perhaps the most prominent of these. Further, her replies to his *Reasons against Independent Government* and *Antapologia* had been effective and damaging. Finally, Samuel Chidley was not only a Separatist but a close associate of Lilburne, Walwyn and the new Leveller party whom more and more he saw as the main danger. He had already mentioned Katharine Chidley with something more than his usual venom,[1] and he must have been delighted to find that in replying to Lanseter he could also hit at the Chidleys. So he wrote, obviously retailing the result of fresh enquiries at Bury:

There is one *Katherine Chidley*, an old Brownist, and her sonne a young Brownist, a pragmaticall fellow, who not content with spreading their poyson in and about London goe down into the Countrey to gather people to them, and among other places have been this Summer at *Bury* in *Suffolk*, to set up and gather a Church there, where (as I have it from good hands) they have gathered about seven persons, and kept their Conventicles together; who being one night very late about their Church-affairs, a mad woman breaking from her keepers and running out of the house she was kept in, happened to light upon the house where this company was, and stood up in the entry of the house; they being upon

[1] *Gangraena*, I, p. 79.

dissolving their meeting, and going to their severall homes, as they were going out, there stood this woman in her smock in the entry speaking never a word, which when they saw, they ran over one another for fear of this white devill, some one way, some another, almost frightened out of the little wit they had. Gaffer *Lanseter* of *Bury* (for so he was, unlesse he hath commenced Master by preaching) whom I have spoke of in the Second Part of *Gangraena*, was a great man with *Katherine Chidley* and her sonne, and is left Preacher to that company of Sectaries in their room; and I have great reason to think by the Epistle to the Reader that *Katherine Chidley* and her son made that book call'd *Lanseters Lance*, because *Katherine Chidley* and her sons Books (for the mother and son made them together, one inditing and the other writing) are highly magnified, and the brazen-faced audacious old woman resembled unto Jael; but as for *Lanseters Lance* for my *Gangraena*, I shall show it to be made not of iron or steele, in no sort able or useful to lance or enter the *Gangraena*, but a lance of brown painted paper, fit for children to play with; and to assure the Reader of it I received this last week a message to this purpose, from one of the Ministers who gave me intelligence about *Lanseter*, that he was perfecting the proofs and particulars about *Lanseters* businesse, and I should shortly hear from him; and within this two or three days a godly understanding man who was present at the meeting when *Lanseter* preached upon *Ezra*, gave me an account of the businesse, of the truth of the whole, and hath put me in a way, whereby, under the hands of persons present at the meeting, I may have it confirmed; and so among the confutations of some other pamphlets, I shall insert this of *Lanseters*.[1]

This further confutation never appeared:

As for that Pamphlet called *Lanceters Lance for Edwards Gangraena*, I have lately received from two godly Ministers in *Suffolk* a large relation by way of justification and proofe of what in my

[1] *Gangraena*, III, pp. 170–1. There is nothing to support Edwards' view that the Chidleys wrote *Lanseters Lance*. The references to their books are much more like those of an enthusiastic admirer than of an author trying to work in a surreptitious puff. And the direct, personal style is quite unlike that of their avowed works and much more like that of the honestly indignant shop-keeper. The Chidleys were professional and competent theological and polemical writers and for them to have gone so far outside their usual manner and to have entered so far into the skin of the Bury Drapier would, if done deliberately, argue a little of the peculiar genius of Swift, of which they certainly show no trace elsewhere. This is not to say they may not have helped Lanseter.

Second Part of *Gangraena* was written of Lanceter, as also some other passages related in those papers concerning Lanceter, one Chidley, and Barrowe,[1] but they containing a whole sheet of paper are too much to be put in a Postscript, and must be reserved for the Fourth Part; and I am of the minde when *Lanceter* shall come to reade them, he will wish he had beene opening his Pack when he was writing his Pamphlet.[2]

Part Four was never written, and it is clear that in 1646 Edwards was a sick, desperate and fear-ridden man. So much appears in the Preface to his last published work:[3]

I proposed to have added to this *Part* further proofs out of the New Testament against Toleration and for the Magistrates power: but these Preparatives and Additionals amounting to about some ten sheets (the reviewing, perfecting, and printing thereof would take up at least twenty days) and not knowing what a Day might bring forth, the Storm comming on so fast, I thought it best, for fear this Book might be suppressed at the Presse and never see the Sun, to send it forth as it was, that the Church of God at home and abroad might have the benefit of it, and to reserve the rest for a second Part (if God spare life and liberty).

This impression is confirmed by other writers. Thus J. Maddocks and Henry Pinnell:

You may guesse at Master Edwards his diet and constitution by his complexion, and so long as his queasey pen no better digesteth those crude, raw and incocted informations, no mervaile if you read his sicknesse in his forehead, as you may the substance of his book in the front of it.[4]

Soon after the publication of *The Casting Down of the last and strongest hold of Satan* in June 1647 Edwards retired to Holland "tradition says for fear of the resentment he had roused",[5] and certainly convinced that the Presbyterian cause was lost. On August 24th of that year he died there.

[1] John and Anne Barrow are among those signing the Covenant of 1646. See below.
[2] *Gangraena*, III, p. 291.
[3] *The Casting Down of the last and strongest hold of Satan. Or a Treatise Against Toleration and pretended Liberty of Conscience.*
[4] *Gangraenachrestum or, A Plaister to Allay the tumor and prevent the spread of a pernitious Ulcer* (Sept. 1646), p. 8. Compare Walwyn, *Prediction*, pp. 1-2, and John Saltmarsh, *Reasons for Unitie*, pp. 46-7, quoted on p. 53 of this volume.
[5] Haller, *op. cit.*, p. 229.

THE CHRISTMAS RIOT IN BURY, 1646

Walwyn had remarked that the worst danger from Edwards' intolerance was that it divided Presbyterians from Independents in a way which could only benefit the Royalists:

> Whosoever doth, or shall endeavour to perswade the godly and honest Presbyters to abandon, discourage or molest their faithfull, helpfull valiant and assured friends of other judgements (whom Mr. Edwards would have to be used worse than dogs) they are at the best, but Wolves, or Wolves friends, and seek the destruction of all honest people, of what judgements soever.[1]

The truth of this appeared on a large scale with the renewal of the Civil War in 1648 but it was perhaps apparent earlier in a smaller way in such events as the Christmas Riot at Bury in 1646.

In few respects did Puritan rule run more completely counter to popular feeling than in the attempts to suppress the celebration of Christmas, and in the public controversy which developed over this issue they were at an obvious disadvantage. They might argue convincingly in serious theological treatises that Christmas was pagan, popish, unscriptural, derogatory to the respect due to the Sabbath and attended in practice with all sorts of abuses and inconveniences,[2] but such arguments can have had little weight except among their own already convinced supporters. Their opponents replied at times in a similiar vein,[3] but more often and more effectively took different ground. There are a number of lively, satirical pamphlets which ridicule the saints and defend the right of the plain man to enjoy his traditional holiday in the traditional way.[4]

Behind the theological arguments and the satire lay another issue: Christmas was both attacked and defended because it helped to preserve and idealise feudal social relations:

> The old use was, that the Rich releived the Poore, the Poore had cause to pray for the Prosperity of the Rich, one Neighbour

---

[1] Walwyn, *Antidote*, p. 13.

[2] See Joseph Heming, *Certain Quaeries Touching The Rise and Observation of Christmas* (1648); and Richard Tomlin, *Responsoria ad Erratica Piscatoris* (1653).

[3] See George Palmer, *The Lawfulness of the Celebration of Christs Birth-day debated* (1648); and Edward Fisher, *A Christian Caveat to the Old and New Sabbatarians* (1650).

[4] E.g. John Taylor, *The Complaint of Christmas* (1646); and (anon.) *Women Will Have their Will: or, Give Christmas his Due* (1648).

Feasted another, everyone in his degree made good cheere, for
Christmas came but once a year.[1]

And a broadsheet ballad dealing with the subject lamented:

> Our Lords and Knights, and Gentry too,
> Do mean old fashions to forgoe:
> They set a porter at the gate,
> That none may enter in thereat.
> They count it a sin
> When poor people come in.

adding that Christmas, with Charity, "was slain at Nasbie fight".[2]

Consequently, attempts to prevent Christmas being celebrated as a
public holiday frequently resulted in disorders. Edwards refers to
such disorders in London and some city unnamed on Christmas Day
1645.[3] After the ending of the war there is sufficient evidence, I think,
that the popular feeling about Christmas was deliberately exploited
by the Royalists. The pro-Christmas pamphlets, especially the satirical
ones, are often openly Royalist. Cakes and ale are identified with kingly
government. This alliance between Royalists and those who liked to
be merry is indicated in the account of the Bury riot, "complotted by
the Malignant Party", but supported by "the Prentices and divers rude
deboyst Fellows".

The same pattern can be seen in the Christmas riot at Canterbury in
1647. Royalist and Parliamentarian accounts of it exist and all make it
plain that a three day riot ended with the seizure of the Town Hall
and a declaration "for the restitution of his Magestie to his Crown and
dignity, whereby Religion may be restored to its ancient splendour and
the known Laws of the Kingdom maintained".[4] Similar events took
place elsewhere. A contemporary newspaper, *The Kingdoms Weekly
Intelligencer* (No. 241), after an account of the Canterbury riot
says:

> the like bold attempt was made at *Ipswich*, in *Suffolke*, and in
> divers other places in the Kingdome. At *Ipswiche* the contestation
> was so great and pursued with so much violence, that sundry men
> were hurt, and two persons slain outright, but the ring-leaders of

[1] *Complaint*, p. 4.   [2] *The World is Turned Upside Down* (1646).
[3] *Gangraena*, I, p. 102.
[4] *The Declaration of many thousands of the City of Canterbury*. This is the Royalist version.
Compare, *Canterbury Christmas: or A True Relation of the Insurrection in Canterbury on
Christmas day last*.

the tumult, and the most active of the Incendiaries are apprehended and are to be tryed by the Law.

The riot at Bury, then, was not an isolated outbreak, but part of a
prolonged and nation-wide struggle, theological, social and political.
That a considerable Royalist party always existed in Bury is indicated
by the scale of the rising there during the Second Civil War in 1648.
Smaller, but no less significant as showing that influential forces were
continually at work below the surface, was the restoration in 1647 of
Dr. Thomas Stephens, an undisguised Royalist, to the post of High
Master of the Grammar School, from which he had been removed two
years earlier. Nor can there be much doubt that the bitter conflict
between Presbyterians and Independents encouraged the growth of
Royalism and left people like Lanseter in a weak and isolated position.
It seems clear, at any rate, that it was against him and his friends that
the main fury of the riot was concentrated.

An account of this riot was given in a pamphlet published in London
a few days later. It is short enough to be reproduced here in full:

A PERFECT
RELATION
OF THE
Horrible Plot, and bloudy Conspiracie
OF
The Malignant party at EDMONDBURY in
SUFFOLK, for the Murdering of Mr. LANCETER, and
divers other eminent and well-affected Persons, for
opening their Shops upon *Christmas-day*.
ALSO
The number of the Conspirators, and the
manner how they were appeased, with the losse on both
sides. Together with a Proclamation thereupon, and
the apprehending of the chiefe Ring-leaders,
and how they are to be tryed the next
SESSIONS
JANUARY, 4. 1647
Printed and Published and to be present-
ed to the Wel-affected Party, through-
out each respective County within the
Kingdome of England.
LONDON, Printed for I. Johnson, 1647.

Sir

The opportunity which I have embrased, and the good Tydings which I have to accompany it, hath moved me to set Pen to Paper, and to acquaint you with the horrid conspiracy and malicious Design of the Malignant Party at Edmondsby in Suffolk, against the People of God and the Members of Jesus Christ, who for their faithfulnesse and zeale to the Gospel of Christ, by endeavouring to maintain the purity of Religion, with the loss and hazard of both lives and fortunes, the inveterate malice and mischivous intentions of those ravening and devouring Spirits began to grow to some maturity, and to appear in a most vild and bloudy shape; for these wicked Members of Sathan, and enemies to God and Religion, had so conspired together, against the people of God, that they were resolved to prosecute their Designe, in case that any of them should presume to open their shops on Christmas day, and to that end had prepared divers weapons for the executing of the same, the particulars, together with the manner of this Conspiracy, I shall here present to the view of all good Christians, as shall manifestly appear by these ensuing lines, Viz.

In Edmondsbury in Suffolk God hath delivered his people from a great and evill Designe, complotted by the Malignant Party in the Town, the manner this:

The Prentices, and divers rude deboyst Fellows of the number of a hundred and fifty, or thereabouts had listed themselves together and had gotten three Captains.

And this was their design, to get together at the Crosse (being the place appointed for to meet) on the 25 of this instant Moneth of December (commonly called Christmas Day.) And their resolutions and determinations were, that whosoever should set open their Shops on the said day, they were resolved to pluck out the owners, and fire their houses, and kill them if they resisted, and pull out their goods, and lay waste and desolate those stately Buildings and Dwelling Houses which are the grace and ornament of the Town.

And the better to accomplish their Design, the Conspirators had provided great Clubs with great nailes crosse the end of each Club, every Naile weighing a pound.

But their mischievous Designs were discovered beforehand, by some Prentices, to whom the Mutineers came for their hands. And on the Wednesday some stirred about it and went to the Magistrates, and informed them thereof. Whereupon to prevent the great danger that might thereby arise Divers of them having skil in the Law found it would bee upon themselves if they suffered such a thing to be therefore the day following they sent for divers of the conspirators, and laid the Law to them, and bound them over to the Sessions.

And on Christmas Day most of the chief Magistrates, and many Constables, and other Officers assembled together.

Afterwards there were about thirty or forty about Mr. Lanseters dore (in the place called Cook-row)[1] his shop being open.

And there proclamation was made, and in severall places more, that those which were not in their own houses within half an houre, should be imprisoned; and some were laid hold on, and frighted; so that there was only a little hurt done, two men being wounded beyond the horse-market towards the end of the Towne; for when the wel-affected Party began to assemble themselves together, for the appeasing of these tumultuous Villians, some of them made at them with their Clubs, and wounded these two, but it is hoped not mortal, though indeed (as yet) they seeme very dangerous, by reason of the deepness of the wounds, and the festering of them.

But after a short time, these viperous Rascals were appeased, and the streets cleansed of these Vermin; so that their bloudy Designes were frustrated and mischievous and machavilian Plot discovered:

For the Great God of Heaven would not suffer his People to bee left as a prey unto the mercilesse Malignants teeth.

And it is to be minded, that above all, they aymed at Mr. Lanceter, who was not possessed with fear of them, but quietly waited upon the Lord, with the expectation of Deliverance from the hands of God, which he had, and was preserved; though he used no outward means to attain it himself. But this the Lord did to give his People more experience of his goodness; and hee is able to do much more, for his hand is never shortened.

And therefore let all the Godly Saints, and praying People, according to the Direction of the Spirit of Christ, from the

[1] Now Abbeygate Street. It will be noted that this confirms Lanseter's contention that he was no pedlar but a mercer owning his own shop.

consideration and experience of Gods former loving kindnesse, and preservations, rest upon him for future times.

Thus having given you a brief and exact Relation of the great and bloudie conspiracie complotted by the Malignant Party at Edmonby in Suffolke, I shall humbly take my leave, and remaine

Your affectionate Servant,

L.M.[1]

Edmondsbury, Jan. I. 1647.

This relation in confirmed by very good Hands, and at the request of many eminent, and wel-affected Persons printed, and presented to the publicke view of all the Free-born Subjects of England.

LANSETER AND HIS FAMILY IN BURY

It will be convenient to conclude with a summary of what I have been able to discover about John Lanseter, his family and his Church from other sources. These give no information about the place or date of his birth; the fact that he was, as he told Edwards, the only man of his name in Bury suggests that he may have come to the town from elsewhere. The first Bury mention records his marriage on July 30th, 1639, to a Mary Atkinson in St. James' Church.[2] On October 25th, 1640, his eldest son, John, was baptised there.[3] Two other children, who followed in quick succession, are not in the Baptismal Register, presumably because their father had by then separated himself from the established Church; if, as seems at least likely, the son was named Samuel after Samuel Chidley, this would indicate that Lanseter knew the Chidleys before they came to Bury. Perhaps he served his apprenticeship in London. The second child was a daughter, Mary. About 1650 Samuel was at the Bury Grammar School (in spite of its Royalist High Master!).[4]

Lanseter's sermon, so contemptuously handled by Edwards, must have been delivered early in 1646; there is no evidence that the

---

[1] These initials do not fit any of the known Bury Independents, unless perhaps they may stand for something like Lanseter, Mercer.

[2] *St. James' Parish Register, Marriages,* p. 35.

[3] *Ibid.,* Baptisms, p. 122.

[4] *Bury St. Edmunds Grammar School List,* p. 225. The same list includes among *Foreigners* (i.e. scholars from outside the town) the name Chiloe. This may well be a corruption of Chidley, and if so this is further possible evidence for a close connection between Lanseter and the Chidleys, as there could be no other reason for them to send a relative to school at Bury.

Chidleys were in Bury before the summer of that year, though they may have been. If not, it seems possible that they were there on the invitation of Lanseter, who was clearly the leading spirit among the little group of Independents in Bury. On August 16th, 1646, Lanseter and seven others[1] signed a Covenant setting up a gathered Church in Bury. Lanseter signed for his three children as well as for himself, and Samuel and Katharine Chidley signed as witnesses. Their statement says:

> . . . we do therefore with our posterity, covenant to become a peculiar temple for the Holy Ghost to dwell in, an entire spouse of Jesus Christ our Lord of Glory, for the enjoyment of all his holy ordinances, according to his institutions, and so to walk in all his ways so far as he hath revealed unto us, or shall reveal hereafter.[2]

On the departure of the Chidleys, Lanseter, as we have seen, was left as Preacher to the little Church, but it evidently met with difficulties, for on December 20th, 1648, a new, shorter and less flowery Covenant was made, indicating that the Church had lapsed and was now reformed. It was signed by ten persons, and of these, three—Lanseter, William Woods and John Thrower—had been among the original eight. Lanseter's was the first signature and the Covenant, which is in his writing, reads:

> We whose names are heare subscribed do resolve and engage by the help of the Spirit of God to walke in al the ways of God so far forth as he hath revealled or shall reveall them unto us by his word, and in all deutays of Love and watchfullness to other as become a Church of Christ.

Mrs. Lanseter was not among the original ten (nor had she been among the eight of 1646) but about fifteen months later she subscribed, making her mark, as did a fair proportion of the members.

We next hear of Lanseter in connection with the preparations for the Nominated (Barebones) Parliament. His name appears with 51 others

[1] Edwards had said that the Chidleys had gathered "about seven" persons—an indication that his information was sometimes quite reliable, even in details. The eight names include three women, an unusual feature which we can certainly attribute to the influence of Katharine Chidley. The addition of children, six in all, signed for by parents, is also unusual.

[2] Some information about Lanseter and his Church is in John Browne, *History of Congregationalism in Norfolk and Suffolk*, pp. 394–5. But for much more I am indebted to Mr. J. Duncan, for whose generous and invaluable help I want to take this opportunity of expressing my warmest thanks.

"in the name and by the appointment of several of the Churches, and many of the well-affected from all parts of the County of Suffolk", as signatories of a letter of May 19th, 1653, recommending as Members for the county Jacob Caley, James Harvey, Robert Duncombe, Edward Plumpstead, Francis Brewster and John Clarke. Others who sign include George Stannard, Thomas Caley, John Burrow (Barrow?) and James Granery (Grundy?) whose names appear in one or other of the Covenants mentioned above.[1]

An undated letter, evidently written slightly later, is signed by John Lampeter [sic] and Henry Leach "in the name and by the appointment of the Church at Bury, and the well-affected there, and the Franchise thereof". There is evidently some feeling in Bury that the town is not sufficiently represented in the nominations made above, as they recommend, in addition to John Clarke, two leading Bury men, Samuel Moody and Thomas Chaplin.[2] All three of these were frequently chosen as Commissioners for Taxes and similar offices, but Moody and Chaplin did not secure places in the Parliament, the five Suffolk places going to the men recommended in the original letter, with the exception of James Harvey.[3]

The Church Book, from which the Covenants given above are taken, contains no more entries till the arrival of a regular Minister, Thomas Taylor, about the beginning of 1653. (He was not formally ordained till 1655.) Entries are then in his writing and tell an interesting story:

> Anno Doṁi
>> 1653 William Woods sometimes a member of this Church and one of the foundation was delivered over into the hands of Sathan and cut off from the body in the name and by the power of the Lord Jesus for the sin of theft about the 10th day of the 2nd month commonly called Aprill in the year of Grace 1653.
>
> Anno doṁi
>> 1654 John Lanseter a member of this Church one of the foundation, for divers yeares an usefull instrument

---

[1] John Nickolls, *Original Letters and Papers of State, Addressed to Oliver Cromwell*, 1743, p. 94.

[2] *Ibid.*, p. 126.

[3] S. R. Gardiner, *History of the Commonwealth and Protectorate*, II, p. 239. Gardiner prints a list in which Brewster and Clarke are described as "Moderate" and Caley, Duncombe and Plumpstead as "Advanced".

for the good of the Church, afterwards falling into the heinous and beastly sins of drunkenness and uncleanness was at length with greate sorrow and lamentation when the whole Church was met together, delivered over into the hands of Sathan and cut off from the body about the 6th day of the fifth month commonly called July in the yeare of Grace 1654.

Anno domi

1655   John Thrower an unprofitable troublesome and un-savoury member of this Church, being one of the foundation, was at length after the exercise of much for-bearance, for the sins of railing, tippling, living perversely and frowardly with his wife, and for despising the Church's admonition, deservedly cast out and cut off from this body and delivered over into the hands of Sathan in the name and by the power of the Lord Jesus when the Church was met together in the 4th month commonly called June, in the yeare of Grace 1655.

Thus, within quite a short time from the arrival of the new Minister every one of the original members of the Church had been expelled on grounds of moral turpitude. It is perfectly possible that Taylor's version is correct, and that the expulsions were solely for the reasons stated, yet the coincidence is considerable and one would give a good deal to have Lanseter's side of the matter. Though expelled he evidently maintained his Independent principles, for his name appears among a number of others presented by the Grand Jury at the Bury Quarter Sessions in January 1675 "for absenting themselves from divine service for three Sundays past, contrary to the Statute". He was similarly presented on October 8th, 1675. And at "the gen'all Sessions and gaole delivery holden for the s'd Burgh the vii of Aprill 1676" was fined (with others) 2s.[1]

Mary Lanseter remained a member, subscribing to the Confession of Faith in the Church Book on January 1st, 1655, where she is said to be "clear on all but that of infant baptism".[2]

[1] Duncan, *The Prosecution of Nonconformists, 1662–1689, in Bury St. Edmunds* (MS.), pp. 3, 6.

[2] That is to say that like many early Independents she held some Anabaptist views. It is tempting to suppose that Mrs. Lanseter had been one of that "great sort of people" who listened to Clarkson preaching Anabaptism from his prison window on the Angel Hill in 1645. This would be almost within earshot of her house in Cook Row. *Proc. Suff. Inst. Arch.*, XXVI, 170.

Nothing more is heard of Lanseter's eldest son, John, in Bury, but I think he must be the John Lanster who has a house with two hearths in the parish of St. Mary Tower, Ipswich, in 1674. At the same date John Lancester has a house with six hearths in St. Mary's Parish, Bury St. Edmunds.[1] He continued in business there with his son Samuel and a farthing token issued by *John Lanseter in Cook Row in Bury* is recorded by Golding.[2] In 1677 Samuel married Sarah Stannard,[3] and in 1689 Lanseter died. St. Mary's Register records the burial of "John Lansetter, milliner" on March 10th.

Samuel and Sarah had five children, of whom only the second, also called Samuel, survived beyond infancy.[4] Samuel Lanseter senior prospered and joined the established Church, being a Church-warden at St. James' in 1707. He died, according to an inscription in that Church, on September 11th, 1731, at the age of 88. Samuel Lanseter junior died, unmarried so far as I can discover, in 1756 at the age of 75[5] and with his death the family came to an end, at least in Bury. The Church which John helped to found has had a continuous life from 1648 and remains as the Congregational Church in Whiting Street.

[1] *Hearth Tax Returns*, pp. 171, 56.
[2] *The Coinage of Suffolk*, p. 36. The token is now at Moyses Hall, Bury St. Edmunds.
[3] *St. Mary's Church Marriages, Bury Post*, 7/11/30
[4] *St. James' Parish Registers, Baptisms*, pp. 196, 198, 202, 207, 211; *Burials*, pp. 161, 164, 173.
[5] Rev. Francis Haselwood, *Monumental Inscriptions at Bury St. Edmunds*, p. 13.

3

John Saltmarsh: A Type of Righteousness

And it was not by his hanging upon the Crosse onely, for that was but one suffering of his love among millions, to teach us to be valient in protesting against that beast of Excess and destroyers of men (to the hinderance of admiration) with a holy and moderate continuation unto death, and dye with love to righteousness (as Mr. Saltmarsh did, a blessed change) protesting against the flitting favor and honor of the greatest of men, abhorring to become implicite members of the Serpants-Tayle, to sting the rest of the silly beasts of the mountains unto death.

John Jubbes, *An Apology.*

Saltmarsh was perhaps the most talented and influential of all the preachers of the antinomian left. Yet little is known of his antecedents or early life, and nothing of that little would lead us to anticipate his later developments.

His family apparently came from the village of the same name in the East Riding of Yorkshire, and Fuller describes them as "right ancient (but decayed)".[1] Wood writes that he "was descended from an antient family living sometime at *Saltmarsh* in *Yorkshire*, but whether born in that County or at *Strubby* in *Lincolnshire*, I know not".[2] The family would seem to have been conservative—one Saltmarsh was involved in the Pilgrimage of Grace, another was a captain in the Royalist garrison at Newark.

The date of his birth is also uncertain. His biographer in the *D.N.B.* says he was about 35 when he died in 1647. Rufus M. Jones says that he was born about 1600.[3] He was a student at Magdalene College, Cambridge, but there is no record of his matriculation, and the first firm date we have is 1636 when he took the degree of M.A. In the same year he published a small volume of Latin and English poems, *Poemata Sacra.*

[1] *Worthies,* 1953 edn., p. 665. [2] *Athenae Oxonienses,* 1669, II, p. 191.
[3] *Mysticism and Democracy,* p. 92.

All this would seem to make the later birth date the more probable.
Thirty-six would be old to graduate, nor is it likely that Saltmarsh,
who for the rest of his life was a polific author, would have waited so
long before appearing in print.

The *Poemata Sacra* have all the marks of a young man's work.
Fuller calls him "no contemptible poet" and this seems a fair enough
judgement. These are metaphysical poems of the kind then in fashion,
devotional in the manner of George Herbert, with something of his
evidence of a genuine religious feeling and a capacity to hit on a lively
and arresting sequence of images. Yet they never go deep enough to
make us regret that Saltmarsh turned thereafter to prose. *The Riddles*,
part of a group entitled *The Picture of God in Man*, is perhaps typical of
his manner at its best:

> Go up and show me where the lightning stood,
> After the first bright kiss upon a cloud:
> Show me the leaves of stone th'Almighties pen
> First writ on in the flaming mount, and then
> Measure the path to Euphrates sad banks:
> Ask for the garden at those weeping tanks;
> Then for the tree and the unluckie bough
> Where the first sin hung and was pluckt: and now
> Gaze up to see the starre the heav'ns did hatch
> To light the Eastern Wisdome to the cratch:
> Do these, I shall believe theres one that can
> Shew me the Picture of a God in man.

In 1639 Saltmarsh became rector of Hasterton in Yorkshire, and
from here, in 1640, came his second book, *Holy Discoveries and Flames*,
devotional meditations on scriptural texts, elegantly ornamented with
emblematic eyes and hearts. Dedicated to King Charles, there is no
hint here of anything but Royalist sentiment. The last "Flame", on the
text "Nation shall rise against nation", is clearly related to the troubles
of the time and ends with an earnest prayer for peace. Even more than
Poemata Sacra, *Discoveries and Flames* shows a sincere and personal
religious sense, but both are cast in the conventional forms of the
Anglican piety of the time, with nothing to suggest that their author
would find his spiritual home in the New Model Army rather than in
Little Gidding.

The change in his outlook seems to have come some time after
1641, and passages in *Free Grace* which appear to be autobiographical

describe a severe spiritual crisis. Here Saltmarsh describes his misery and the failure of orthodox preachers to satisfy him. He found it hard to believe that his repentance was real and not caused merely by fear of hell. He tells how he gradually became assured of his calling through the spirit, though still suffering from doubts. At times he had tried to destroy himself:

> I was tempted to *make away myself*, least the longer I lived, the more I should dishonour Religion. Satan came again to me, to eat something with pins in it, to choak myself, that it might not appear how I died, which I did, but in mercy found no harm; the Lord prevented it, I know not how. . . .
>
> The Lord once when I thought to have *stabbed* myself, sent a *wicked fellow*, who brought a book to read, by which I was mercifully prevented. I found still, in all my *temptations*, I was prevented by some *providence*, and upheld.[1]

His writings suggest that he only came to his antinomian convictions by degrees, and some time after his political conversion to the parliamentary cause. In his last published work, written in June 1647, he declared that while he was with the Army as a chaplain:

> I never made State-businesse any *Pulpit-work*, I never preached anything but Christ. Indeed, formerly I was a stickler in *Yorkshire* for the *Parliament*; but I have since been taught (I blesse God) onely to pray for them and obey them.[2]

There was, as will be seen, a sense in which his religious beliefs strengthened his political convictions in the broadest sense. They were never firmer than in the last few months of his life. But it is certainly true that his early writings, immediately after he espoused the parliamentary cause, were politically polemical in a style quite absent from his later work. Thus, the first product of his new period was a short reply to Thomas Fuller's *Sermon of Reformation*, published in August 1643, in which Fuller was criticised for saying that a thorough Reformation was utopian, that private men must wait upon the supreme authority, that is the Monarch, to begin a Reformation and that it should be conducted with "carefulness not to give any just offence to the Papists".

Fuller replied with *Truth Maintained* in March 1644, of which he says:

[1] *Free Grace*, p. 52.   [2] *A Letter from the Army*, pp. 4–5.

I . . . challenged him to an answer, who appeared in the field no more, rendering his reason thereof, that "he would not shoot his arrows against a dead mark," being informed that I was dead at Exeter.[1]

This is incorrect. Saltmarsh did reply in *Dawnings of Light*, but so moderately that it is possible that his zeal was tempered by some report of Fuller's death. It was arising from some remarks in Saltmarsh's first pamphlet against Fuller that questions were raised in the House of Commons about its attacks on the Royal Family. Saltmarsh was defended so outspokenly by Henry Marten that the latter was expelled from the House and committed to the Tower.[2]

Another polemic, appearing in October, was *A Peace but No Pacification*, arguing against a compromise and for continuing the war to a victorious conclusion. The King, Saltmarsh urged, would respect no oath, nor could any means be devised to force him to do so:

> The Machiavellisme of later times have made a Maxime in the science of Politicks, how to overwrest their own obligations, and have made it one part of the perfection of a Statist to be too wise for engagements.

Peace can be secured

> not so much by inventing any new engine to binde *our Kings in chaines, and our Princes in fetters of iron*, but by endeavouring such an extirpation of *Popery*, *Prelacie*, and *Malignity*, as our Peace may be rather secured by a *disability of contending*, than by any new *Oaths* or possibility of resisting.[3]

In 1643, having come to the conclusion that tithes were unchristian, he gave up the living of Hasterton, and, after an interval during which he is said to have been preaching in Northampton, was appointed Rector of Brasted in Kent, a good living, worth, according to Walker, £200 a year.[4] However, as he later made clear in a controversy with the Presbyterian John Lay, he refused to take any of this income. Ley had written:

> Concerning the unlawfulnesse of Tythes, if his Tenet now be right, his taking of them before was wrong; and the same constitution of conscience, which makes him now to renounce them,

---

[1] *Loc. cit.*   [2] Gardiner, *Civil War*, I, p. 202.   [3] *A Peace*, pp. 9, 12.
[4] *Sufferings of the Clergy*, p. 202.

may make him at least to doubt whether he be not bound to
returne what he hath received of the Parishioners of Brastead in
that kinde into their hands againe, by vertue of that received rule
of Augustine in his Epistle to Macedonia. The sinne is not remitted,
unlesse the goods that be unlawfully taken be restored.[1]

To this Saltmarsh retorted:

For my restoring of *Tythes,* now unlawful to me; I have done it;
I have returned to the State my property for a full years Arrearage:
nor did I take Tythes since I was in *Kent,* but the peoples free
composition from the first; and being even convinced against that
too, a yeer since, I forbore it. But take heed how you put forgiveness of *sin* upon *restitution*; for that is not only *Popery* but
like the *Pope* you would *sell pardons* onely to the *rich,* and none to
the *poor*; and you would put more upon *Sacrifice* then upon
Mercy.[2]

The last of Saltmarsh's books in this political-controversial vein,
but with suggestions of a new approach, is the appropriately titled
*Dawnings of Light: Wherein the true Interest of Reformation is opened . . .
And Many other things inpartially Hinted, to a Further Discovery of Truth
and Light* (January 1645). This was the first of his books to be published
by Giles Calvert, whose name on a title-page was in itself almost a
political and religious manifesto. He was, from this time, Saltmarsh's
usual publisher.

An interesting passage considers the relation of divine and human
forces in the working out of historical events:

God improves Reformation by *created means,* and *entities,* which
are like wheels and springs, and God moves by these, sometimes
in the way of his *omnipotence,* sometimes more connaturally, and
according to his way of moving, the improvements are; if he
move in a connatural way, he works with the creature little
further then in its own capacity, and then things move slowly on,
because he puts not out his hand to bring on the creature faster
then its own strength will carry it.[3]

He goes on to argue for a general toleration, rather cautiously as
compared with his later outspokenness, and claims the toleration of

---

[1] *Light for Smoke,* pp. 4–5.   [2] *An End of One Controversie,* p. 5.
[3] *Dawnings of Light,* p. 27.

opposed standpoints within the parliamentary camp will strengthen and not weaken the cause:

> the more we dispute, in our intemperancy and unnaturall heats, in which we spend as much Labour as in the Cause itself, and I am sure in some differences I could name, the truth stands by, while we wrangle beside it, and the dust that we raise in arguing, makes the truth less discernible, and that which is considerable amongst us here, is the exceeding prejudice raised against *difference of judgement, and divisions,* not considering that it is Gods secreet or engine for discovery, as well of truth, as errour, and for advantaging the one, as well as disadvantaging the other.[1]

It was, however, in *Free Grace: or the Flowing of Christs Blood freely to Sinners* (December 1645) that Saltmarsh's characteristic doctrines first found their full expression. Its title-page describes it as

> Being an Experiment of *Jesus Christ* upon one who hath been in the bondage of a troubled conscience at times, for the space of about twelve years, till now upon a clearer discovery of *Jesus Christ,* and the Gospel: Wherin divers secrets of the soul, of sin and temptation, are experimentally opened, and by way of Observations, concerning *a natural condition* and *a* mixed condition of *Law* and *Gospel*: With a further revealing of the Gospel in its glory, liberty, freshnesse and simplicity for Salvation.

Rejecting the Calvinist doctrine of election by which in practice salvation was reserved for a tiny minority of the human race, Saltmarsh argued that the grace of God, freely available to all, not only offers them the prospect of salvation in the world to come but sets them free from the bondage of the moral law in this. He denied that this would lead to "looseness and libertinism" and was careful to distinguish his doctrine from that of those who made God's grace an excuse for sin, as some antinomian extremists were certainly then doing:

> Can the *Free-grace* of *Jesus Christ* tempt any one to sin of itself? *Can a good tree bring forth evil fruit?* And shall we call everyone *Antinomian* that speaks *Free grace,* or a little more freely than we do? If any man *sin* more freely because of *forgiveness of sins,* that man may suspect himself to be *forgiven*; for in all *Scriptures* and

[1] *Dawnings of Light,* p. 57.

Scripture-examples, the more forgiveness the more holinesse; Mary *loved much because much was forgiven to her.*[1]

The first part of *Free Grace* describes the process by which Saltmarsh reached his new-found assurance, and this is followed by a general exposition of his views, mainly in short numbered paragraphs each elaborating a particular proposition. Typical headings are:

VIII.   They that are under Grace revealed, are no more under the Law.

X.   A justified person is a perfect person.

XXX. All the sins of beleevers done away on the Crosse.

Under the heading "A Beleevers glorious freedom" he writes:

The Spirit of Christ sets a *beleever* as *free* from *Hell,* the *Law,* and *Bondage,* as if he was in *Heaven,* nor wants he anything to make him *so,* but to make him *believe* that he is so.[2]

And under the heading "The Law is now in the Spirit, and in the Gospel for a beleever to walk by" he outlines the characteristic antinomian doctrine of successive and higher revelations of truth, each abrogating the partial truth of earlier revelations:

The Gospel is both a *perfect law* of life and *righteousnesse,* of *grace* and *truth*; and therefore I wonder at any that should contend for the ministry of the *Law* or *Ten Commandments* under Moses. . . . And although the *Law* be a beam of *Christ* in *substance* and *matter,* yet we are not now to live by the *light* of one *beam* when the *Sun of righteousness* is risen himself; that was a fitter light to those who lived in the region and shadow of death.[3]

Free Grace, and subsequent books in which the same doctrines were developed, naturally drew upon Saltmarsh the fire of the big guns of the Presbyterian establishment, equally alarmed by his condemnation of tithes, his advocacy of toleration, the threat of his antinomianism to the structure of dogma and discipline they were trying to set up and the democratic implications of his ideas. His opponents included John Ley, Thomas Gatacre, and, heaviest gun of all, the Scottish theologian Samuel Rutherford. For the remaining two years of his life Saltmarsh was constantly involved in controversies in which, it must be said, most of the acrimony came from his opponents. Thomas Edwards also cast a jaundiced eye in his direction.

[1] *Free Grace,* An occasional word.   [2] *Ibid.,* p. 140.   [3] *Ibid.,* p. 146.

In *Groanes for Liberty . . . with . . . some Quaeres For the better under-standing of Mr. Edwards last Book called Gangraena* Saltmarsh made an effective case against Presbyterian intolerance by quoting passages from the group of divines who had written under the name Smectym-nus in 1641 when they were protesting against episcopal rule. "Why", he asked, "are Divines more jealous of conscientious and unoffensive liberty now that the Government is coming into their hands, than when it was in their predecessors?"[1]

Of Edwards he wrote:

> Your trampling upon your Brethren as the mire in the streets, have forced my *Spirits* into these few queries: *for Sion sake I cannot hold my peace.*
>
> The Designes of your book seem to be these;
> 1. A Designe of *Provocation* to the Magistrate against your Brethren.
> 2. of *Accusation* under the old Project of Hereticks and Schismaticks.
> 3. of *Historicall Recreation* to the people, that they may make themselves sport with the *Beleevers* that differ from ye, as the *Philistines* with Sampson upon the Stage.

And he concluded:

> I had said more to ye, had you printed more *Reasons* and less *Reviling*, and something more than *Stories* and *Winter Tales.*[2]

This evidently went home, since Edwards, in the second part of *Gangraena*, singled Saltmarsh out as one of those who ought to be silenced:

> But we see what sad times we are fallen into, and that the Sectaries are grown fearlesse, that they dare come abroad, and plead their desperate cause, as Master Saltmarsh, Walwyn . . . which symp-tome, among many others, makes me fear the night and darkness is at hand, when as the wolves and the wild beasts dare come out of their dens.[3]

In the last three pages of *Reasons for Unitie, Peace, and Love*, in the main part of which Saltmarsh replied to Gatacre and others, he con-demned Edwards for his lack of charity and justice, compared him to Archbishop Laud and described a meeting and conversation:

> Is it any other *ground* or *bottom* you stand upon in this your way

[1] *Groanes for Liberty*, p. 5.   [2] *Ibid.*, pp. 31-2.   [3] *Gangraena*, II, p. 137.

of *accusing* the *brethren*, but, *Paul* you say named some, and the *Fathers* named some so, and *Calvin*, as you told me the other day when I met you? And was there ever *crime* without some *Scripture*, or *Shadow* of the *Word*? Did not *Canterbury* on the scaffold preach a Sermon of as much *Scripture* and *Story* for what he did as you can for yours, if you should ever preach there? He thought ye all *Hereticks*, as you do us; he thought he might persecute you, as you do us. . . .

Poor soul! Is your *conscience* no better seated then in such aiery apparitions of *Scripture*, and failings of *Fathers*? Do you not hear the *Prayers* of those *souls* you wound, pleading with *God* against your *sin*? Are you not in the *gall of bitterness* and *bond of iniquity*? Is not your *spirit* yet flying, where none pursues you? Are not your dreams of the *everlasting burning*, and of the *worm* that never *dies*? Have you no *gnawings*, no *flashings*, no *lightenings*? I am afraid of you. Your face and complexion shews a most sadly *parched*, *burnt* and *withered spirit*. Methought when I called to you the other day in the *street*, and challenged you for your unanswerable Crime against me, in the third page of the last *Gangraena*, in setting my name against all the *Heresies* you reckon, which your *soul* and the *world* can witnesse to be none of *mine*, and your confession to me when I challenged you: how were you troubled in *spirit* and *language*? Your sin was, as I thought, upon you, scourging you, checking you, as I spoke. I told you at parting, I hoped we should overcome you by *prayer*. I believe we shall pray you either into *Repentence* or *Shame* or *Judgement*, ere we have done with you. But Oh might it be *Repentence* rather, till Master Edwards *smite his thigh, and say What have I done?*[1]

Edwards saw the matter somewhat differently:

. . . for his two stories he relates of discourse with me upon two severall times speaking together, they are deceitfully and falsely related, the greatest part concealed, and what is related not justly set down: I writ them both down in my Diary, especially the last immediately after I left Master *Saltmarsh*, and so can give a just and good account of them, but they are too long to be inserted in a *Postscript*, and of the first, that being at Master *Vicars* house and in his hearing, he hath given the Reader already a good part of it in his *Schismatick Sifted*, little (I think) to M. *Saltmarshs* credit.[2]

[1] *Reasons for Unitie*, pp. 46–7.   [2] *Gangraena*, III, p. 295.

John Vicars spoke of *Groanes for Liberty* as

> full fraught . . . with very false, falacious and grosly misapplyed
> parallels, and unsavorie comparisons, between the cases or con-
> ditions and times of the *domineering* Prelates over the truly *tender*
> *consciences* of the (then) truly godly *Nonconformists*, and our (now)
> pious *Presbyterians* in their gracious and most moderate desire of
> *unity* and *uniformity* in *sound Doctrine* and *Scripturall discipline*, with
> his *Schismaticall Sectaries*, in their most ungodly and ungrounded
> grones, or rather grunts, for abominable, yea damnable Libertie of
> Conscience, forsooth.[1]

He goes on to relate how, having persuaded Saltmarsh to hear Edwards
preach:

> Master Saltmarsh gave Master Edwards such high and honourable
> Testimony both of his godly, sound, and satisfactory preaching,
> and also for his gravity, solidity and sweetly tempered moderation
> in conference, as that I am confident, he is not able to give better
> testimony and commendation to any *Independent* or *Sectarie*
> whatsoever.[2]

Edwards and Vicars complained that John Bachiler not only licensed
the pamphlets of Saltmarsh and other Sectaries but added flattering
commendations and even helped in their composition:

> There is one Master John Bachiler, Licencer-General of the
> Sectaries books, Licencer to *Master Saltmarsh, Cretensis, Walwin,*
> *Webb* and divers other Sectaries; who hath been a man-midwife
> to bring forth more monsters begotten by the Divill, and borne
> of the Sectaries within the three last years than were brought to
> light in England by all the former Licensers of the Bishops and
> their Chaplaines for fourscore years.[3]

Bachiler did indeed play an important part in enabling controversy to
proceed on something like equal terms, and some of his comments on
Saltmarsh's books are interesting. Of *An End of One Controversie* he
wrote:

> The *Law* of *Nature* giving a man leave to speak fairly in his owne
> just defence, and the *Law of Grace* requiring him to speak zealously

---

[1] *Schismatick Sifted*, p. 29.   [2] *Ibid.*, p. 31.
[3] *Gangraena*, III, p. 102. It may be noted that all three parts of *Gangraena* had
highly eulogistic commendations from another Licenser, James Canford.

in defence of *Truth*, I think it equal that this answer to Mr Ley should be printed.

And, giving his imprimatur to *Reasons for Unitie*, he wrote, "I conceive thou hast a taste both of the Sweetnesse and Glory of the Gospel."

An End of One Controversie (April 1646) was a reply to Ley's *Light for Smoke*, itself a reply to Saltmarsh's *Smoke in the Temple*. Ley calls Saltmarsh "late Preacher at Brasted in Kent, now revolted both from his Patronall calling and charge", from which it may be inferred that he had now left the parish to which he had been appointed at the beginning of 1645. Ley clearly recognised the democratic implications of Saltmarsh's doctrines, which encourage:

> wild and wicked fancies, that every man may beleeve what he list, and live as he beleeveth, and so may doe what is right in his own eyes, that is, whatsoever is wrong in the eyes of God and all good men, as if there were no King in Israel, that is no Government.[1]

It is significant that he attributes to Saltmarsh the characteristic Leveller principle of popular sovereignty, in which the people are superior to Parliament itself:

> You give up the Magistrates Authority to the peoples liberty, leaving it their choice to receive, or refuse Church-Government, as they like or dislike it; for thus you would have it propounded unto them, "People, here is a Government, which to some of us seemeth to be a Government according to the Word of God, take it and examine it, if you be so perswaded, and if the Word of God hold it forth clearly, embrace it; if not, doe not obey anything in blinde and implicite obedience; thus were fair dealing with conscience." But it were foul dealing with the Magistrate, yea and the people too, for it would bring all to Anarchie and confusion, as Judg. 17.6. If you say you meane it in respect of the Assembly of Ministers, they present it not untill the Parliament have ratified it by their Authoritie; and so your meaning must be, that they should put that to the peoples choice, which the Parliament hath concluded in their Votes, and imposed both on the Ministers, and people, by their civill Sanction; and what is this but to subject the Supreme Authority to the popular liberty?[2]

[1] *Light for Smoke*, Dedicatory Epistle.   [2] *Ibid.*, p. 46.

Saltmarsh's reply, which appeared on April 17th, was short and restrained. His statement on tithes has already been quoted, and he went on to defend religious liberty:

> Nor would I have *men believe as they list,* as you say of me: I would onely not have men forced to *believe* as *others* list, as you and your *Brethren* list: I would have *Faith* wrought by the *Spirit of God,* not by the *spirites of men,* who have no dominion over *Faith.*[1]

An End of One Controversie had the air of a final reply, but two days later a further and really extraordinary reply appeared. Its character is indicated by its title: *Perfume Against the Sulphurous Stinke of the Snuffe of the Light for Smoak, called, Novello-Mastrix. With a Check to Cerberus Diabolus, and a whip for his barking against the Parliament and the Armie.* It is jesting and abusive in tone, and so unlike anything else that Saltmarsh ever wrote that, though it appeared under his name, it is tempting to wonder if it may not have been written by someone wishing to discredit him. In this connection it may be significant that, unlike his other writings, it was unlicensed and was issued by a publisher with whom Saltmarsh was not otherwise associated.

A month later *Reasons for Unitie, Peace and Love,* in which Saltmarsh dealt with Gatacre and Edwards, appeared. *Shadows Flying Away,* the section of the book answering Gatacre, illustrates clearly some of the characteristics of his method of thought, rational and lucid in spite of his sometimes fanciful and hyperbolic language. To Gatacre's suggestion that God might be angry with his people he replied that all human conceptions of God could only be partial and allegorical, and that much that is said in the Bible, expecially in the Old Testament, must be interpreted as the best approximation to truth possible to men in any particular age:

> Is he said to *chastise* as *Fathers,* otherwise then in expressions after the *manner of men;* because of the *infirmities of our flesh,* must we conceive so of God as of one another? Can he be provoked for sins done away and abolished? Hath Christ taken away all the sin of his? Hath he born all upon his body or no? Speaks he of anger otherwise then by way of *Allusion* and *Allegory?* . . . Or speaks he not in the Old Testament according to the Revelation of himself then, and in the New Testament of himself now, only because

[1] *An End,* p. 5.

our infirmity, and his own manner of appearing which is not yet so.[1]

He rejected a literal interpretation of Scripture, still more the then common practice of quoting isolated texts, often out of context, to prove some point or other:

Yea, but will you take the Doctrine of the Gospel from a *part*, or *summary* of it, as you say, and not from the Gospel in its *fulness*, and *glory*, and *Revelation*: Will ye gather Doctrines of Truth, as *Ruth* for a while did *gleanings*, here one *ear of Corn*, and there another; and not rather go to the full sheaf, to Truth in the Harvest and Vintage? Will you pick up *Truth* by pieces and parcels, in *Repentence*, and *Obedience*, and *Self-denial*? . . . Will ye Preach Doctrines as they lie in the *Letter* or in their *Analogy* and inference of Truth?[2]

This was to be Saltmarsh's last polemical work, and it was almost a year before he appeared again in print. It will be convenient here to anticipate a little and dispose of the weightiest and certainly the most exhausting attack on him, by the famous Scottish divine, Samuel Rutherford. *A Survey of the Spiritual Antichrist. Opening The Secrets of Familisme and Antinomianisme in the Antichristian Doctrine of John Saltmarsh, and Will Dell, the present Preachers of the Army . . . and others* is a volume of almost 600 closely printed pages in the grand manner of Scottish theological controversy in which every last point is pressed home to the uttermost. Rutherford uses hard language at times, but, unlike Edwards and others he was concerned with doctrine and ideas rather than with personalities. However, he was obviously alive to the political dangers of men with the views of Saltmarsh and Dell being in a position to infect the Army. He was not alone in his fears. As Professor Haller writes:

Baxter, Edwards, and other contemporary witnesses supply us with a considerable list of men whose sermons and tracts were eagerly heard or read by the soldiers and populace directly after Naseby. Two in particular Baxter found holding sway at head-quarters, namely John Saltmarsh and William Dell, and of these the former seemed the prime source of that antinomianism which, he thought, led to the anarchy that presently ensued. Baxter was indeed moved to write because he saw Saltmarsh's "Flowings of

[1] *Shadows*, p. 11.   [2] *Ibid.*, p. 12.

Grace" (*Free Grace: or the Flowings of Christs Blood freely to Sinners*) "so exceedingly taking both in the Country and the Army", "especially when I saw how greedily multitudes of poor souls did take the bait, and how exceedingly the Writings and Preachings of *Saltmarsh* and many of his fellows did take with them".[1]

In general it may be said that Rutherford seems to have given a fair if hostile account of Saltmarsh's teachings, always with the proviso that no set of words used by two men of such entirely different cast of mind could ever have the same meaning to both of them. Saltmarsh and Dell, he alleged:

> deny the Scriptures to be an obliging rule to the Saints, but only the word written in the heart.[2]

And he interpreted the Scriptures figuratively rather than literally:

> Saltmarsh cleareth his mind touching personall mortification as faintly, and holdeth many other points of Familisme, as of Christ crucified, risen, ascended to heaven in a figure, or in the spirit, not really in his true man-head.[3]

A large section of the first part of Rutherford's book deals in system and detail with Saltmarsh's errors. They include:

> Praying a law-bondate to Saltmarsh and Familists.
> Saltmarsh holds that neither written Law, nor written Gospel is an obliging rule, but only the Spirit, as did the Libertines.
> Saltmarsh with H. Nicholas teacheth that every creature is God, or a substantial part of God.
> Saltmarsh and the Familists teach that there is salvation in all religions.[4]
> Saltmarsh divises a new union between God and Man, Divills and Angels.[5]

Rutherford describes Part II of his polemic as "A Modest Survey of the Secrets of Antinomianism; with a brief refutation of them from the word of truth." Modest and brief are hardly the words one

---

[1] *Liberty and Reformation in the Puritan Revolution*, p. 198.
[2] *Spiritual Antichrist*, p. 191.   [3] *Ibid.*, p. 194.
[4] Compare *Smoke from the Temple*: "Consider that we may be one in Christ though we think diversely, and we may be friends, though not brethren, and let us attain to union though not to unity." Quoted from Woodhouse, *Puritanism and Liberty*, p. 182.
[5] *Op. cit.*, pp. 223–77.

would use to describe either Rutherford or his works, and this particular survey runs to no less than 239 pages.

About June 1646 Saltmarsh took what was perhaps the most important step of his life when he went to the Army as preacher. He was not an entire stranger to it. We know that he preached to the General and Army besieging Oxford on May 25th, 1645, but this would seem to have been only a visit, since in *A Letter from the Army*, written in June 1647, he speaks of "this whole year I have been with them". His absorption with this new work was doubtless the reason for the long and unwonted gap in his writings which followed the appearance of *Reasons for Unitie*. And there can be no doubt that he both gave and received much in his contact with the bursting life, intellectual energy and democratic resolution of this new kind of citizen army. To it he brought a conviction that all men were on the road to heaven if they would but follow it. This led him to a deep respect for the gifts and capacity of ordinary men, so different from the contemptuous attitude of orthodox Calvinism for the reprobate multitude. Under the heading *No despising for too much learning, or too little*, he had written:

> Let not one despise another for gifts, parts, learning. Let the Spirit be heard in the meanest; let not the scribe or disputer of the law despise the fisherman, nor they despise them because scribes and disputers. The Spirit is in Paul as well as Peter, in both as well as one.[1]

This was a double-edged statement, rejecting both the Presbyterian claim that only the learned and duly qualified can understand and should presume to expound the word of God, and the view, held by some sectaries, and from which Walwyn was not entirely free, that learning was an actual impediment and the ignorant were *more* likely to have received the truth. For Saltmarsh the liberating truth came direct from God and could come equally to all.

This Christian liberty, offered freely to all by the love and grace of God, was not, of course, identical with the civil liberty demanded by the Army democrats with whom Saltmarsh was now in close and sympathetic contact, but the two liberties were complementary and in practice those who valued the one were likely to value the other.

In *Sparkles of Glory*, written after he had been with the Army about a year, he wrote:

[1] *Smoke in the Temple, op. cit.*, p. 182.

The *Sons of men* taken into this *glory* of the *Son of God*, are that new or second Creation, that *new Jerusalem*, which came down from God, the *city of the living God*, the Spirits of just men made perfect, the new creature, the heavenly men; as is the *Lord from Heaven* so are they that are heavenly.[1]

We shall find him shortly identifying the heavenly men, the saints, with the Levellers imprisoned and persecuted by the Grandees. This new creation and fellowship was for all men, forming an invisible Church whose unity strongly resembled that which was developing in the Army itself:

> And into this Church all are admitted through the *Spirit* of Christ, and all are discerned *members* in the same *Spirit*, and trayned by the *Spirit*. And this Church of Christ being *baptized by Spirit* into one *body*, is not to be divided by any outward things which are of this *Creation*, which are *visible, outward* and *perishing*; or by any *fellowship* and *ordinance* below the *glory* of the Spirit.[2]

The people had an active, positive part to play in events:

> The interest of the people in Christ's kingdom is not only an interest of compliancy and obedience and submission, but of consultation. of debating, counselling, prophesying, voting, &c. And let us *stand fast in that liberty wherewith Christ hath made us free*.[3]

It is clear that such doctrines were welcome to the Levellers and no less clear that Saltmarsh's personality, his sincerity and the unworldly simplicity which was reflected in his refusal of tithes and neglect of the many opportunities to advance his fortunes that were offered to the popular preacher, a quality by no means universal among his colleagues even on the Left, made him generally loved and respected. His year with the Army must have been a time not only of constant preaching but of discussion and thought. Something of this can be seen in *Sparkles of Glory*, which is less polemical, more contemplative, than any of his writings since *Free Grace*. Something of this is suggested by its sub-title: *Some Beams of the Morning Star Wherein are many discoveries as to Truth, and Peace*. It has the appearance of a collection of occasional reflections, jotted down as they came or arising as by-products of some other activity, rather than a systematically constructed treatise. It

[1] *Sparkles of Glory*, p. 10.   [2] *Ibid.*, p. 18.   [3] *Smoke from the Temple, op. cit.*, p. 184.

opens with an Epistle, significantly directed to Parliament, on the theme of religious liberty:

> There are two *Principles* in the world, which have these sad, and dark conclusions *attending* them, the two Principles are these:
> 1. That such as conforme not to the *Doctrine*, and *discipline* established; and yet as to the *State* are *good Subjects* and *peacably* affected, shall be *proceeded* against by *fines, imprisonment,* etc.
> That such as shall *speak* upon the *Scriptures*, or open them, *Publikely*, or in *Private*, and are not *ordained* by the laying on of *hands* of that present established *ministery* of a *kingdome*, shall be proceeded against by *fines, imprisonments*, etc.[1]

The evil consequences of these two principles are expounded in some detail.

Of especial interest is a section (pages 289–98) dealing with the Seekers, the group with which Saltmarsh had perhaps most in common. Rutherford alleged that in *Sparkles of Glory* "he professeth himself a Seeker". This is incorrect. After a sympathetic summary of Seeker doctrines, Saltmarsh criticises them, and it would appear that he was prepared to go rather further along the same road. The Seekers, he writes,

> wait in this time of the Apostacie of the *Christian Churches*, as the *Jews* did in the time of their *Apostacie*, and as the *Apostles* and *Disciples* at *Jerusalem*, till they were endued with power from on *high*, finding no practice for *worship*, but according to the first *pattern*. . . .
> They wait for a *restauration* of all things, and a setting up of all Gospel *Officers, Churches, Ordinances*, according to the *patern* in the *New Testament* . . .
> This is the highest of their Attainment.

Saltmarsh, however, argues that this pattern,

> was but a more *purely-legal Dispensation*, or a discovery of the *Gospel* rather as to *Christ* after the *flesh* then after the *Spirit*. . . .
> That to wait in any such way of *Seeking* or expectation, is *Antichristian*, because there is no *Scriptures* to warrant any such restauration. . . .
> That the *truth* is, Christ is already in all *his* in *Spirit* and *truth*,

[1] *Sparkles of Glory*, p. 2.

and as the *eternal seed,* and his *fulnesse* is already in the *Saints,* or all true *Christians.*

In the absence of any actual sermons preached during this year with the Army, *Sparkles of Glory* has a special value in giving us some idea of the nature of his teaching in its final development.

In his next, and last, published work he appears in a new role, that of the voice of the Army, defending and explaining its conduct and policy. *A Letter from the Army, Concerning the peaceable temper of the same,* was written when the strength and unity of the Army was at its highest point. At the end of May 1647 officers and men alike rejected Parliament's order to disband. Fairfax, apparently much against his will, was compelled to go with the rest. "It is incredible," an Agitator wrote on May 29th, "the Unitie of Officers and Soldiers." At a rendezvous on Newmarket Heath, on June 4th and 5th, officers and men adopted *A Solemn Engagement of the Army,*[1] binding themselves not to disband till all their grievances had been met, and setting up an Army Council which included elected representatives of the regiments sitting with full voting rights. On June 4th, too, Cornet Joyce took the King from Holdenby and brought him to Army headquarters. Salt-marsh's *Letter,* which refers to the King's arrival, must have been written immediately after it, since it was sent to London, printed, and appeared not later than June 10th according to Thomason's dating.

In it Saltmarsh stressed the peaceable and reasonable temper of the Army, but no less their determination to secure justice for themselves both as soldiers and citizens:

> Since I came to the Army, I blesse God, I have seen no temper there, but intendency to peace, and the preservation of the Kingdom; and they professe unanimously, That when their just grievances are satisfied, and they estated in a free and cleer capacity as *Subjects,* as well as *Souldiers,* because they say, that will flow down upon all their fellow subjects in the Kingdome, who may be secured by Parliament as to their Civill rites and just liberties, they shall freely disband, or be commanded as the Parliament shall think fit in their wisdomes.[2]

Saltmarsh, like the Levellers, realised, and was anxious to guard against, the danger that the civilian population, heavily taxed and suffering from the effects of years of war, would turn against the Army

[1] See Wolfe, *Leveller Manifestoes,* pp. 142–53.   [2] *A Letter,* pp. 1–2.

and support its disbandment on any terms. He therefore stressed the common interests of soldiers and civilians and insisted that the Army was the most powerful defender of the people's liberties:

> There is a general cry in the Counties as wee march, that the Army would help them, and be their *Mediatours* to the *Parliament* for *Justice* and *Righteousness*: they are generally much troubled about the burning of some Petitions.[1] The Army are very sensible of the Counties grievances, being under a grievance themselves.
>
> The Counties cry, *Peace*, *Peace*, let us have no more Forces raised to make new Warres. I hope the LORD will give a right understanding amongst the people, that the Army are wholly for Peace too,
>
> There is a Solemn Ingagement the whole Army hath entered into in order to their just grievances, at the last Rendezvous. There is a mighty spirit raised up in the Army for Justice and Righteousness. We admire at it.[2]

He declared that the *Solemn Engagement* showed that the Army had no intention of destroying civil government, or imposing Independency or anything else upon the country,

> for truly that were wholly to oppose their owne *Principles*, if they should have thoughts to any such thing, who desire that they should not be *compelled* themselves.[3]

The King, he wrote, had been brought to the Army without its foreknowledge, but this was done to avert the danger of a new war, and he was, "confident that nothing will be done as to this by the Armie, but that which may become honest men".[4]

The unity which *A Letter* reflects was short lived. Once Parliament had retreated over disbandment and arrears of pay, Cromwell, Ireton and the senior officers generally were anxious to compromise and had little sympathy with the wider political demands for which the rank and file and a good proportion of the junior officers were pressing. Saltmarsh's sympathies were clearly with this latter party. By the end of June the political lines were already drawn. The Grandees were, in effect, repudiating the *Solemn Engagement* and wanted to restore what they regarded as normal discipline. The Levellers were increasingly concerned to secure the endorsement of their political programme.

---

[1] The Leveller *Petition* of March 1647 and its successors. See pp. 163–5 of this volume.
[2] *A Letter*, p. 2. [3] *Ibid.*, p. 3. [4] *Ibid.*, p. 4.

Early in October the conflict came to a head with the appointment of new and more militant Agitators by several regiments and the publication of *The Case of the Armie Truly Stated*. Shortly after this the first draft *Agreement of the People* was drawn up. On October 28th and 29th the two documents were debated by the Army Council at Putney.

By this time, and very possibly soon after writing *A Letter*, Saltmarsh had left the Army and gone to live at Laystreet, Ilford, Essex. Wood's account suggests that his retirement may have been due to ill-health, and he was certainly now in the last months of his life. It is not impossible, however, that he may have been under some pressure from the Army authorities. Though now at a distance he must have kept a keen eye on Army developments and remained in touch with his friends there. Late in October, with the forthcoming Putney discussions evidently in his mind, he wrote three letters, to Fairfax, to Cromwell and to the Council of War. These were published after his death with the title *Englands Friend Raised from the Grave* (July 1649). It was presumably the third of these that Captain Bishop, a Leveller supporter, demanded should be read at Putney on October 29th:

> You have met here this day to see if God would show you any way wherein you might jointly preserve the kingdom from its destruction, which you all apprehend to be at the door. God is pleased not to come in to you. There is a gentleman, Mr. Saltmarsh, did desire what he has wrote may be read to the General Council. If God do manifest anything by him I think it ought to be heard.[1]

All three letters are similar in content. That to Fairfax refers to his ill-health (God has "raised me up from the power of the grave"). He declared that:

> There is a mighty noise of unrighteousness and injustice in the proceedings at your Councels as to the Kingdom: And truly Sir, this not in most Counties onely amongst the people, but amongst the choicest, most conscientious Christians: . . . God hath at present brought a dark cloud over you, and the Lord show you a way out of it, which is presented to me to bee this onely way, stop not the breathings of God in meane private Christians; the counsells of God flow there, when the greater persons sometimes

---

[1] *Woodhouse, op. cit.*, p. 81.

JOHN SALTMARSH

(for his glory) are left naked without a word of advice from him.
I found this desolating evil beginning in your meetings. Be Faithfull to your ingagements for Justice to the Kingdome: you have
many, and you promised speedy redresse of many things. Consider
and compare in the light of God impartially, how your first
principles, and publike promises and proceedings answer each
other.[1]

He accused the Army leaders of failure to carry out their promises,
writing in terms which show that the *Solemn Engagement* was in his
mind. The letter to Cromwell has, perhaps, a more personal note than
the other two, suggesting that his intimacy with Cromwell may have
been closer than with Fairfax:

Sir, it is the voice of the people, but that which sounds loudest
is the voice of choice and spirituall desiring Christians, that your
proceedings have much injustice, great delays, and the hearts of
many good people are turning from you, as you are in these wayes,
you are much accused of unfaithfulnesse to solemn Ingagements:
Sir, I was moved long since, you may remember, to tell you what
would follow in stopping the breathings of God in private
and poor Christians. . . . Sir, break off this sin by righteousness,
return to your communion with Christians, let not the wisdom of
the flesh intice you under the disguise of Christian prudence, for
that wisdom is not from above which is not pure and easie to be
intreated.[2]

The general implication of these letters is unmistakable: the Army
should return to the unity of the June days, when the high officers
listened to the voice of the rank and file, the "meane private Christians". With them is a short note from Saltmarsh's widow, saying:

These Letters were written, and sent according to the super-
scriptions, by the Author a little before his departure; they might
have continued in silence, as they have done ever since, but
providence hath otherwise disposed, through the desires of many
friends; and you have them printed according to the original
copies.[3]

Their publication, over eighteen months after his death, is one among
many indications of the continuing interest Saltmarsh aroused and the

---

[1] *Englands Friend*, p. 1.   [2] *Ibid.*, pp. 3–4.   [3] *Ibid.*, p. 6.

E

extent of his influence, and this interest was undoubtedly stimulated by the dramatic circumstances attending his death.

The Putney debate, with its apparent Leveller victory, was followed by the reassertion of the Grandees' authority at the Corkbush rendez-vous, the execution of Arnold, a number of arrests and the extinction, for the time at least, of Leveller hopes. Meanwhile Saltmarsh was at Ilford watching events attentively in spite of his increasingly poor health, and with something like despair. What followed is described in *Wonderfull Predictions Declared in a Message, as from the Lord, to Sir Thomas Fairfax and the Councell of his Army. By John Saltmarsh Preacher of the Gospell.* [1]

The account is introduced by a Preamble by "an eminent person at Headquarters":

> Whilst *Mr Saltmarsh* was in the Army he walked unblamable, kept himself to his text, in labouring to beat down sin: and exalt Christ. . . . He appeared at the Headquarters as one risen from the grave, his eyes almost fixed in his head, or rather as if he had come out of a Trance with feare and trembling to expresse his dreame . . . he did not come with bitter revilings and reproaches, but rather with wholesome admonitions to flye that danger which he apprehended was hanging over the Army.[2]

On Saturday, December 4th, 1647, he told his wife that he had been in a trance, had seen a vision and had received a command from God to declare to the Army what had been revealed to him. He set out immediately and in London informed "Sir H. M. a worthy Knight (a member of the House of Commons) his deare friend (and divers others)" about his mission.[3] He reached the Army headquarters at Windsor early on Monday morning. There:

> He met with Mr. A. (one of the Adjutators) who saluting him, he said, Mr. A. depart from the Tents, lest you perish with them, for the Lord hath revealed to me, that he is very angry with this Army because they have forsaken him.[4]

He then spoke to the Army Council saying that God had now for-saken them and would not prosper their cause because they had im-

---

[1] Other accounts, similar in essentials but in less detail, in Rushworth, *Historical Collections* and Wood, *Athenae Oxonienses.*
[2] *Wonderfull Predictions*, p. 1.
[3] *Ibid.*, p. 2. According to Wood, this was Sir Henry Mildmay.   [4] *Ibid.*, p. 3.

prisoned his Saints. To Fairfax, before whom he pointedly appeared
with his head covered, he declared that he had formerly so much doted
upon his person that he had offended God thereby, but that he had now
no command from God to honour him.

When he had parted with his Excellency he went to L. G. [the
Lieutenant-General, Cromwell] whom he met in the Hall, who
asked him how he did, Mr. Saltmarsh put not off his hat to him
neither; but told him that the Lord was angry with him, for
causing those Godly men to be imprisoned, sleighted, and abused,
for those Engagements which he had formerly owned, and the
persons such as he knew faithfull to the Cause of God: that the
Armies falling off from their former principles, it would be their
ruine, and destruction; and would raise up such fractions among
themselves, as would undo them. And much other discourse to
that purpose.

L. G. told him that some things were not so well as he could
wish: but that he wondered at those passages that fell from
him. . . .

On *Tuesday* morning December 7. Mr. Saltmarsh went (againe)
to L. G. telling him that he had one thing yet to deliver to him;
which God required of him which was this: That he would
(immediately) take effectual course for the inlargement of the
members of the Army, that were committed for not complying
with the Generall Councell: And that he do not prosecute against
those who have been so faithfull. . . .

Mr. *Saltmarsh* further declared that he was sorry to see such
obstinacy. And that although some tenderness was upon his
spirit (the day before) yet now he saw that his heart was hard-
ened. . . .

That Morning Mr. *Saltmarsh* declared to C. B. and others, the
same things again, which he had done before at the Generall
Councell. C. B. asked him, whether he would advise all honest
faithfull members to leave the Army, and lay down Armes, and
quite leave off the military practice. To whom he answered,
No; for, saith he, God hath yet a great work to be done: in
which he will make use of Members of the Army, to do great
things for the glory of his Name.[1]

This seems inconsistent with his earlier advice to Mr. A., but two

[1] *Ibid.*, pp. 4–6.

explanations may be suggested. Saltmarsh may have been advising
Mr. A. to leave the Council not the Army. Or, if, as is most probable,
Mr. A. was William Allen, Saltmarsh may have been shrewd enough
to read his character and to see him already on the way to becoming
Cromwell's Adjutant-General to the deadly peril of his soul. Perhaps
the most striking thing about the narrative is the deference with which
Saltmarsh was listened to by everyone from Fairfax downward.

His mission was now concluded:

> After he had taken leave of the Officers, telling them, That he
> had done his errand, and must leave them, never to see the Army
> more: he came that night to *London*. . . .
> On Friday Decemb. 10. he told his wife that he had now finished
> his course; and must go to his Father: and in the afternoon he
> complained that his head did ake, desiring to lie down upon his
> bed, where his wife took all possible care she could of him. But
> whatsoever he received for sustenance, he could not retain it; yet
> he rested well, all that night.
> On Saturday Decemb. 11. in the morning, he was taken speech-
> lesse. And in the afternoon, about four or five a clock, he dyed very
> peacably and quietly. And his soule is, no doubt, at rest with the
> Lord.[1]

Saltmarsh's journey to the Army from his death-bed undoubtedly
attracted widespread attention and may have had some weight in
impressing upon the Grandees the advisability of the reconciliation
that took place with the Levellers on December 21st, though, in fact,
the whole logic of events was forcing this decision upon them. Yet
they were more susceptible to this sort of moral influence than we
today can easily realise, and Saltmarsh's saintly character, his ability
as a preacher and his devoted service as an Army chaplain gave his
words a peculiar impressiveness.

After his death he became for a time a symbolic figure, a type of the
righteous preacher through whom God speaks. The regard in which he
was held is shown by the publication at the end of December of
Wonderfull Predictions, and, later still, of *Englands Friend*. It is shown no
less by the way Colonel John Jubbes referred to "pretious Mr. Saltmarsh", and by such publications, of little value in themselves, as
Twelve Strange Prophecies . . . with the Predictions of John Saltmarsh
(May 1648) and Samuel Gorton's *Saltmarsh Returned from the Dead.* . . .

[1] *Wonderfull Predictions*, p. 6.

Or the Resurrection of James the Apostle (1655).[1] The coupling of Saltmarsh and James, whose Epistle was such a favourite among the
radicals of the time, is significant, even though Saltmarsh does not
actually refer to it very often in his own writings.

Saltmarsh's reputation extended far beyond those who shared or
sympathised with his doctrines. Fuller speaks of his old antagonist with
something like affection, but perhaps the most remarkable tribute came
from Anthony Wood, who seldom had a good word for any Puritan
divine:

> He was a Chaplain in the Parliament Army under Sir Tho.
> Fairfax, where he always preached the bonds of love and peace,
> praying that he might be the cord to unite Christians in unity.
> He meddled not in the pulpit with Presbytery and Independency,
> but solely laboured to draw the soule from sin to Christ.[2]

On the other hand, the publication of John Brayne's *The Smoak of the
Temple cleared* in July 1648 suggests that even after his death his arguments still seemed to opponents to need a reply.

At first sight it might seem strange that this most unworldly, and,
in a sense, apolitical of preachers should be the one most in sympathy
with the Levellers, and, in fact, the only really prominent established
cleric to espouse their cause actively. Yet perhaps it was just these
qualities which gave him a view of the conflict that was both deeper
and broader than that of most of his colleagues. Though he early took
the side of Parliament with the enthusiasm which marked all his
activities, he had a strong streak of pacifism, like Walwyn, and like
Walwyn felt that the war could only be morally justified if it could be
seen as a struggle for a true Commonwealth, a new order of love,
freedom and justice. Without such objectives it could only seem to
him a sordid brawl, a fight for narrow material interests. And in the
Levellers he came to see a practical attempt to secure such ends. For
him as for them, freedom was indivisible and free grace had as a
logical consequence people's freedom.

---

[1] Gorton, whom Rutherford calls a disciple of R. Beccon and a denier of the Incarna-
tion, was a leader of the Familists in New England, where he had a stormy career and was
perhaps the only man whom Roger Williams found himself unable to tolerate.
[2] *Athenae Oxonienses*, II, p. 192.

4

The Ranters

The Ranters formed the extreme left wing of the sects which came into prominence during the English Revolution, both theologically and politically. Theologically these sects lay between the poles of orthodox Calvinism, with its emphasis on the power and justice of God as illustrated in the grand scheme of election and reprobation, with its insistence upon the reality of Hell in all its most literal horrors and upon the most verbal and dogmatic acceptance of the Scriptures, and of antinomianism with its emphasis upon God's mercy and universality, its rejection of the moral law, and with it, of Hell in any but the most figurative sense, and its replacement of the authority of the Scriptures by that of the inner light. The Ranters pushed all these beliefs to, and sometimes even a little beyond, their furthest logical conclusions, which, when acted upon, soon brought them into conflict with law and authority. The conviction that God existed in, and only in, material objects and men led them at once to a pantheistic mysticism and a crudely plebeian materialism, often incongruously combined in the same person. Their rejection of scripture literalism led sometimes to an entirely symbolic interpretation of the Bible and at others to a blunt and contemptuous rejection. Their belief that the moral law no longer had authority for the people of a new age enjoying the liberty of the sons of God led to a conviction that for them no act was sinful, a conviction that some hastened to put into practice.

The political views of the Ranters were the outcome of this theology. God existed in all things:

> I see that God is in all Creatures, Man and Beast, Fish and Fowle, and every green thing, from the highest Cedar to the Ivey on the wall; and that God is the life and being of them all, and that God doth really dwell, and if you will personally; if he may admit so low an expression in them all, and hath his Being no where else out of the Creatures.[1]

[1] *The Light and Dark sides of God*, Jacob Bauthumley, quoted from N. Cohn, *The Pursuit of the Millennium*, p. 336.

But man alone could be conscious of his Godhead and this gave to all men a new and equal dignity. The poorest beggars, even "rogues, thieves, whores, and cut purses" are "every whit as good" as the great ones of the earth.[1] The Ranters, and they alone at this date, spoke for and to the most wretched and submerged elements of the population, the slum dwellers of London and other cities, though to what extent their message reached these depths it is now hardly possible to say.

In Coppe and Clarkson, in Foster and Coppin there is, in different degrees and forms, a deep concern for the poor, a denunciation of the rich and a primitive biblical communism that is more menacing and urban than that of Winstanley and the Diggers. Like the Diggers, and unlike Lilburne and his followers, they were ready to accept the name of Leveller in its most radical implications, but with the difference that for them God himself was the great Leveller, who was to come shortly "to Levell with a witnesse, to Levell the Hills with the Valleyes, to lay the Mountaines low".[2] It is hardly accidental that the Ranters began to come into prominence soon after the Leveller defeat at Burford and would seem to have attracted a number of embittered and disappointed former Levellers. Where Levelling by sword and by spade had both failed what seemed called for was a Levelling by miracle, in which God himself would confound the mighty by means of the poorest, lowest and most despised of the earth.

Such, briefly, was the nature and setting of the Ranter Movement, which came into sudden prominence towards the end of 1649, reached its peak in the following year and thereafter seems to have survived only in fragments. The purpose of this essay is to give some account of Ranter ideology and then of the rise, fortunes and decline of the Movement.

I

The ideas of the Ranters were, of course, not new. They may be traced across Europe and across the centuries from the time, to go back no further, of Joachim of Fiore in the twelfth century, with his doctrine of the three ages, in the last of which, shortly to be expected, the sons of God would enjoy perfect spiritual liberty. To trace the course of these ideas in any detail would take me far beyond my present

---

[1] A. Coppe, *The Fiery Flying Roll*, II, p. 2.   [2] *Roll*, I, p. 4.

scope—a few salient points only may be noted.[1] A generation or so after Joachim, the Amurians in France added to his doctrine of the three ages a neoplatonic pantheism which declared that "all things are one because whatever is, is God". Later, in Germany, the loosely connected groups which are known under the general name of the Brethren of the Free Spirit turned this idea into a way of living. While Joachim had expected the age of the spirit in the near future, the Brethren claimed that it was already here and exercised themselves the promised liberty of the sons of God. Sharing the perfection of God all that they did must of necessity be good: sin for them ceased to have a meaning. In the sixteenth century these beliefs received a new social dimension from Thomas Munzer, the leader of the great peasant insurrection of 1525, and among the Anabaptists of Munster. Through various channels they began to reach England, especially the artisans of London and East Anglia. As early as 1646 Thomas Edwards was denouncing those who declared,

> That by Christs death, all the sins of all men in the world, Turks, Pagans, as well as Christians committed against the moral Law and the first covenant, are actually pardoned and forgiven, and this is the everlasting gospel.

and that

> there is a salvation that shall be revealed in the last time which was not known to the Apostles themselves.[2]

But it was among the Ranters above all that such beliefs and others related to them are found in the fullest and most uncompromising forms. What made them different in kind from their medieval predecessors was the fact that they were the heirs of a successful revolution which they still hoped to see carried to a victorious end. This is why Clarkson wrote on the title-page of *A Single Eye* that it was printed "in the Year that the Powers of Heaven and Earth Was, Is and Shall be, Shaken, yea Damned, till they be no more for Ever", and Coppe that his *Fiery Flying Roll* was a "word from the Lord to all the Great Ones of the Earth" printed "in the beginning of that notable day when the secrets of all hearts are laid open". Many Ranters and their hearers

[1] See Norman Cohn, *The Pursuit of the Millennium*, 1957, especially Chs. VII and VIII. Whatever may be argued against Prof. Cohn's conclusions, his book is a most valuable compilation of material on popular heresies of the Middle Ages. See also A. L. Morton, *The Everlasting Gospel*, 1958.

[2] *Gangraena*, I, pp. 23, 28.

had been in the forefront of the revolution and their sense of participation gave their message a force and universal applicability previously absent.

The central Ranter doctrine, from which all else logically flows, concerns the nature of God and man and their relationship. John Holland, whose book, *The Smoke of the Bottomlesse Pit*, though hostile, contains perhaps the clearest and most objective account of Ranter doctrine, writes:

> They maintain that God is essentially in every creature, and that there is as much of God in one creature, as in another, though he doth not manifest himself so much in one as in another: I saw this expression in a Book of theirs, that the essence of God was as much in the Ivie leaf as in the most glorious Angel. . . . They say there is no other God but what is in them, and also in the whole Creation, and that men ought to pray and seek to no other God but what was in them.
>
> The titles they give God are these: They call him The Being, the Fulnesse, the Great Motion, Reason, the Immensity.[1]

The passage already quoted from Bauthumley's *The Light and Dark side of God*, on which Holland obviously drew to a considerable extent confirms this. Holland also says that the Ranters believe, concerning man,

> That man cannot either know God, or beleeve in God, or pray to God, but it is God in man that knoweth himself, believes in himself and prayeth to himself . . . hence they alledge that man differeth in nothing from the bruit beast, but onely that God doth manifest himself more in man than he doth in the beast.[2]

Richard Coppin who, while denying that he was a Ranter, was very close to their ideas, influenced at least Coppe considerably, and gave Ranter theology a sophistication it often lacks, emphasised the unity and indivisibility of God under the diversity of his appearances:

> Thus this spiritual man, which thus knows all things, and judgeth all things, can be no less than God, who is all things; it can be no part or peece, as broken from God, for God cannot be divided or broken asunder . . . and where he is he is perfect; and in whom he is, he is perfect. . . .

[1] *Op cit.*, p. 2.   [2] *Op. cit.*, p. 5.

But some will say, Is God all in one and none in another? or is he all in every one?

I answer, that God is all in one and so in everyone; the same all which is in me, is in thee; the same God which dwels in one, dwels in another, even in all; and in the same fulnes as he is in one, he is in everyone: But there is this difference, everyone hath not a like manifestation of him; the first man hath the same fulness and the same God, but not the same manifestation of that fulness; the same God but not the same knowledge of God.[1]

Clarkson, looking back on his Ranter period after a gap of ten years, wrote:

For this I conceived, as I knew not what I was before I came in my being, so for ever after I should know nothing after this my being was dissolved; but even as a stream from the Ocean was distinct in itself while it was a stream, but when returned to the Ocean was therein swallowed and become one with the Ocean; so the spirit of man while in the body was distinct from God, but when Death came it returned to God, and so became one with God, yea God itself.[2]

This image of river and ocean was common to the Ranters and to their medieval ancestors. It can easily be seen how completely it excluded all orthodox beliefs in personal immortality and especially those in a material Heaven and Hell. For their theologians Hell was no more than a state of mind in which they existed before, as Bauthumley put it, "God . . . brought me into the glorious liberty of the Sons of God, whereas I was before in bondage to sin, law, an accusing Conscience which is Hell."

The identification of God with man and with the natural universe had two apparently opposite consequences. It might lead to a mysticism which found God everyone: equally it might lead to a virtual materialism which in practice dispensed with him altogether. If God existed everywhere in general he could be said to exist nowhere in particular. In fact, both these tendencies are found in the Ranters, sometimes oddly combined in the same person. This did not disturb them, since they loved to present truth as reconciliation of opposites. This comes out in the characteristic titles of a number of Ranter works—in Clarkson's *A Single Eye, All Light, No Darkness; or Light and Darkness One,* in

---

[1] *Divine Teachings,* pp. 8–9.   [2] *The Lost Sheep Found,* p. 28.

Bauthumley's *The Light and Dark sides of God,* or in Salmon's *Heights in Depths and Depths in Heights.* Coppe stresses the diversity and unity of God in his Preface to Coppin's *Divine Teachings*:

> Thus saith the Lord, I am Alpha and Omega, the beginning and the ending, the first and the last; and now the last is reaching the first, and the end the beginning.
>
> All things are returning to their Original, where all parables, dark sayings, all languages, and all hidden things, are known, unfolded and interpreted.

God is at once,

> A jealous God, and the Father of Mercies; in him (I say) the Lyon and the Lamb, Servant and Lord, Peace and War, Joy and Jealousie, Wrath and Love, etc. are reconciled and all complicated in Unity. . . .
>
> And all those seemingly cross Denominations do sincerely and secretly declare him to be all in all, and one in all, according to the Scriptures.

If there was a Light and Dark side of God, so there may be said to have been a Light and a Dark side of Ranterism. It brought together two very different traditions—that of pantheistic mysticism which we have traced briefly, and, almost equally ancient if not quite so venerable, that of rude scepticism and anticlericalism that was certainly no less marked in England than in other lands.[1] Anticlericalism arises inevitably out of the role of the Church as exploiter. Long before the Reformation the luxury and corruption of the higher clergy and the monastic orders were arousing hostility, and, if many parish priests were poor, their very poverty made it all the more a necessity for them to curse for their tithes, which involved them in a perpetual war with their parishioners. There were few demands more strenuously pressed by the radicals in the English Revolution than the abolition of tithe. Alongside this anticlericalism went a crude, and, to the orthodox, hideously blasphemous rejection of Christianity and of religion itself. Christopher Marlowe is alleged to have said, among many other things, that the first beginning of Religion was only to bring men in awe, that Christ was a bastard and deserved to die more than Barrabas and that of all the Apostles only Paul had wit and he was a timorous fellow for

---

[1] This tradition is discussed by C. Hill in "Plebeian Irreligion in 17th Century England" in *Studien über die Revolution* (Berlin, 1969).

bidding men to be subject to magistrates. Whether Marlowe actually said any of these things is unimportant. The fact that he was accused of saying them shows that such views were current at the time. It is possible to find many of the same accusations, sometimes in almost the same words, made against the Ranters.

Thus John Holland, whose accounts are relatively restrained, reports:

> I have heard some say, that if Christ was on earth now he would be ashamed of what he did before; I heard one of them say, it is a question whether Christ was born of a virgin, nay, saith another, he was a bastard sure enough. . . .
>
> I heard one of them say, the day of Judgement was begun already, and that the world had been made many thousand millions of years before we read of its creation, and that it shall continue many millions longer than we expect.[1]

Some of the more sensational accounts of Ranter utterances are considerably more startling, though they should not be entirely rejected on that account. One tells how, as some Ranters were at dinner,

> eating a piece of beef, one of them took it in his hand, tearing it asunder said to the other, *This is the flesh of Christ, take and eat.*
>
> The other took a cup of Ale and threw it into the chimney corner, saying, *There is the bloud of Christ.* And having some discourse of God it was proved that one of them said, *That he could go into the house of Office, and make a God every morning,* by easing his body.[2]

Perhaps even more revealing is the tale of a journeyman shoemaker in St. Martins who,

> when he heard any mention of God, he used to laugh, and in a disdainful manner say that he believed *money,* good *clothes,* good *meat and drink, tobacco and merry company* to be *Gods:* but he was little beholding to any of these: for his God allowed him but eight pence or ten pence a day, and that he made him work for; and he knew not of any thing that could be gotten from him by fair means, therefore he would have a saying to him, and force what he pleased. . . . But at another time in his Ranting mood . . . the Shoemaker replied to this effect (yet in broader language) *that*

---

[1] *Op. cit.*, pp. 3, 6.   [2] *Strange Newes from Newgate*, pp. 2–3.

the Divil was nothing but the backside of God, and that it was but a scarecrow.[1]

This Ranter who spoke of the Devil as the backside of God was only expressing in a homely way a common Ranter doctrine. To God, Clarkson wrote in *A Single Eye*, "Light and Darkness are both alike", so that to the truly enlightened, "Devil is God, Hell is Heaven, Sin Holiness, Damnation Salvation". Putting the same idea in a different way the Ranters were fond of arguing that God *made* the Devil, an argument that according to Fox the Quakers found it difficult to dispose of. He records that two Quakers in Cornwall were converted to Ranterism because they could not meet this point.[2] And in fact there was really very little room in Ranter theology for the Devil in any form that the seventeenth century could recognise. He became merely an aspect of the all-pervasive God. A Ranter told John Holland

that the Divil could do no evill at all, if God did not give him a power to do it, and therefore the Divil is not so much in the fault as men think he is . . . one of them said he hoped to see the poor Divil cleared of a great many slanders that had been cast upon him.[3]

And with the Devil went sin, as a logical consequence of Ranter views on the character of God and the relation of God and man. Since God is man and man God, they argued, and since God is altogether good, all that we do is done by him and is good also. As Clarkson put it:

Sin hath its conception only in the imagination; therefore, so long as the act was in God, or nakedly produced by God, it was as holy as God: but after there was an appearance in thee, or apprehension to thee, that this act is good, and that act is evil, thou hast with *Adam* eat of the fruit of the forbidden Tree, of the Tree of knowledge of good and evil, then thou hast tasted of that fruit, which is not in God, for saith the Text, *Out of the mouth of the most High proceedeth not evil, and good*: good but not evil; for God is good and good is God: therefore it was he made all things good: yea that which by you is imagined evil, he made good.[4]

For the Ranters, as for all antinomians, this created problems of

[1] *Arraignment and Tryall . . . of the Ranters.*   [2] *Journal*, 1952 edn., p. 443.
[3] *Op. cit.*, p. 6.   [4] *A Single Eye*, p. 8.

conduct which could be faced in different ways. For some, like Salt-marsh, it necessitated an even more scrupulous code of behaviour.[1] And Tobias Crisp's solution was similar:

> The grass and pasture is so sweet that he [God] hath put a beleever into, that though there be no bounds in such a soule, yet it will never goe out of this fat pasture to feed on a barren common.[2]

Some Ranters, like Bauthumley, were evidently not quite happy about the implications of this doctrine and attempted to find a com-promise position:

> And whereas some may say, then men may live as they list, because God is the same, and all tends to his glory, if we sin or if we do well:
>
> I answer them in the words of the Apostle: Men should not sin because grace abounds; but yet if they do sin, that shall turn to the prayse of God, as well as when they do wel. And so the wrath of man praises God as well as his love and meekness, and God is glorified in the one as well as the other. And however this may seem to countenance that God is the Authour of sin, and wills sin; yet to me it is plain, that there is nothing that hath a being but God, and sin being a nullity, God cannot be the Authour of it, and so falls not within the decree of God. . . .
>
> These things I write, not to countenance any unseemly act or evill in any man.[3]

Others, like Clarkson, were prepared to face the logic of their position, though even he found himself forced to draw the line at murder:

> yet the very motion of my heart was to all manner of theft, cheat, wrong or injury that privately could be acted, though in tongue I professed the contrary, not considering I brake the law in all points (murther excepted:) and the ground of this my judge-ment was, God made all things good, so nothing evil but as man judged it; for I apprehended there was no such thing as theft, cheat or a lie, but as man made it so.[4]

Yet antinomianism was not merely a claim upon personal liberty —it was also a positive weapon against the hypocritically righteous, the Calvinist elect who were trying to force a "reprobate" majority

---

[1] See this volume, p. 50.   [2] *Christ Alone Exalted*, Sermon II, p. 39.
[3] Cohn, *op. cit.*, pp. 338–9.   [4] *The Lost Sheep*, p. 27.

into conformity to the pattern of living which they thought proper. The great flowering of antinomianism at the end of the Civil War was in part due to a widespread feeling that a new age had brought a release from old bondages. It was also a reaction against the new bondage of Presbyterian discipline. The Church had always claimed to regulate conduct over a wide field, but the pre-revolution Church Courts, irritating as they often were, were still limited in their operations. The rich were too dangerous to be interfered with under ordinary circumstances, and the fact that the Courts were mainly interested in revenue from fines rather than with morality, meant that those who were too poor to be worth fining also tended to escape. The Presbyterians, who were genuinely concerned with enforcing moral standards, extended the inquisition further down the social scale. Overton wrote scathingly of their activities:

> Friends and Country-men, where are you now? . . . sure you must have the banes of Matrimony re-asked at the Conventicle of Gallants at White-hall, or at least you must thence have a Congregational Licence, (without offence be it spoken to true Churches) to lye with your wives, else how shall your wives be chast or the children Legitimate? they have now taken Cognizance over your wives and beds, whether will they next? Judgement is now come into the hands of the armed-fury Saints. My Masters have a care what you do, or how you look upon your wives, for the new Saints Millitant are paramount [to] all Laws, King, Parliament, husbands, wives, beds, &c.[1]

It was to the urban lower orders that the Ranters undoubtedly made their greatest appeal and there were elements in their theology which attracted many who did not fully understand it but who disliked being dragooned by the "armed-fury Saints". It was in the writings of Abiezer Coppe that the Ranter attitude to good and evil was most powerfully developed. His gospel, he wrote, is,

> To the Scribe folly; to the Pharisee blasphemy, who hath [ad unguem] at's fingers ends, he blasphemeth, is a friend of Publicans and Harlots, he is a glutton, and wine-bibber; and say we not well, that he hath a divil?
>   Which Pharisee, in man, is the mother of harlots, and being the worst whore, cries whore first: and the grand blasphemer,

---

[1] *The Picture of the Councel of State*, p. 31.

cries out blasphemy, blasphemy, which she is brimfull of. . . .

But the hour is coming, yea now is, That all his carnal outward, formal religion, (yea of Scripturaly cognizance, so far as its fleshly and formal) and all his fleshly holiness, zeal and devotion shall be, and is, set upon the same account as outward drunkeness, theft, murther and adultery. . . .

Yea the time is coming, that zealous, holy, devout, righteous, religious men shall (one way) dye, for their Holiness and Religion, as well as Thieves and Murtherers for their Theft and Murther. . . .

But once more, the time is coming, that Thieves and Murtherers shall scape, as well as the most zealous and formal professors; and men shall be put to death (or be murthered by men) no more for the one than for the other.[1]

In *A Fiery Flying Roll* he urges the pious to give up their formal religion and so-called Gospel Ordinances, under which lies nothing but "snarling, biting, besides covetousnesse, evil surmising". He explains his unconventional conduct:

Kisses are numbered among transgressors—base things—well! by base hellish swearing, and cursing . . . and by base impudent kisses . . . my plaguely holiness hath been confounded, and thrown into the lake of fire and brimstone.

And then again, by wanton kisses, kissing hath been confounded, and externall kisses have been made the fiery chariots, to mount me swiftly into the bosom of him whom my soul loves, [his excellent Majesty, the King of Glory].[2]

Coppe regarded swearing as having a positive value, saying that he would rather

heare a mighty Angell (in man) swearing a full-mouthed Oath . . . cursing and making others fall a swearing, than heare a zealous Presbyterian, Independent or spiritual Notionist pray, preach, or exercise.

Well! One hint more; there's swearing ignorantly, i'th darke, vainely, and there's swearing i'th light, gloriously.[3]

It is not surprising that he was accused of every kind of misconduct. One anonymous pamphlet wrote,

he is one that not long since assumed the pulpit in a noted Church

<hr />

[1] R. Coppin, *Divine Teachings*, Preface.　　[2] *Roll*, Pt. II, Ch. 5.　　[3] *Ibid.*, Pt. I, Ch. 2.

in London, and in a most wicked manner blasphemed and curst for an hour together, saying, a pox of God take all your prayers, preaching, reading, fasting &c.[1]

And another:

> their Ring-leader, *Copp* (when he was fitter to have gone to bed and slept, than to have spoken in a public place) bestowed an hours time in belching forth imprecations, curses, and other such like stuffe, as is not fit to be once named among Christians: and when he perceived that he should be called to answer . . . he took two of his she-Disciples, and went to the Citie of Coventrie, where it was soon dispersed abroad, that he commonly lay in bed with two women at a time.[2]

The truth of such stories, which come from pamphlets of the lowest, muck-raking type, must be doubtful, but it would hardly be surprising if many of the more ignorant Ranters, for whom the subtleties of their doctrines may have had little meaning, interpreted them literally as dispensations from all customary standards of conduct. Much of the evidence is, of course, hearsay and grossly prejudiced. We may well doubt the report that at a meeting in Shoemakers Alley their time was spent "in drunkenness, uncleanness, blasphemous words, filthy songs, and mixt dances of men and women stark naked",[3] though passages in Clarkson's *The Lost Sheep* do suggest that such accounts may not be entirely without foundation and that at times a ritual nudism may have been practised as a symbol of their liberation from the bondage of the moral law. Another story, of which differing versions exist, has suggestions of a ritual undertone:

> They taught, That they could neither see Evill, know Evill, nor Act Evill, and that whatsoever they did was Good and not Evill, there being no such thing as sin in the world: Whereupon Mistris E. B. striking fire at a Tinder-box lights up a candle, seeks under the Bed, Tables, and stooles, and at last comming to one of the men, she offers to unbutton his Cod-piece; who demanding of her what she sought for? She answereth, For sin: whereupon he blows out her candle, leads her to Bed, where in the sight of all the rest, they commit Fornication.[4]

[1] *The Ranters Ranting*, p. 5.   [2] *The Routing of the Ranters*, p. 3.
[3] *Ibid.*, p. 2.   [4] *The Ranters Last Sermon*, p. 3.

And it is certainly possible to find some justification in Ranter writers for the statement that,

> they affirms that God is so far from being offended at the crying sins of drunkenes, swearing, blaspheming, adultery etc that he is well pleased therewith, and that (O strange and horrid impiety) it is the only way of serving him aright.[1]

A similar situation may be seen in Ranter views about the Scriptures. Naturally, believing themselves directly instructed by the word of God within themselves, they tended to minimise the importance of the written, external word. As sons of the new age of spiritual liberty and knowledge they felt themselves in possession of a fuller truth never before enjoyed. So Coppin wrote:

> So you see, that the holy Apostles and Prophets which were before us, knew nothing of the Mystery of Salvation, but what was revealed to them by the Spirit, and what they knew was but in part, and not in full possession, for they had but the Spirit of Prophecy given them. . . . Here we see that these things which the Prophets, and Apostles, and the Angels themselves have desired to look into, yet could not find the depth of them, but God hath revealed them more fully to us in this later age by his Spirit.[2]

In so far as the Scriptures were a guide they could only be so when symbolically interpreted by the inner light. Their attitude was much like that of Blake, who, according to Crabb Robinson,

> Warmly declared that all he knew was in the Bible, but then he understands by the Bible the spiritual sense. For as to the natural sense, that Voltaire was commanded by God to expose.[3]

Both Salmon and Coppe speak of the History and the Mystery as conflicting forms of truth:

> He is not a Christian indeed, that doth by the power of Nature, believe what is Naturally and Historically reported of Christ in the Scripture, but he that by the power of the Spirit beleeves all this History to be verified in him in the *Mystery*; for there is a History and a *Mystery* of Christ; the History is *Christ for us*, the Mystery is *Christ in us*.[4]

---

[1] *The Ranters Religion*, p. 4.   [2] *Divine Teachings*, pp. 23–4.
[3] Quoted from Symonds, *William Blake*, 1907, p. 267.   [4] *Anti-Christ in Man*, p. 27.

From this it is no long step to total rejection. Holland shows us the process at work:

> The best they say of the Scripture is; That it is a tale, a History, a Letter, and a dead Letter, and more, the fleshly History; They call it a bundle of contradictions. I heard one sweare it was the archest piece of Witchcraft that ever was invented. Another said it was the greatest curse that ever came into the world, for, said he, the Scripture hath been the cause of all our misery . . . and there would never be any peace in the world, till all the Bibles in the world were burned.[1]

A poem quoted in *The Ranters Religion* declares,

> such lies
> Cannot be found in any Histories,
> Save in that booke of fallacies, they name
> The Bible, which from some fooles fancy came.[2]

And *The Ranters Last Sermon* includes among their beliefs

> That the sacred BIBLE was but a meer Romance, and contradictory to itself; only invented by the Witts of Former Ages, to keep People in subjection, and (as they term it) in Egyptian slavery; likewise, That there was as much truth in the History of Tom Thumb, or The Knight of the SUN, as there was in that Book.[3]

This rejection of scriptural literalism and the sometimes very forcible language in which it was expressed was one of the main reasons for the horror the Ranters aroused and the ferocity with which they were persecuted. It is also very much at variance with most modern conceptions of Puritanism, yet it is indeed only an exaggeration of a constant trend within Puritanism such as can be seen in Saltmarsh and Walwyn, and in Quakerism a little later. It is closely connected with the rejection of orthodox views of Heaven and Hell as actual places and any belief in a personal immortality. Again, as with Walwyn, if in a cruder way, we can see how mysticism does not, at this stage, conflict with the use of reason and common sense as criteria for commonly accepted beliefs.

The social ideas of the Ranters, like their theology, cannot be separated from Joachite beliefs in the new (usually the third) age of spiritual liberty. This they related directly to the progress of the Revolution in

[1] *Op. cit.*, p. 3.   [2] P. 8.   [3] P. 4.

England: for them the fall of monarchy was only the first stage in vast
changes by which the whole social order would be turned upside
down. Richard Coppin, in whom so many Ranter ideas found their
first expression, wrote:

> God now comes forth from the great and learned of the world,
> and exalts himself in the poor and ignorant; as *James* saith, *Hath
> not God chosen the poor of this world?* Not only poor, as touching the
> world; but poor and ignorant in the things of God.[1]

The conception of a series of progressive and higher revelations
found its most detailed political expression in J. Salmon. In *A Rout,
A Rout: or some part of the Armies Quarters Beaten Up, By the Day of the
Lord Stealing upon them*, which appeared on February 10th, 1649,
he first outlines in much the usual way the three successive manifesta-
tions of God. First in the Jewish Ceremonies, then in "the flesh of the
Son, as being a more true pattern", but now,

> God (having hitherto walked under this form) is now (and hath
> been these last dayes) come to rend this vail in pieces, to shake this
> form, to lay it waste, and cloath himself with another.

He then ingeniously applies a similar pattern to contemporary events:

> The power and life of the King, and in him the very soul of
> Monarchy sunk into the Parliament, and here it lost its name
> barely, but not its nature, its form but not its power, they making
> themselves as absolute and tyrannicall as ever the King in his
> reign, dignity and supremacy; yet the Lord ascended a little
> nearer himself, by taking of this form (the Parliament) and
> hereby made way for his after-design.
>
> We see in a short time, he layes aside that glorious shew and
> Idol (the Parliament) and cloaths himself with the Army: and
> thus both King, Monarchy and Parliament, fell into the hands
> and upon the swords of the Army. . . .
>
> Thus far we see God hath moved from party to party, and sits
> down at present in the Army: and here also God makes darkness
> his secret place, living under a poor, low, carnal form, and few
> can behold his beautifull presence under the power of the Sword.[2]

God's will is now, he proceeds to explain, that the Army too should
lay aside its power and cast itself upon him. He will give victory

[1] *Divine Teachings*, p. 3.   [2] *A Rout*, pp. 1–10.

out of suffering and humility and only then will the new age really commence:

> You are afraid to lay down your Swords, lest you should lose your Liberties; but the Lord will recompense this seven-fold into your bosme, he is coming to make you suffer a blessed Freedom, a glorious Liberty, a sufficient recompense for the loss of all outward glories. . . . When you are become children of the new birth, you shall be able to play upon the hole of the Aspe, and to dwell with the Cockatrice in his den, oppression and tyranny shall be destroyed before you.[1]

This note of extremely radical, and, if the phrase may be allowed, *active* pacifism is characteristic of Ranter political writing. It came partly from the nature of their theology, with its emphasis on the inevitable coming of the new age of liberty and brotherhood. God, they felt, was abroad in the land and they needed only to proclaim his purpose. But it came also from the precise political situation in which Ranterism developed. In February 1649 when *A Rout, A Rout* was written, Charles had just been beheaded and the Council of State was in effective control. In the two parts of *Englands New Chains Discovered* we can sense the feeling of the Levellers that they had been outwitted and betrayed. In a few weeks their leaders would be in prison: in a couple of months their last hope would be destroyed at Burford. Already a sense of defeat, that something had gone wrong with the expectation of a new England, was in the air. It was in this situation, with the left in retreat and the turning point of the Revolution already passed, that the Ranters became prominent. With ordinary political calculation failing, many people began to look for a miraculous deliverance.

For Abiezer Coppe and George Foster, God the Great Leveller was about to manifest his power:

> the mighty God of Jacob is at hand, and will come of a sudden when thou art not aware of, even that mighty Leveller, for to Levell and lay mountaines and hils low, even you that are greater and richer than your fellow-creatures, even as low as may be, and so will make all equal with the plaines.

So Foster wrote in *The Sounding of the Last Trumpet*, "declaring the

[1] *Ibid.*, p. 11.

universall overturning and rooting up of all Earthly Powers in England".

The combination of pacifism with Leveller principles is especially marked in Coppe, who, as he insisted,

> never drew sword, or shed one drop of any mans blood . . . all things are reconciled to me, the eternall God (IN HIM) yet sword levelling, or digging levelling, are neither of them his principles.
>
> And now thus saith the Lord:
>
> Though you can as little endure the word LEVELLING as could the late slaine or dead *Charles* (your forerunner who is gone before you—) and had as live heare the Devil named as heare of the Levellers (Men-Levellers) which is, and who (indeed) are but the shadowes of the most terrible, yet great and glorious good things to come.
>
> Behold, behold, behold, I the eternall God the Lord of Hosts, who am that mighty Leveller am coming (yea even at the doores) to Levell in good earnest, to Levell to some purpose, to Levell with a witnesse, to Levell the Hills with the Valleyes, and to lay the Mountaines low. . . .
>
> *For lo I come (saith the Lord) with a vengeance, to levell also your Honour, Riches etc. to staine the pride of all your Glory, and to bring into contempt all the Honourables (both persons and things) upon the earth, Isa. 23. 9.*
>
> For this Honour, Nobility, Gentility, Propriety, Superfluity etc hath (without contradiction) been the Father of hellish horrid pride, arrogance, haughtinesse, loftinesse, murder, malice, of all manner of wickedness and impiety, yea, the cause of all the blood that ever hath been shed, from the blood of the righteous *Abell*, to the blood of the last Levellers that were shot to death. *And now as I live (saith the Lord) I am come to make inquisition for blood.* . . .
>
> And maugre the subtilty, and sedulity, the craft and cruelty of hell and earth: this Levelling shall up;
>
> Not by sword; we (holily) scorne to fight for anything; we had as live be dead drunk every day of the weeke, and lye with whores i'th market place; and account these as good actions as taking the poor abused, enslaved ploughmans money from him . . . we had rather starve, I say, then take away his money from him, for killing of men.[1]

---

[1] *Roll*, Pt. I, pp. 1–5.

Levelling as Coppe and Foster understood it involved a far greater social upheaval than the political changes advocated by Lilburne and his associates, or Winstanley's quite limited proposals for joint cultivation on the commons and waste land. It was linked with a passionate denunciation of the rich and with a primitive type of Communism which looked back both to the early Apostolic Church and to the teachings of John Ball.

The rich, Foster declared, grudge the poor even a piece of bread, but "all things are the Lords" and he is coming shortly to bring down their pride, who "because of your riches have thought yourselves better than others; and must have your fellow-creatures in bondage to you, and they must serve you, as work for you, and moyle and toyle for you, and stand cap in hand to you, and must not displease you, no by no meanes".[1] Coppe, who like Foster drew much of his imagery from the Epistle of St. James, addressed himself to the poorest and most depressed strata of society, at a time when the slum population of London was suffering terrible hardships as a result of the wartime dislocation of trade and industry. In an extraordinary passage, whose meaning is clear if its grammar is sometimes confused, he declares that God, in whose name he writes, will come upon the rich like a highwayman, saying:

> Thou hast many baggs of money, and behold I [the Lord] come as a thief in the night, with my sword drawn in my hand, and like a thief as I am—I say deliver your purse, deliver sirrah! deliver or I'l cut thy throat!
>
> I say (once more) deliver, deliver my money which thou hast to him, and to poor creeples, lazars, yea to rogues, thieves, whores, and cut purses, who are flesh of thy flesh, and every whit as good as thy self in mine eye, who are ready to starve in plaguy Gaols, and nasty dungeons. . . .
>
> The plague of God is in your purses, barns, houses, horses, murrain will take your hogs (O ye fat swine of the earth) who shall shortly go to the knife, and be hung up i'th roof, except— blasting, mill-dew, locusts, caterpillars, yea, fire your houses and goods, take your corn and fruit, the moth your garments, and the rot your sheep, did you not see my hand, this last year, stretched out?
>
> You did not see.

[1] *Last Trumpet*, p. 2.

My hand is stretched out still.

Your gold and silver, though you can't see it, is cankered, the rust of them is a witnesse against you, and suddainly, suddainly, suddainly, because of the Eternal God, myself, its the dreadful day of Judgement, saith the Lord, shall eat your flesh as it were fire James 5.1–7.

The rust of your silver, I say, shall eat your flesh as it were fire.[1]

Coppe felt himself one with God, to the extent that in his writing it is sometimes impossible to say whether his "I" is God or Abiezer Coppe. But no less he felt that he was one with all men, and especially with the poor and miserable. This comes out most dramatically in the story of the beggar which occupies Chapter III of the second part of the *Roll*. On September 30th, he writes, he met a "most strange deformed man". Coppe was filled with love and pity for him:

> Whereupon the strange woman who flattereth with her lips, and is subtill of heart, said within me, Its a poor wretch, give him two-pence.

The woman, whom elseshere he calls the "wel-favoured harlot" and the "holy Scripturian Whore" is the formal righteousness which exalts prayer, gospel ordinances and conventional morality at the expense of mercy and justice. He rejects her temptations, but she returns to the attack, saying, "Its a poor wretch give him 6d. and that's enough for a Squire or Knight to give to one poor body." He almost falls, but in the end,

> the plague of God fell upon my pocket, and the rust of my silver rose up in judgement against me, and consumed my flesh as with fire . . . and the 5 of *James* thundered such an alarm in mine ears, that I was fain to cast all I had into the hands of him, whose visage was more marr'd than any mans that I ever saw.
>
> This is a true story, most true in history.
>
> Its true also in the mystery.

He put off his hat to the beggar, bowed seven times, and, finally, "rode back once more to the poor wretch, saying, because I am a King, I have done this, but you need not tell any one".

Coppe's conduct can be paralleled by that recorded by Professor N. Cohn of a certain Loy Pruystinck a century earlier in Antwerp. Pruystinck demanded that his richer disciples should publicly embrace the thieves, prostitutes and beggars who formed the bulk of his following. He is said also to have symbolised this uniting of opposites by himself dressing in rags which were sewn with jewels.

Professor Cohn speaks of Pruystinck and similar religious leaders as regarding themselves as "an élite of amoral supermen", who accepted no obligations to ordinary mortals and whose "communism" was no more than an arrogation of their own right to dominate and exploit the unenlightened. Whatever may have been the truth in these other cases it must be said that in the writings of Coppe and other Ranters the main emphasis is not on such privilege but on giving and sharing, on the human dignity of the poor and despised, and on the imminence of a day of liberty, brotherhood and social justice.

Coppe was, no doubt, unbalanced, and by the extravagance both of his conduct and language deprived himself of the chance of a hearing, yet there is a genuine nobility in much of his writing, not least in the passages where he states his belief in the need for common ownership:

> I know there's no Communion to the Communion of Saints, to the inward Communion, to communion with the spirits of just men made perfect, with God the Judge of all.
> No other Communion of Saints do I know.
> And this is Blood-life-spirit-communion.
> But another Communion also do I know, which is water, and but water, which I will not be without; my spirit dwells with God, the Judge of all, dwells in him, sups with him, in him, feeds on him, with him, in him. My humanity shall dwell with, sup with, eat with humanity; and why not [for a need] with Publicans and Harlots? why should I turn away mine eyes from mine own flesh? Why should I not break my bread to the hungry, whoever they be? . . .
> Howl, howl, ye nobles, howl honourable, howl ye rich men for the miseries that are coming upon you.
> For our parts we that hear the Apostle preach will also have all things in common; neither will we call anything that we have our own. . . . Wee'l eat your bread together in singleness of heart, wee'l break bread from house to house.[1]

This aspect of Ranter doctrine is strongest in Coppe, though it can be seen also in Foster, and, in a perhaps more intellectualised way, in

[1] *Roll*, Pt. II, pp. 18–19.

Clarkson. But there is evidence that it was widespread. *The Ranters Last Sermon*, for example, states

> They taught, That it was quite contrary to the end of Creation, to Appropriate anything to any Man or Woman; but that there ought to be a Community of all things.[1]

There is plenty of evidence, too, for the social and, indeed, convivial nature of their gatherings. They ate together and drank wine, smoked tobacco (still regarded by most as an act of doubtful morality), danced and sang. Hostile pamphlets print three alleged Ranter hymns—one a drinking song, one advocating sexual liberty and a third ridiculing orthodox religion. It is tempting in this connection to recall the importance of singing among the American I.W.W., who were also fond of irreverant parodies of hymns. Under the Commonwealth the old laws of settlement had broken down and one of the very real if temporary freedoms the Revolution had brought was the freedom to move about in search of work. It may well be that among these migratory workers, unattached and prepared to break with tradition, the Ranters found many of their supporters. This would at least help to explain the rapidity with which they seem to have spread to all parts of the country.

Charges of sexual promiscuity as a matter of principle were frequently made against them. Thus, Holland says:

> They say that for one man to be tied to one woman, or one woman to be tied to one man, is a fruit of the curse; but they say, we are freed from the curse; therefore it is our liberty to make use of whom we please.[2]

No doubt there was much malice and exaggeration in such charges, but they are not really at variance with declared Ranter principles. Edward Hide Jun., a hostile but not on the whole unfair critic, explains that they believe "that all the women in the world are but one mans wife in unity and all the men in the world are but one womans husband in unity; so that one man may lie with all the women in the world in unity, and one woman may lie with all men in the world, for they are all her husband in unity".[3]

They seem to have used the expression "fellow creature" as the usual mode of address among themselves, thus emphasising not only their social equality but their position in a chain that stretched from

---

[1] P. 4.   [2] *Op. cit.*, p. 4.   [3] *A Wonder*, p. 42.

God to the lowest form of life. They were fond, also, of coarse jests that emphasised the animal nature of man. Samuel Shepherd calls them "The Joviall Crew", while Ephraim Pagitt, having declared that, "the *Ranter* is an unclean beast, much of the same make with our *Quakers* . . . only the *Ranter* is less sowre, professes what he is, and as he has neither Religion nor honesty, so he pretends to none", nevertheless adds with what looks like a measure of unwilling admiration:

> They are the merriest of all devils, for extempore lascivious Songs, not extempore Prayer, but as absurd and nonsensicall, for healths, musick, downright baudry and dancing, the two last of which commonly proceed and follow the conjunction of the fellow creatures, which is not done in corners.[1]

Such comparisons between Ranters and Quakers were not uncommon at this time, in spite of the strong hostility between the two sects. Baxter wrote:

> But the horrid Villainies of this Sect did not only speedily Extinguish it, but also did as much as ever anything did, to disgrace all *Sectaries*, and to restore the Credit of the Ministry and the sober unanimous Christians: So that the Devil and the Jesuits quickly found this way served not their turn, and therefore they suddenly took another.
>
> And that was the fourth Sect, the *Quakers*; who were but the Ranters turned from horrid Prophaness and Blasphemy, to a Life of extreme Austerity on the other side. Their Doctrines were mostly the same with the Ranters: they make the Light which every man hath within him to be his sufficient Rule, and consequently the Scriptures and Ministry are set light by.[2]

It seems reasonable to conclude that these festive Ranter meetings were not merely an expression of fellowship and rough good spirits, though these were present and important. They had also a ritual character. The joint meal was a sharing of bread, perhaps even a kind of sacrament, and the stories in which the Ranters on such occasions are said to have parodied the Christian sacraments in what seemed to their contemporaries a blasphemous manner are in fact evidence for this. The rank and file Ranter was not a poet or mystic like Coppe or Salmon, and what began as poetry could in their hands become clowning, just as the metaphysical subtleties of Ranter doctrine could

[1] *Heresiography*, 6th edn., pp. 259–61.   [2] *Reliquiae Baxterianae*, p. 77.

coarsen into nonsense and paradox. If there was such a thing as the typical or average Ranter he was probably something very like Robert Wilkinson of Leicester as he is presented to us by the Quaker Richard Farnworth:

> He said he was both God and Devil, and he said there was no God but him and no Devil but him, and he said whom he blest was blest, and whom he curst was curst, and he said he was a serpent, and so he is, and he said the Apostles were lyers and deceivers, and I gave him a Bible to prove that, and he said the Bible was a pack of lyes, and there was neither heaven nor hell but here, and yet he was both in heaven and hell, and he had as lieve be in hell as in heaven, and he said he was a serpent and a whoremaster, and before he said he was born of God, and could not comit sin.[1]

II

It would probably be incorrect to speak of the Ranters as a church, or even as a sect. There is no evidence for any formal organisation or generally received body of doctrine. Gilbert Rouleston, who claimed to be a converted Ranter, speaks of seven different sorts of Ranters, to whom he gives such fancy names as Shelomethites, Clements, Athians (whose beliefs as he describes them appear to be those of the Mortalists) and Nicholantenes. For such elaborate sub-divisions there is no evidence elsewhere, but they may perhaps represent some differing trends within a loose grouping of people with broadly similar views. The term Ranter seems to have been used in a rough and ready way to describe not only people like Coppe and Salmon but a rather different type of group like that around John Robins in London or William Franklin and Mary Gadbury in Winchester.

While the Ranters properly so-called identified themselves with God only in the sense that all men and even all living things shared in the divine nature, Robins and Franklin claimed to be Gods, or to be inspired by God, in a special and personal sense. Each formed a small, self-contained group around its own prophet or messiah, with a chosen woman disciple who filled the role of Mary—in the case of the Robins group at least she claimed that a child she was about to bear would be a new Christ. These groups, in their nature exclusive, do

---

[1] *Ranters Principles*, p. 19.

not seem to have had any connection either with one another or with the Ranters as a whole, and though some of their teachings were similar, it is not necessary to discuss them here in any detail.

If, however, we cannot speak of a Ranter sect, it is possible to speak of a Ranter Movement, and this Movement has a history which can be traced, at least in broad outline. Many uncertainties must remain because of the nature of the evidence—the writings of the Ranters themselves are, as has been shown, primarily concerned with doctrine, and any historical details they may contain are incidental. On the other hand the literature about the Ranters, though quite extensive, is uniformly hostile and frequently nothing but the lowest type of gutter journalism. Its statements have always to be weighed against one's estimate of what is credible as well as against what the Ranters say about themselves. And this again must be considered in relation to the fact that they were constantly persecuted and were forced to express themselves with great caution.

Yet, when allowance has been made for all this, it is possible to follow the careers of the leading figures as well as the rise and decline of the Movement as a whole. Of these leaders, Clarkson is dealt with elsewhere in this volume. The fate of Coppe, who is perhaps the most central as well as the most spectacular figure, can best be followed in connection with the general history of Ranterism. The other two, whose writings have survived at least in part, can conveniently be discussed separately and more briefly.

Most of what we know about Joseph Salmon we learn from his recantation *Heights in Depths*, which is, like many such books of its kind and time, a form of spiritual autobiography. He was, apparently, when he wrote *Anti-Christ in Man* (December 1647) and *A Rout, A Rout* (February 1649), an officer in the Army. Something has already been said about these—the first is antinomian, but not perhaps specifically Ranter, the second, which as we have seen, applied Joachite principles to the contemporary political situation, may perhaps be regarded as his farewell to the Army. It must have been soon after this that he wrote *Divinity Anatomized*, a book which has disappeared but which is mentioned in *Heights in Depths* as the main place in which his Ranter views had been "vented", As a result of this, and probably of his preaching, he was arrested and imprisoned at Coventry, where Fox found him, together with other Ranters, towards the end of the year. Fox has described his argument with these Ranters, "who said they were God".

I asked them, if they knew whether it would rain tomorrow. They said they could not tell. I told them God could tell. Again, I asked them if they thought they would be always in that condition, or should change, and they answered they could not tell. Then said I unto them, "God can tell and God doth not change. You say you are God and yet you cannot tell whether you shall change or no." So they were confounded and quite brought down for that time. Then . . . I perceived they were Ranters, and I had met with none before.[1]

Fox says that "not long after this" Salmon put forth a paper or book of recantation, upon which he was set at liberty. However, it seems clear from *Heights in Depths* that Salmon was released shortly before its publication in August 1651, and upon promise of writing it. He says that while he was in prison he had time to reflect, had been helped by conversations with a Major Black and that finally Colonel Purefoy arrived in Coventry with an order from the Council for his release. He then proceeds to account for his ideas and their develop-ment. He had found the world a chaos, in which he had sought for some assurance:

> Behold the Lord maketh the earth empty and voyd; he layeth it waste: it reels to and fro like a drunkard: all its Foundations are out of course.[2]

He forsook his home and kindred to become successively Presbyterian, Independent and Baptist, and this, "in the hottest time of persecution: I was made one eminent both in holding forth this way to the world and also in an open suffering for the same".[3] He is thought to have preached in and round Rochester and later he served in the Army.

But all this gave him no comfort and he heard "a voice from the throne of the heavenly Almightiness: arise and depart for this is not your rest". This was the beginning of a deep inner crisis that seems to have been a characteristic stage in the development of most of the Ranter prophets. First came a period of exaltation:

> I saw heaven opened unto me and the new Jerusalem (in its divine brightness and corruscant beauty) greeting my Soule by its humble and gentle discensions. . . . I appeared to my selfe as one confounded into the abyss of eternitie, nonentitized into the

[1] *Journal*, p. 47.   [2] *Heights in Depths*, pp. 3–4.   [3] *Ibid.*, p. 11.

being of beings; my Soule split, and emptied into the fountaine and ocean of divine fulness: expired into the aspires of pure life.[1]

This, however, was only temporary, and soon he "turned from a King to become a Beast".

> I was now sent into a strange land, and made to eat unclean things in *Assyria*; walked in unknown paths, and became a mad man, a fool among men. . . .
>
> Being then clouded from the presence of the Lord, I was violently posted through most dark paths, where I ever and anon stumbled and fell into the snare of open error and profaneness, led and hurried (by what power let the wise judge) in a principle of mad zeal; to tear and rend the very appearances of God, which I had formerly cherished in my brest.[2]

This is a characteristic account, but it must be remembered that it was written after a long and severe imprisonment, and, assuming that his recantation was sincere, as it has every appearance of being, after he had come to believe that the views he had once held were erroneous. As he wrote he felt a new peace in a quietism that had perhaps been partly foreshadowed by the pacifism of *A Rout, A Rout*:

> I am now at rest in the silent deeps of eternity, sunk into the abysse of silence, and (having shot this perilous gulf) I am safely arrived into the bosome of love; the land of rest. . . .
>
> I see there is nought that can satisfie under the Sun. . . .
>
> My great desire (and that wherein I most delight) is to see and say nothing.[3]

The last pages of his recantation are devoted to:

> A Sincere Abdication of certain Tenets, either formerly vented by, or now charged upon the Author.
>
> I am daily accused as one that holds these horrid opinions. *Viz* That there is no God; no Devil; no Heaven; no Hell; as one that denies the Scripture, and the blessed Trinity of the God-head; that saith there is no Sin; or otherwise that God is the author of Sin; these (among others of less consequence) are chiefly alledged against me.

Salmon denied having held these views, or, in some cases, admitted that

---

[1] *Ibid.*, p. 15.   [2] *Ibid.*, pp. 18, 23.   [3] *Ibid.*, p. 28.

he had been in error. Even so, his explanation of his doctrines was still far from orthodox: he wrote, for example:

> That God is that pure and perfect being in whom we all are, move and live; that secret blood, breath and life, that silently courseth through the hidden veins and close arteries of the whole creation.[1]

Salmon is obviously trying here to express his beliefs in a way that would not give offence, but what is said is really not at all inconsistent with the usual Ranter idea of God.

"Silence", Salmon wrote, "hath taken hold of my spirit", and in fact he seems to have taken no further part in public affairs.

The story of Jacob Bauthumley or Bottomley was similar. He was a militantly Puritan cobbler in Leicester, where, we learn, "At one Bury's house 2 ministers Mr. Higginson and Mr. Burdin stood by while Bottomley the shoemaker of Leicester prayed." He was also in trouble for causing a disturbance in All Saints Church.[2] Like Salmon he served in the Army and there wrote *The Light and Dark Sides of God*, for which he was punished by being burned through the tongue. The town authorities of Leicester were sufficiently alarmed by this book to send it to London for advice, since it seemed to them to be "of a very dangerous consequence and lets open a very wide dore to Atheisme and profanes".[3] He too hints at a spiritual struggle, though in much less detail than Salmon or Coppe:

> I was continually suffering the torment of Hell, and tossed up and down, being condemned of my self. . . . And this is that I found til God appeared spiritually, and shewed me that he was all glory and happiness himself, and that flesh was nothing . . . God . . . brought me into the glorious liberty of the Sons of God, whereas I was before in bondage to sin, law, an accusing Conscience which is Hell.[4]

He continued as an active Ranter in Leicester, to which he returned after his Army service, and Fox met him at nearby Swannington in 1655:

> And the next day Jacob Bottomley came from Leicester, a great Ranter, but the Lord's power stopped him and came over them all. . . .

---

[1] *Heights in Depths*, pp. 37-8.
[2] Joan Simon, *The Two John Angels*. Trs. Leics. Arch. and Hist. Soc., XXXXI, p. 39.
[3] Simon, *op. cit.*, p. 48.   [4] Cohn, *op. cit.*, p. 339.

And we sent to the Ranters to come forth and try their God, and there came abundance who were rude, as aforesaid, and sung and whistled and danced, but the Lord's power so confounded them that many of them came to be convinced.[1]

By about 1660, however, he appears to have become sufficiently respectable to be appointed library keeper and sergeant-at-mace in Leicester.[2]

One other name should be mentioned here, that of Richard Coppin. Coppin denied being a Ranter, indeed, he claimed that the Ranters, like other sects, had "persecuted" him in some unspecified way, but his *Divine Teachings*, published in September 1649, was a quarry in which all Ranters seem to have mined and few of their books are without ideas and phrases taken from it. Its publication coincided roughly with the opening of the main period of Ranter activity and prominence.

Coppin, unlike most of the Ranters, was a man of considerable theological training and sophistication. Originally an Episcopalian, he reached his final positions in the customary way, being in turn Presbyterian, Independent and Anabaptist. In the later 1640s he was preaching around Rochester, evidently with some effect, since Wood says that after 1644 William Sandbrooke "was appointed by the Presbyterian Party one of the three Lecturers in the Cathedral there, purposely to preach down the Blasphemies and Heresies of *Rich Coppin* and his besotted and begotted followers".[3] About 1648 he had a crisis of faith of which *Divine Teachings* was the outcome. From that date he became an itinerant preacher and was constantly in trouble for his views, being placed on trial twice at Worcester, twice at Oxford and once at Gloucester. The indictment at Worcester, as he gives it, shows how nearly his views coincided with those of the Ranters:

> First, that I should say, That they were evil Angels (meaning the Ministers who preach the Gospel of Christ) that told people of damnation, and that such ought not to be heard or believed.
> Secondly, That all men whatsoever should be saved.
> Thirdly, That those that heard me were all in heaven, and in glory.
> Fourthly, That God was as much in me as in Christ. . . .
> Sixthly, That there was no general Day of Judgement.

[1] *Journal*, pp. 182–3.　　[2] Information from Mr. G. A. Chinnery.
[3] *Athenae Oxonienses* II, p. 149.

Seventhly, That there was no heaven but in man.

Eighthly, That he that thought there was a hell, to him there was a hell, but he thought there was no hell, to him there was no hell.[1]

On the whole he escaped lightly, though in December 1655 he was imprisoned for six months at Maidstone. The impression given in *Truths Testimony* is that, while juries were hostile, judges were sympathetic and inclined to stretch the law as far as possible in his favour. He does not deny holding the beliefs with which he was charged.

There can be no doubt that the autumn of 1649, when *Divine Teachings* appeared, marked a coming together in Ranterism of a number of former Levellers and others of the politically defeated left wing of the commonwealth forces. Giles Calvert, who published it, had issued the final version of *An Agreement of the People*, and it is worth noting that immediately it appeared *Divine Teachings* was commended in the Leveller journal *The Moderate*, as "an excellent book". William Larner, the usual Leveller printer, issued both Bauthumley's *The Light and Dark Sides of God* and works by Clarkson. It is clear that from the way Clarkson describes his introduction to the Ranters by Calvert that the latter, if not actually a Ranter (and he seems always to have been cautious of identifying himself too completely with anyone) at least enjoyed their full confidence. Clarkson found among the Ranters no less a Leveller than Major William Rainborough, brother of the recently murdered Thomas.[2] A final pointer in the same direction is the fact that Clarkson, Rainborough and others gathered at the house of a Mr. Walis or Waddis of Ilford, where John Saltmarsh had lived during the last month of his life. Saltmarsh and the Ranters differed in many ways, but they were all branches upon the great tree of Free Grace, and Saltmarsh would certainly have sympathised with the Ranter conception of God as the Great Leveller.

Divine Teachings came out with a long Preface by Abiezer Coppe, his first public appearance of which we have actual knowledge, though Anthony Wood speaks of a book called *John the Divines Divinity* by J.F., to which he also wrote a Preface and which appeared on January 13th, 1648. This does seem to have survived. Coppe was born in

---

[1] *Truths Testiminony*, p. 31.

[2] It may not be without significance that Major Rainborough had been frustrated in all his efforts to obtain justice upon his brother's murderers. *Second Part of Englands New-Chaines*, p. 11.

Warwickshire and in 1636 went to Oxford, first to All Souls and then to Merton. Here, according to Wood,

> all lectures or examples could not reform, or make, him live like a Christian: And it was then notoriously known that he would several times entertain for one night or more a wanton huswife in his Chamber . . . in the little or old quadrangle, to whom carrying several times meat, at the hour of refection, he would make answer, when being asked by the way, what he would do with it, that *it was a bit for his cat.*

Wood is hardly an unbiassed witness, but since Merton was his own college and he matriculated only eleven years after Coppe, this anecdote may well be based on first-hand information. This is more than can be said of his further statement that after he had turned Ranter,

> 'twas usual with him to preach stark-naked many blasphemies and unheard of villanies in the day-time, and in the night to be drunk and lye with a wench that had been also his hearer stark naked.[1]

Such accusations are typical of many that were made against him and which he repudiated with what seems genuine indignation. Pamphlets written against the Ranters, he writes,

> are scandalous and bespattered with Lyes and Forgeries, in setting me in front of such actions which I never did, which my soul abhors; such things which mine eyes never beheld, such words which my tongue never spake, and mine ears never heard.
>
> All like that false aspersion—Viz, that I was accompanied to Coventry with two she-disciples, and that I lay there with two women at once. Which two she-disciples were Captain Blak, and other Souldiers, who have hurried me from Gaol to Gaol; where I sing Hallelujahs to the Righteous Judge, and lie in his bosome, who is everlasting loving kindness.[2]

His development followed a pattern with which we are by now familiar. After leaving Oxford he turned Presbyterian, then Anabaptist, preaching widely in Warwickshire. He was in prison in Coventry in 1646. Finally after a prolonged spiritual convulsion he became a Ranter. This crisis he has described more vividly and in greater detail than any other Ranter writer:

[1] *Op. cit.*, p. 367.   [2] *A Remonstrance . . . of Abiezer Coppe*, p. 6.

First, all my strength, my forces were utterly routed, my house I
dwelt in fired; my father and mother forsook me, the wife of my
bosome loathed me, mine old name was rotted, perished; and I
was utterly plagued, consumed, damned, rammed and sunk into
nothing, into the bowels of the still Eternity (my mothers wombe)
out of which I came naked, and whereto I returned again naked.
And lying a while there, rapt up in silence, at length (the bodys
outward forme being awake all this while) I heard with my outward eare (to my apprehension) a most terrible thunder-clap,
and after that a second. And upon the second thunder-clap, which
was exceeding terrible, I saw a great body of light, like the light
of the Sun, and red as fire, in the forme of a drum (as it were),
whereupon with exceeding trembling and amazement on the
flesh, and with joy unspeakable in the Spirit, I clapt my hands,
and cryed out, *Amen, Halelujah, Halelujah, Amen.* And so lay
trembling, sweating and smoking (for the space of half an houre)
at length with a loud voice (I inwardly) cryed out, Lord what wilt
thou do with me; my most excellent majesty and eternall glory
(in me) answered and sayd, Fear not. I will take thee up into my
everlasting Kingdom. But thou shalt (first) drink a bitter cup, a
bitter cup, a bitter cup; whereupon (being filled with exceeding
amazement) I was throwne into the belly of hell (and take what
you can of it in these expressions, though the matter is beyond
expression) I was among all the Devils in hell, even in their most
hideous crew.

And under all this terrour and amazement, there was a little
spark of transcendent, unspeakable glory, which survived, and
sustained itself, triumphing, exulting and exalting itself above all
the Fiends.[1]

This conversion seems to have taken place in Warwickshire about the
middle of 1649 and to have included a command, "Go up to *London*,
to *London*, that great City". There Coppe, who emphasised the social
aspect of his teaching more, perhaps, than any other Ranter, began in
the autumn of that year an appeal to the London poor, in a series of
sermons in the streets in which the rich were denounced. The substance
of these outbursts was probably incorporated in *A Fiery Flying Roll*,
where he speaks of himself as,

charging so many Coaches, so many hundreds of men and women

[1] *Roll,* I, Preface.

of the greater rank, in the open streets, with my hand stretched
out, my hat cock't up, staring on them as if I would look thorough
them, gnashing with my teeth at some of them, and day and night
with a huge loud voice proclaiming the day of the Lord throughout London and Southwark.[1]

No doubt this is the episode referred to by Clarkson in *The Lost
Sheep*, which states that shortly before his own conversion Coppe "had
lately appeared in a most dreadful manner". Coppe's campaign in the
streets, soon to be followed by the publication of *A Fiery Flying Roll*
(January 1st, 1650) marked the beginning of the period of maximum
Ranter activity and was followed almost at once by a campaign of
persecution and abuse directed against them.

A Fiery Flying Roll, from which a number of extracts have already
been given, described itself as "A Word from the Lord to the Great
ones of the Earth". With it was bound *A Second Fiery Flying Roule*,
addressed "To all the Inhabitants of the Earth". The violent and provo-
cative tone of the *Roll*, together with Coppe's unconventional
behaviour, attracted a great deal of attention and led to an immediate
reaction. The Ranters, hitherto almost ignored, began to be written
and talked about. A glance at the bibliographical note appended to this
essay will show that almost half the items listed date from the year 1650
and more than half the remainder from 1651.

Coppe, who had either left London after the publication of *A Roll*,
or been taken from it under arrest, was soon in prison in Coventry.
On February 1st Parliament issued an Order declaring that passages
from *A Roll* had been read before it and contained "many horrid
Blasphemies, and damnable and detestable opinions, to be abhorred by
all good and godly people". It was ordered that copies be publicly
burnt "by the hand of the Hangman, at New-Pallace-Yard at West-
minster, the Exchange, in Cheapside and at the Market-place in
Southwark". Search was to be made and all copies that could be found
were to be destroyed.

One of the first attacks on the Ranters came from the Anabaptists.
Heart-Bleedings of Professors Abominations appeared on February 28th
and this was signed by sixteen of their ministers. These included a
number—Kiffin, Spilsbury, Patience and Drapes—who less than a year
ago had signed *The humble Petition and Representation of Several
Churches of God in London* directed against the Levellers. On both

[1] *Roll*, II, Ch. 5.

occasions they were eager to disavow any connection with what they regarded as an unpopular group. Here, though the Ranters are not mentioned by name, their familiar tenets are all outlined and repudiated. The pamphlet deals at length with the argument "that those who have faln into such desperate abominations, were sometimes members of our Congregations, and from thence are apt to condemn our profession, and question whether our way be of God or no, saying, you see what your judgement leads to". They reply that, "Many if not most of them were never members with us", and that in any case no flock can be condemned for having had a few black sheep.[1]

That these fears were not without foundation was shown by the publication a fortnight later of *A Blow at the Root, Or some Observations towards A Discovery of the Subtilties and Devices of Satan*, a production of the Presbyterian establishment in which the excesses of the Ranters serve as an excuse for an attack on all the Sects. Its anonymous author contends that one thing leads inevitably to another:

> An over-curious questioning of some things appertaining to *Religion* (against which yet I conceive, no cleare evidence can be given) disposeth to *Separation*: *Separation* is an ordinary step to *Anabaptisme*; *Anabaptisme* perfects itself in *Seeking*, being above *Ordinances*, and *Questioning* everything revealed in the *Scriptures*, and in high *Raptures* and *Revelations*. This determinates in *Levelling*, and (through that) runnes compasse (with some) to that strange and fearfull *straine* declared and taught in the late *Fiery flying Roll*; which state's the *perfection* of all Religion expressly [in perfect Libertinisme]. So that Profaneness ye may perceive, is the Devils *Alpha* and *Omega*.[2]

The main Ranter doctrines are then attacked in some detail.

Meanwhile the Ranters appear to have been growing in strength and Clarkson's *A Lost Sheep* describes the increasing boldness of their activities. In April George Foster published *The Sounding of the Last Trumpet*, with social and political ideas very similar to those of Coppe and Clarkson.[3]

In June Parliament set up a Committee to enquire into the Ranters and other heretical groups. On June 21st it reported "on the several abominable Practices of a Sect called Ranters", and a Bill was prepared

---

[1] *Op. cit.*, p. 12.   [2] *Op. cit.*, pp. 151–2.

[3] In November this was reprinted with a similar work, *The Pouring Fourth of the seventh and last Viall upon all Flesh*.

which was debated on several days during June and July. On August
9th Parliament passed its Act for the Punishment of Atheistical, Blasphemous and Execrable Opinions. This Act declared a number of
heresies to be punishable by six months' imprisonment, with banishment for a second offence. These included maintaining that God
"dwells in the creature and nowhere else", that "the acts of uncleanness,
Prophane Swearing, Drunkenness, and the like Filthiness and Brutish-
ness, are not unholy and forbidden in the Word of God", that such
actions and "the like open wickedness, are in their nature as Holy and
Righteous as the Duties of Prayer, Preaching or giving of Thanks to
God", "that such men and women are most perfect, or like to God or
Eternity, which do commit the greatest Sins with least remorse or
sense", and that "there is no such thing really and truly as Unrighteous-
ness, Unholiness or Sin, but as a man or woman judgeth thereof;
or that there is neither Heaven nor Hell, neither Salvation nor Damnation, or that those are one and the same thing".

This Act was the signal for paper polemics to be followed up by
organised police action. Some Ranters, like Coppe and Salmon, had
already been imprisoned. Now began systematic police raids, often
made on evidence provided by informers. The Ranters, however,
were by no means silenced or quickly defeated. *A Single Eye* by
Clarkson appeared in September 1670[1] and Bauthumley's *The Light
and Dark sides of God* in November. Opposition to the Act was also
shown by William Larner's publication in 1651 of *The Petition of
Divers gathered Churches, and others wel affected, in and about London, for
declaring the Ordinance of the Lords and Commons for punishing Blasphemies
and Heresies, null and void*. This Petition was reprinted in 1655.

Soon after the passing of the Act Coppe was brought from Coventry
to London and examined by a Parliamentary Committee, as were
Clarkson and William Rainborough soon after. Both Clarkson and
Coppe proved difficult subjects. Clarkson, like Lilburne and Overton
before him, stood on his rights as a free citizen, refusing to answer any
questions that might incriminate him. Coppe adopted different tactics.
The Weekly Intelligencer for October 1st–8th mentioned "the arrogant
and wild deportment of Mr Copp the great Ranter, who made the
Fiery Roll, who being brought before the Committee of Examinations,
refused to be uncovered, and disguised himself into a madnesse,
flinging Apples and Pears about the roome, whereupon the Committee

[1] Thomason, whose datings I have usually followed, gives the date as October 4th. but
the Parliamentary Order for it to be burnt was dated September 27th.

returned him to Newgate whence he came". A similar account of the
incident is given in *The Routing of the Ranters.*

In December and January 1650–1 appeared a whole swarm of
anti-Ranter pamphlets, many anonymous, crudely printed, mostly
apparently from the same press, and for the most part of the most
scurrilous and witch-hunting character. Not only are they full of allega-
tions of obscene orgies and suggestions that the Ranters were Royalist
agents or concealed Jesuits, but such even greater absurdities as that the
Devil in person attended their meetings,

> and taking them by the hands very familiarly, he leaves the print
> of his *fowl Paws* behinde him, which the Ranter can never get
> out, it remaining black and *Blue*; they being fearfully tormented
> thereat.[1]

Another pamphlet tells how a Ranter preacher, when his audience
turned against him, "called for . . . a pissepot, and in an instant, upon a
great flash of fire, vanished, and was never seen more".[2] In a third, one
Kendall of Drury Lane, having made an assignation with a she-Ranter,
"was suddenly strook dead in the place to the great amazement
and astonishing of many beholders".[3]

These pamphlets do, however, give some interesting details,
especially of the suppression and persecutions of the Ranters. In the
Arraignment and Tryall . . . of the Ranters we read of an Army Ranter
being hanged by the thumbs, in *The Ranters Recantation* of one W.
Smith, hanged at York "for denying the Deity, *Arian*-like", and of a
number of police raids and imprisonments.

Clarkson's coolness in avoiding arrest during such a raid is described
in *The Routing of the Ranters.* A meeting in Whitechapel was surprised
"by the officers of the place":

> Amongst this company was that Claxton (before mentioned)
> who with undaunted boldness and audacious carriage, spake to the
> Officers, that came with authoritie to apprehend them, to this
> effect.
>
> *Gentlemen,* I perceive you are come to seize on us, your fellow
> creatures, for what cause I know not; I pray use not any violence,
> or terrifie and affright those of our fellow creatures here, that
> are of a weak and tender constitution: if we have offended

---

[1] *Ranters Last Sermon,* p. 7.   [2] *The Ranters Recantation,* p. 5.
[3] *Strange Newes from Newgate,* p. 6.

the Law, we shall readily and willingly submit to be tried by it. And taking up his cloak, he said *Gentlemen*, I will not leave you as I am ready to go along with you. And forth he went with the first; and as the others were coming forth (about thirty in numbers) he framed an excuse to return back into the house, pretending he had left something of great use behind him, and so escaped away at a back door; but is re-taken, and at this day in prison.

The same pamphlet, describing a raid on the house of one Middleton, at the sign of *David and the Harp* in Marsh Lane, supplies an illuminating detail:

> one of the men took a candle, and went up and down the room, as if he had been seeking a needle; and after a while, one asked him what he sought after? to whom he answered, *That he lookt for his sins but they were not there, he could not find them.*

Mrs. Middleton, who at about this time was Clarkson's mistress, escaped, but most of those present were arrested. This is probably the same episode as that referred to in *The Ranters Ranting*, when also Mrs. Middleton is said to have escaped arrest, but the names of some of the others are given as John Collins, I. Shakespeare and Thomas Wilberton. These, and five others were brought before Sir John Wolaston and sent to the Compter.

Strange Newes from Newgate and the Old-Baily describes the "Proofs, Examinations and Confessions of J. Collins and T. Reeve, two of the Ranters taken in Moor-Lane, at the General Sessions of Gaol-Delivery, holden in the Old-Baily the twentieth day of this instant January". Each was sentenced to six months' imprisonment under the Act of August 9th. Elsewhere there are accounts of the dispersal and arrest of groups at York, Uxbridge, King's Lynn and other places. Other pamphlets speak of large numbers of Ranters who have repented, and, as *The Ranters Declaration* puts it, "now live civilly in their respective places and habitations".

In all this proliferation of slander and abuse two pamphlets written in these months stand out as at least attempting serious argument. One is *The Smoke of the Bottomlesse Pit* by John Holland, already referred to, whose attempt to give a fair account of Ranter doctrine belies its catch-penny title and justifies its author's claim that it was written, "not with any intent . . . to make their persons odious unto any, much lesse to stir up any to persecute them barely for their judgements; for when I consider what the Scripture saith, I find it not Gods method to deal with spiritual enemies with carnal weapons". The other was *A Wonder and Yet no Wonder* by Edward Hide Junior, published in December, and, most surprisingly, by Giles Calvert.

While a publisher is not, of course, necessarily identified with all the views of the authors he publishes, this must reflect a deliberate intention by Calvert to retreat from his recent Ranter connections. This may have been mere natural caution in the face of persecution and possible damage to his business interests. On the other hand he continued to publish radical and dangerous books (including the last speeches of many of the Regicides) right up to his death in 1663, and his widow Elizabeth continued the same policy afterwards. But about this time Calvert was to begin his long association with the Quakers, scores of whose books he was to publish in the next dozen years, and it seems more probable that this is mainly an indication that he was moving from the Ranter to the Quaker standpoint and perhaps wished to emphasise the fact.

Hide (more usually Hyde) was a Royalist, related to the future Chancellor, who had been sequestered from his living of Brightwell in Berkshire, but he is described by Wood as "an enthusiastical person". His book certainly contains much cloudy stuff about Great Red Dragons and the like, but his criticism of the Ranter position, though hostile, is not entirely unsympathetic. People like the Ranters, he argues, err,

> by ushering in Error with these six glorious truths following; that is to say
> God Doth all things.
> Is all things.
> All things are in God.
> All things are of God.
> All things are through God.
> All things are to God.
> From these excellent premises they draw such rotten and unsound Principles as that they are very God and infinite and Almighty as the very God is. . . . That Heaven and all happiness consist in the acting of those things which are sin and wickedness; That those are most perfect, and like to God and Eternity, which do commit the greatest sins without least remorse or sense . . . and that there

is neither Heaven nor Hell . . . and that there is not any distinction between them, or between light and darkness; that Reason is God.[1]

It will be noted that Hide, like other writers, tends to use the actual words of the Act of August 9th, and these will also be found to colour the language of subsequent Ranter retractions.

The combination of legal prohibition, police repression and adverse propaganda in the last months of 1650 and the first of 1651 did not destroy the Ranter movement, but it certainly checked its growth, drove it underground and forced it to shun rather than court public notice. From this time Ranterism ceases to be news and references to its activities decrease sharply. Meantime the most prominent Ranter spokesmen, Coppe and Clarkson, like many of their followers, were in prison. Clarkson was released after about a month and the sentence of banishment passed on him was never enforced. However, he left London for East Anglia and soon abandoned his Ranter activities if not his beliefs. His colleague Rainborough was only "discharged and disabled of and from bearing or executing the Office of a Justice of Peace in the County of *Middlesex*, or any other County within *England* and *Wales*".[2]

Coppe remained in prison, and in January 1651 issued a partial recantation—*A Remonstrance of the sincere and zealous Protestation of Abiezer Coppe Against the Blasphemous and Execrable Opinions recited in the Act of Aug 10 1650*. Apart from complaints that he had been slandered, this consisted mainly of denials that he had ever held the views attributed to him. This evidently did not satisfy the authorities and he was kept in prison for another five months till he wrote a second and fuller recantation, *Copps Return to the wayes of Truth: . . . Or Truth asserted against, and triumphing over Error; And the Wings of the Fiery flying Roll clipt*. It is dated:

$$\text{May } 30 \begin{cases} \text{The day of} \\ \text{my nativity} \end{cases} 1619 \\ \begin{cases} \text{And the day of my} \\ \text{new birth} \end{cases} 1651^3$$

In the Preface Coppe addresses Parliament, asking pardon for his

---

[1] *Op. cit.*, pp. 36–42.   [2] *Parliamentary Resolution* of 27/9/50.
[3] Thomason gives the date 11/7/51: perhaps there was a gap between its writing and publication.

sins and errors, but saying that many errors not his own have been
maliciously attributed to him. He has been in prison a year and a
half, during which his wife's health has suffered and "my poor innocent
children scattered here and there in several places to our great care,
Grief and charge". His fall, like that of Nebuchadnezzar, had been
due to spiritual pride:

> In a mystical sense I built a great Babel. And (in the pride of my
> heart) I walked in the Palace of the Kingdome of Babylon,
> i.e. recreating and priding myself, in the pleasures of . . . Babel,
> i.e. Confusion.

On pages 1 to 13 he proceeds to disown the following errors and
assert their opposites:

1. That there is no sinne.
2. That there is no God.
3. That Man, or the meer Creature, is very God.
4. That God is in Man, or in the creature onely, and no where else.
5. That Cursing and Swearing, is no sin.
6. That Adultery, Fornication and uncleannesse is no sin.
7. That community of Wives is lawful.

In view of the provisions of the Act, and the penalties it contained, he
could hardly have done otherwise, and apparently the authorities were
sufficiently convinced since they released him. He did not convince
everyone. In September he preached a recantation sermon at Burford
which was attacked by John Tickell in an appendix to *The Bottomles
Pit Smoking in Familisme*. Tickell accused Coppe of deceit and equivo-
cation. The Ranters "use to speak one thing and mean another. . . .
Before the late Act they spake boldly, now they dare not." When
they speak of Christ and his crucifixion they regard Christ as a type,
not as an historical figure—a charge justified to a certain extent by
Ranter insistence on the primacy of the mystery over the history in
the Scriptures.

How far Coppe's enforced recantation was sincere it is difficult to
say. But he seems, as far as possible, to have held to the essence of his
beliefs. Thus, while denying that there was no sin, he expressed the
view that all men are equally sinful in the eyes of God:

> Thieves, little thieves, and great thieves, drunkards, adulterers,
> and adultresses. Murtherers, little murtherers, and great murther-

ers. All are sinners. Sinners All. What then? Are we better than they? No, in no wise.[1]

Most significant of all, far from denying any of the social views advanced in A Fiery Flying Roll he reaffirmed them almost defiantly:

As for community, I own none but that Apostolical, saint-like Community, spoken of in the Scriptures.

So far as I either do, or should own community, that if flesh of my flesh, be ready to perish; I either will, or should call nothing that I have, mine own.

If I have bread it shall, or should be his, else all my religion is in vain. I am for dealing bread to the hungry, for cloathing the naked, for the breaking of every yoak, for the letting of the oppressed go free. . . .

Yet,

Know all men by these presents, that I am utterly against the community which is sinful, or destructive to soul or body, or the well being of a Common-wealth. . . .

I own none other, long for none other, but that glorious (Rom. 8) liberty of the sons of God.

Which God will hasten in its time.[2]

The sting of his recantation was certainly in its tail.

After his release Coppe remained in London, but it is uncertain how far he resumed his Ranting activities, since little is heard of him after this. Wood says that he "was kindly entertained among those of his own opinion". Fox reports a meeting with him in 1655 which suggests that there had been no great change, provided that his date is correct:

During the time I was prisoner at Charing Cross abundance of professors, priests, and officers, and all sorts of people came to see me . . . and there came one Cobbe, and a great company of Ranters came in that time also, and they began to call for drink and tobacco; and I desired them to forbear it in my room; if they had a mind to it they could go into another room. And one of them cried, "All is ours", and another said, "All is well": but I replied, "How is all well when thou art so peevish and envious and crabbed?"[3]

Of Coppe's later years Wood writes that "the name of Coppe

[1] Op. cit., p. 4.   [2] Ibid., p. 14.   [3] Journal, p. 195.

being odious, he did at the Kings restauration change it to *Higham*, and practising Physick at *Barnelms* in *Surrey*, and sometimes preaching, went for divers years under the name of Dr Higham". He died in August 1672 and was buried "on the south side of the church there, under the seats".

Under all these blows Ranterism ceased to exist as a coherent social and religious movement, but its decline was slow and prolonged. All over the country small, more or less isolated groups, and, no doubt, many individuals, remained. Apart from its specific theology, there was something about its intransigence, its blunt nonconforming irreverence, its rough materialism and perhaps its appeal to an ancient, deep-rooted peasant communism that made a strong appeal to many Englishmen of the lower orders. The best evidence for its persistence in all parts of the country in this period, and for its character, comes from Fox's *Journal*. Fox reports Ranters as late as 1668, and in New England, 1672. From his first sight of them in 1649 he emphasises their rough, unmannerly conduct. They "took tobacco and drank ale" at their meetings. They "fell a-swearing", they "made a disturbance and were very rude", they "sung and whistled and danced". Yet this was essentially a negative type of appeal, not of the kind on which a wide national movement could be built.

What, actually, was the size and strength of the Ranters? It is not easy to answer such a question with any assurance. Fox quoted, with some complacency, a statement by Justice Hotham that the Quakers had saved England from being engulfed by them:

> Justice Hotham was glad that the Lord's power and truth was spread and so many had received it. . . . And moreover he said, if God had not raised up this principle of light and life, the nation had been overspread with Ranterism and all the Justices in the nation could not stop it with all their laws, because they would have done and said as they commanded them and yet kept their principle still. But this principle of Truth overthrows the root and ground of their principle . . . which they could not have done with all their laws.[1]

This judgement should be treated about as seriously as the even more famous one that Methodism saved England from revolution in the nineteenth century. Equally untrustworthy are some contemporary estimates of vast numbers of Ranters being converted—3,000 at one

[1] *Journal*, p. 90.

time according to *The Ranters Declaration*, 700 at another according to *The Ranters Bible*. All reliable evidence suggests that Ranter meetings were quite small, perhaps ten or a dozen or a score of people meeting privately or semi-privately in a member's house. On the other hand they were probably both more numerous and more influential than has sometimes been supposed.

No doubt their main strength lay in the poorer quarters of London, among the impoverished artisans and labourers, suffering the effects of the war, and they appealed also to a number of former Levellers inside and outside the Army. But they were certainly not confined to London or even to its neighbourhood. Ranter activities of various kinds are reported from Abingdon, Leicester, Coventry, York, Berkshire, Kent, King's Lynn, Uxbridge, Ilford and Winchester. Fox supplies many more localities: Cleveland, Ulverston, Holderness, the Peak area, Nottingham, Horsham, Bristol, Weymouth, Norwich, Cornwall, Southampton, among others. Such a list, drawn from only a few haphazard sources, must mean that there was no part of England where their influence was not felt. It suggests also, if less conclusively, what might in any case be expected, that this was a mainly urban movement, drawing support from the wage earners and small producers in the towns rather than from the peasantry.

It is not surprising that it caused alarm in orthodox and propertied circles and was savagely attacked the moment it appeared. Yet it is also clear that it can never have been a real threat to the established order. If it seemed so, it was perhaps because the rich had an uneasy conscience. It arose, as we have seen, at a time of the political defeat of the radical, plebeian element in the revolution, and, indeed, as a consequence of that defeat. It had therefore to face a ruling group that had fully consolidated its position and had a firm grip on the Army and the State machinery. What the Levellers had failed to do with considerable mass support, organising ability, and an attractive programme based on a well considered political theory in a time of exceptional political fluidity was far beyond the powers of groups of confused mystical anarchists, at a time of political retreat, whose programme really amounted to little more than awaiting the day when "God the Great Leveller" would come upon the rich and mighty "as a thief in the night, with my sword drawn in my hand, and like a thief as I am—I say deliver your purse, deliver sirrah! deliver or i'l cut thy throat!"[1]

[1] *Roll*, II, Ch. 2.

The Levellers, again, had behind them a solid class basis to which their programme made a definite appeal. The Ranters could appeal only to the defeated and declassed, the lower strata of the urban poor, and upon these no substantial movement could possibly be built. While individual ex-Levellers might turn to them this could only be out of despair and such recruits were likely to be only temporary. The more substantial and balanced of those who had supported the Levellers were more likely to be repelled by the wild language and wilder conduct of the Ranters. These, in their turn, were largely a reflection of their own despair and demoralisation. A logical contradiction developed here between the ideologues and the mass of their followers. The former might well believe that the day of the Lord was at hand and they were indeed in the very year that the Powers of Heaven and Earth should be shaken and damned, and that therefore their actual actions were a matter of little importance.

Their followers might believe this too, with the surface of their minds. But such conviction is really only possible for a few and for most the practical outcome seems to have been a feeling that they might as well eat, drink and be as merry as their conditions allowed, since they had little more to expect either here or hereafter. For a few critical weeks or months in 1650 expectations may have been pitched rather higher, but when the test came, and it was obvious that the Powers were so far from being shaken that they had the situation well in hand, a rapid disillusion set in. In a sense the fall of the Ranter movement was as swift as its rise—but it was incomplete. Without leadership except at the local level, Ranter groups persisted for a number of years, carrying on familiar procedures as a matter of habit, perhaps, like Margaret Hollis in 1654, who "singing antiquely, and in rude postures, said *That was Religion*".[1]

A tough nonconformism remained, but the millennial expectation was over. So was the passion, the poetry, the vision, the attempt at a comprehensive world outlook, however confused, which gave the Ranters a firm and peculiar place in the English Revolution and in the list of English heresies, and which established them as a main link in the chain that runs from Joachim of Fiore to William Blake.

---

[1] *A List of Some of the Grand Blasphemers.*

BIBLIOGRAPHICAL NOTE

The works listed below fall into three main groups: books or pamphlets by Ranters, books or pamphlets attacking them, and books of a more general character in which they are referred to. They are arranged chronologically, and where precise dates are given these are usually as supplied by Thomason. Though some of these are no doubt inaccurate they are still sufficiently correct to make such a list a useful guide to the development of the Ranter movement.

Very little of this material has ever been reprinted. Professor N. Cohn gives useful extracts from a number of these works in an appendix to *The Pursuit of the Millennium*, and extracts from *Heights in Depths* and *The Light and Dark sides of God* are in an appendix to Barclay's *The Inner Life of the Religious Societies of the Commonwealth*.

Anti-Christ in Man. J. Salmon. 12/12/47.

A Rout, A Rout. J. Salmon. 10/2/49.

A Vindication . . . Or some Reasons given against . . . Ranting. Gerrard Winstanley. 20/3/49.

Divine Teachings. Richard Coppin. Preface by A. Coppe. 18/9/49.

A Fiery Flying Roll. A. Coppe. 4/1/50.

Parliamentary Resolution on F.F.R. 1/2/50.

A Censure upon the Flying Roule (MS. poem). February 1650.

Heart-Bleedings for Professors Abominations. 28/2/50.

A Blow at the Root. 4/3/50.

Pseudochristus. Humphrey Ellis. 7/3/50.

The Sounding of the Last Trumpet. George Foster. 24/4/50.

Act for Punishment of Atheistical etc. Opinions. 9/8/50.

A Single Eye all Light, no Darkness. Laurence Clarkson. 4/10/50.

Parliamentary Resolution on *A Single Eye*, etc. 27/9/50.

Pouring Fourth of the . . . last Viall. George Foster. 15/11/50.

The Routing of the Ranters. 19/11/50.

The Light and Dark sides of God. Jacob Bauthumley. 20/11/50.

The Ranters Ranting. 2/12/50.

The Ranters Bible. Gilbert Roulston. 9/12/50.

The Ranters Religion. 11/12/50.

The Arraignment and Tryall . . . of the Ranters. 17/12/50.

The Ranters Declaration. M. Stubbs. 17/12/50.

The Ranters Recantation. 17/12/50.

A Wonder and yet no Wonder. E. Hide Jun. 21/12/50.

A Remonstrance. A. Coppe. 3/1/51.

The Joviall Crew. Samuel Sheppard. 6/1/51.

Bloudy Newes from the North. Samuel Tilbury. 9/1/51.

Strange Newes from Newgate and the Old-Baily. 20/1/51.

H

The Smoke of the Bottomlesse Pit. John Holland. 22/1/51.

The Ranters Creed. May (?), 1651.

The Declaration of John Robins. 2/6/51.

Ranters of both sexes. John Taylor. 3/6/51.

Copps Return to the wayes of Truth. A. Coppe. 11/7/51.

Heights in Depths. J. Salmon. 13/8/51.

The Bottomles Pit Smoking in Familisme. John Tickell. 23/9/51.

Hell broke Loose: or, the notorious Design of the wicked Ranters. 1651.

The Character of a time-serving saint (1652), in H. E. Rollins. *Cavalier and Puritan Ballads.* 1923.

The Black and Terrible Warning Piece. 29/11/53.

Baby Baptism meer Babyism. Samuel Fisher. 1653.

A List of some of the Grand Blasphemers. 23/3/54.

The Ranters Last Sermon. J.M. 2/8/54.

Divine Essays and Considerations. Isaac Pennington Jun. 1654.

The Ranters Principles and Deceits Discovered. Richard Farnworth. 16/3/55.

The Serpents Subtilty Discovered. Walter Rosewell. 20/6/56.

The Lost sheep found. Laurence Clarkson. 1660.

Heresiography (6th edn.). E. Pagitt. 1661.

The Journal of George Fox. 1694.

Reliquiae Baxterianae. Richard Baxter. 1696.

5

Laurence Clarkson and the Everlasting Gospel

No novelist, setting out to create a typical figure to illustrate the development and variety of religious life in the seventeenth century, would have dared to invent anything so fantastically made-to-measure as Laurence Clarkson.[1] In the course of about twenty years he passed through the whole range of the religious experiences possible in his age, progressing from the Anglicanism in which he was brought up, through Presbyterianism, to become in succession Independent, Antinomian, Baptist or Dipper, Seeker and Ranter, till he found his final home among the Muggletonians.

He recorded his adventures, physical and spiritual, in an autobiography: *The Lost Sheep found: or the Prodigal Returned to his Fathers House, after many a sad and weary Journey through many Religious Countreys. . . . Written by Laur. Claxton, the onely true converted Messenger of Christ Jesus, Creator of Heaven and Earth* (1660), a book almost unknown, but in my judgement of greater intrinsic interest than Bunyan's *Grace Abounding*. In the first place, it covers the period (1640–60) when the sects were at the height of their prosperity and influence. Secondly, it introduces us not merely to one sect, but to the whole range of the advanced religious life of that period, and, third, it is written with an extraordinary frankness and with a fullness of vivid detail which throws much light on the inner life of the sects. Clarkson never hesitates to show himself in an unfavourable light and the assurance with which he embraces each new creed is only equalled by the decision with which he rejects all his previous convictions. Yet with all his constant changes, there seems to be a single thread which he follows, a fixed goal upon which he is bent. What that goal was I will try to show in the course of this essay.

Clarkson was born at Preston, Lancashire, in 1615, of an Anglican family which appears to have been of an average and orthodox piety.

---

[1] His earlier pamphlets are signed Clarkson, the later ones Claxton. I have adopted the earlier form throughout.

This did not satisfy him and at an early age he began to go secretly to hear "godly" ministers in neighbouring towns:

> however, I being under my fathers tuition, he cast a strict eye over me, and would force me to read over the prayers in the book of *Common Prayer* and *Practice of Piety* which I have done till they have fallen asleep and myself, this was our devotion in those days . . . and then the next thing I scrupuled, was asking my parents blessing, that oftentimes in the winter mornings, after I have been out of my bed, I have stood freezing above, and durst not come down till my father was abroad, and the reason I was satisfied, the blessing or prayer of a wicked man God would not hear, and so should offend God to ask him a blessing.[1]

Later he became a Presbyterian, and, on the outbreak of the Civil War, came to London, "where I found them more precise than in our Popish Countrey of *Lancashire*". In London he went to hear the most approved ministers—Calamy, Case and Brooks—but soon grew tired of the Presbyterian thunder and intolerance and became an Independent. Their doctrine he found "clearer and of a more moderate spirit", but "still enquiring after the highest pitch of Light then held forth in London" he was converted to Antinomianism by Simpson and Randel. Presently he made the acquaintance of Paul Hobson, a preacher who

> brake forth with such expressions of the in-comes and out-goes of God, that my soul much desired such a gift of preaching, which after a while Hobson and I being acquainted, he had a Captains place under Colonel *Fleetwood* for Yarmouth, so that thither I went, and there tarried a soldier with them, at which time I had a small gift of preaching, and so by degrees increased into a method that I attempted the Pulpit at Mr *Wardels* Parish in *Suffolk*.[2]

Leaving the Army he became an itinerant preacher, gaining such a reputation locally that he was soon

> invited to preach at *Pulom*, which was a great Parish; so upon liking I went, and was well approved by all the Godly, so there for a time I was settled for twenty shillings a week, and very gallantly was provided for, so that I thought I was in Heaven upon

---

[1] *Lost Sheep*, p. 5. All quotations for which no reference is given are from this pamphlet.
[2] William Wardell was rector of Burgh Castle, 1617–60, and of Belton 1624–60, when he was succeeded in both parishes by Samuel Fleete. Suckling, *Hist. of Suffolk*, I, pp. 301, 340.

earth, judging the Priests had a brave time in this world, to have a house built for them, to tell the people stories of other mens work. Now after I had continued half a year more or less, the Ministers began to envy me for my Doctrine, it being Free Grace, so contrary to theirs, and that the more, their people came from their own Parish to hear me, so that they called me *Sheep-Stealer* for robbing them of their flocks, and to that end came to catch and trap me at several Lectures when I was called, that at last they prevailed with the Heads of the Parish to turn me out.

It was this doctrine of universal salvation which divided the more advanced sects from the Presbyterians and very many of the Independents, who held the orthodox Calvinist views of predestination and the rigid division of mankind into the reprobate and the elect. The non-Calvinist sects tended to hold that since Christ died for all men and not only for the elect, salvation was open to all. The further implications of this are obvious and it is no accident that it was among those professing Free Grace that we find the first signs of modern ideas of democracy and of civil and religious liberty. The Levellers, for example, who came very largely from these sects, drew the conclusion that if all men were capable of salvation all should be capable of voting and taking part in political life. As a result of all this the Presbyterians began to find themselves outbidden both politically and theologically. Hence the fury of Clarkson's rivals and the bitterness with which the Presbyterian Thomas Edwards recorded that:

> An Independent Antinomian Libertine Preacher here in London said *That a poore whoremonger, or a poore drunkard cannot look into your Churches* (speaking of the Presbyterian Preachers) *but hell must be flashed and thrown into their faces.*[1]

Expelled from Pulham, Clarkson resumed his vocation of itinerant preacher along the Norfolk–Suffolk border. He became friendly with Robert Marchant of Weybread and began to court one of his daughters, Frances. Presently he met John Taylor of Colchester, a Baptist, who "brought me to believe that the baptism of the Apostles was as much in force now, as in their day". He then went to London, where he was "baptised in the water that runneth about the Tower" on November 6th, 1644.[2]

Then for *Suffolk* again I travelled through the Church of the

[1] *Gangraena*, II, p. 144.   [2] *Gangraena*, I, p. 72.

Baptists, and was of *Robert Marchant's* family received with joy, for I had the love of all the family, and though he had four daughters marriageable, yet there was one I loved above any in that Countrey, though I was beloved of other friends daughters far above her in estate, yet for her knowledge and moderation of spirit, I loved her.

It is clear from all that follows that Frances Clarkson was a woman of great courage and spirit, as well as remarkably tolerant of her husband's unusual ideas about marriage.

Clarkson now became one of a whole group of Baptist preachers who were extremely active in Suffolk for several months. Perhaps the best known was Hanserd Knollys, of whose activities Edwards gives us a picture. After preaching in the Earl of Manchester's army and in London, where he was imprisoned,

he getting free went down into *Suffolk*, and there played his Rakes, not only for preaching strange Doctrine, but in such a tumultuous, seditious, factious way. . . . Preaching in the Church-yard when he could not get into the Church, and getting up the Pulpits when the Sermon or Lecture had been ended, against the will of the Minister and Parish, so that there were several Riots and Tumults by his means, so that he was sent for by some in Authority in the County, and Articles and Complaints against him to a Committee of Parliament.[1]

Knollys, in a volume of three sermons which mentions Debenham and Stradbroke as scenes of his activities, declares that the disorders were created by his opponents, and that

for this Doctrine [he] had the Meeting-house doores shut against him, and was stoned out of the Pulpit (as he was preaching) by a rude multitude; who were gathered together, and set on by a Malignant *High-Constable*. Which hath been proved by divers witnesses of Good reputation, before the Honourable Committee of Examination at London.[2]

Much later, in a posthumously published autobiography, he gave a short account of the whole affair:

Not long after I was brought before the Committee of Examina-

[1] *Gangraena*, I, pp. 97–8.
[2] *Christ Exalted . . . Being the summe of divers Sermons Preached in Suffolk*, 1646 (title page).

tions, being accused by them that I occasioned great disturbance to Ministers and People in *Suffolk*: which I gave so good and satisfactory an account to them, that upon their report thereof to the House of Commons, they Ordered that I might preach in any part of *Suffolk* where the Minister of that place did not preach: which was all I got for £60 which that trouble cost me to clear my Innocence and the Honour of the Gospel.[1]

That Knollys' preaching had considerable popularity and some lasting effect may be deduced from a commission given him by Parliament in 1649 to preach in Suffolk as a result of a petition from the inhabitants of Ipswich.

Another Baptist preacher was:

> *Andrew Wyke* of the County of *Suffolk*, a Mechanick, but turned a great preacher and Dipper, who for his preaching and Dipping being brought before the Committee of that County, carries himself like *Lilburne, Overton* and other fellow Sectaries . . . reproving the Committee, as *You may think to speak what you please now*, with other such language. This *Wyke*, or some other Sectary, hath printed a pamphlet call'd *The Innocent in Prison Complaining; or, a True Relation of the Proceedings of the Committee at* Ipswich, *the Committee at* Bury St. Edmunds *in the County of* Suffolk, *against one* Andrew Wyke, *a Minister of Jesus, in the same County; who was committed to Prison June 3, 1646.* In which Pamphlet . . . the Committee is exclaimed upon fearfully.[2]

The religious situation in East Anglia in the middle 1640s was clearly peculiar. Since the area had been a Parliamentary stronghold from the outbreak of the war, Episcopacy had been eliminated as a social and religious force and the Presbyterians were in control of the governmental apparatus in the County Committees, and, generally, in the Parishes. At the same time, the sects were winning wide support, especially in the Army. The threat of Royalism, which in other areas still forced all Puritan groups to preserve some sort of unity, hardly existed here and the struggle between the Presbyterians and the sects was already in full swing. Early in 1645 the authorities took steps to check the activities of the Baptists in Suffolk, and Clarkson was one of the first to suffer:

[1] *The Life and Death of Mr Hanserd Knollys. . . . Written with his own Hand in the Year 1672*, 1691, pp. 21–2.
[2] *Gangraena*, III, p. 10.

There was no small stir among the priests what to do with me, which afterwards they got a Warrant from the Parliament to apprehend Mr. *Knowles* and myself, for then *Knowles* was about *Ipswich* preaching that doctrine, and baptising certain people into that faith; now they apprehended Mr. *Knowles* in *Ipswich* Gaol, and from thence Warrants came to secure me, so in the week day being privately assembled in a friends house, within three miles of *Ay*, there came an Officer from the Parliament with certain soldiers and two Constables, with some of the Parish, having clubs and staves surrounded the house, I being very earnest in my doctrine, and at that time was very much pressing the people, that without submitting to Baptism all their profession was nothing . . . in which time some of the Officers hearing me, interrupted my doctrine, and told me I must leave off, and go along with them, shewing me the authority that they had from the Parliament; however, some of our friends would have opposed them, but I saw it was in vain, and so desired our friends to be quiet, and said, we must not only profess Christ but also suffer for him; so it being in the winter time, and almost night, they hasted me to *Ay*, though I, with my friends, desired but so much liberty as to go to my wifes fathers house for linnen and other necessaries, and they would engage for my appearance before the Committee at *Bury*; but all in vain, then my wife told them they should provide a horse for her, for whither ever I went, she would go: at which they were very much incensed, but all to no purpose, so at last a Trooper would have her ride behind him, but she with scorn refused, then they got her furniture to ride behind me, so taking leave of our friends, to *Ay* that night we were carried;[1]

Now one of them went before to provide a Lodging, so the Town having intelligence that they had taken a great Anabaptist, there was no small waiting for my coming, that when I entered the Town, the inhabitants had beset both sides of the streets to see my person, supposing an Anabaptist had bin a strange creature, but when they beheld me, with my wife, they said to one another He is like one of us, yea they are a pretty couple, it is a pity I should suffer: so to the Inne I came, where a great company was in the yard to behold me; so being unhorsed, they guarded me to our Lodging, and a great provision was made for supper, and many a

[1] For convenience I have broken this long quotation into paragraphs; Clarkson rarely opens a new paragraph for anything less than a change of creed.

pot was spent that night to see my face; so to bed we went, and
in the next room by soldiers guarded, so in the morning we were
hasted for *St Edmunds Bury*, which morning Captain Harvey gave
out many sad and grievous words, what the Committee would do
with me, but the devil was deceived; however I said little, so they
came out to me with a Bill what I had to pay for Beer, Wine
and Meat; unto which I said, I had none, but if I had, I would pay
none, it was sufficient I was wrongfully deprived of my freedom,
and not to pay for their rioting; however they told me, I must
before I go; then keep me here still: surely, I said, your Masters
that set you on work, are able to pay your wages: Well, they
said before I came out of prison, if I were not hanged, I should
pay it; then said I, rest yourselves contented till that day:

So towards Bury we took our Journey, and one was gone before
to inform the Committee I was taken; against my appearance
they were assembled in a full Committee, of which I take it
Captain *Bloyes* of *Woodbridge*¹ was their Chair-man. So to the
Hall² I was guarded, the room being full, I was conveyed up
to the Chair-man, who asked my name? To which I replied,
this is strange that you had a Warrant to take me, and know
not my name: Well, that was no matter, do you tell us your
name; so I told them: What Countrey man are you? I said
Lancashire. What made you travel so far to these parts? The like
motions that moved others, moved me. How long have you
professed this way of dipping? Not so long as I ought to have
done, had my understanding been enlightened. What then, you
approve of what you do? Otherways I should not do it. How
many have you dipped in these parts? I being a free born subject
of this Nation ought not to accuse myself; but you are to prove
your charge, by sufficient witness against me; but however I
being brought before you for my obedience to the Commands of
Christ, I am neither afraid nor ashamed to tell you what I have
done: but to give you an account of how many I have dipped, that
I cannot tell. Then you have dipped some? Yea, that I have.
After what manner do you dip them? After a decent order. We
are informed that you dip both men and women naked? As to

¹ William Bloyse: J.P. during the Long Parliament, Colonel of a Regiment of Foot
during the siege of Colchester and M.P. for Suffolk in the Parliaments of 1654 and 1656.
² No doubt the Guildhall. Clarkson's narrative is the fullest and most lively account
existing anywhere of the proceedings of a County Committee.

that, you are not rightly informed. Where is your *Jordan* you dip them in? Though it is not *Jordan*, yet there are several places convenient. Do you not dip them in the night? Yea. And why do you not dip them in the day, it being an ordinance of Christ, as you say? Because you are not able to bear the truth. Then said Sir William Spring but Mr *Claxton*, have you not force some in the water against their wills? That is contrary to Scripture. Did you not one time, being on horseback, with a switch force some into the water? Let them that so informed you, affirm it before you to my face. But Mr *Claxton*, who were those you dipped about *Framlingham*? At this time I cannot remember, but several I have dipped thereaways. Did you not dip six sisters there abouts at one time? I have never dipped six at one time. Then said Sir *John Rowse*, we are informed that you dipped six sisters one night naked. That is nothing to me what you are informed, for I never did such a thing: Nay further, it is reported that which of them you liked best, you lay with her in the water? Surely your experience teaches you the contrary, that nature hath small desire of copulation in water, at which they laughed. But, said I, you have more cause to weep for the unclean thought of your heart.

Mr *Claxton* have you not a wife? One that brought me, said she is in the town. Where is she? Fetch her hither: she being without the door came in quickly and took me by the hand. Well, said the Chair-man, you are a loving woman, is this your husband? Yes, he is my husband. How long have you been married? About two moneths. Where were you married? At *Waybread* in my fathers house. Who married you? My husband, with the consent of my parents, and the Church. At that there was a great laughter, and one said, your husband marry you himself, that is against the law; I being vexed at their folly, answered, Marriage is no other, but a free consent to love each other before God, and who was sufficient to publish the Contract as myself? Nay but Mr *Claxton*, you are not rightly informed as touching a true Marriage. I say I was married according to truth: then if your Marriage be lawful, we are not lawfully married. I question not yours, look ye to that; but this I know, and can prove, I am married according to the word of God; neither can your law repeal the contract of that couple, that hath their parents consent, and the Church confirming the same. Well, well, we shall give you the hearing but how many were present when you took your wife? About twelve. What did you say to her and the Church? First I sought the Lord by prayer for a blessing upon that Ordinance, and then I declared unto her parents and the Church what had passed between she and I, and that before them all I took her by the hand, and asked her if she was not willing to take me for her husband during life? To which she assented, and her parents also approved of it, and gave her to me with the confirmation of the Church.

Then said the Chairman, What think you Gentlemen, of this Marriage? They said this was a strange Marriage. What then Mrs *Claxton*, you look upon this man as your lawful husband? Yea, I deny all other men in the world. Then you have lain with him? I ought to ly with no other. But Mrs *Claxton*, did your husband dip you before or after he became your husband? Before I was contracted in public. How or after what manner did your husband dip you? in your clothes or naked? Sir, we defie any undecent carriage, if you were dipped in your clothes you would spoil them, and besides it you might endanger your life with cold: we have clothes for both men and women provided for the purpose. What were you plunged in over head and ears? So saith the Scripture. What Mr *Claxton*, did you go with her into the water? No I stood on the bank side. Mrs Claxton, were you not amazed or almost drowned? No Sir, the obedience to the Command of God did shut out all fear and cold. What did you not go to bed after dipped? I had a warm bed with dry linnen provided. Did not your husband lodge with you that night? There is no such wickedness among us. Why what matter, you were married before God. Till we were publicly before witness we had no such matter, and let me tell you, if it be the practice of your Church, it is not so in ours. Nay woman, be not angry. I do not say you did so, for truly I am as much against sin as you are. But Mrs *Claxton*, we have an order to secure your husband, and there to endure the pleasure of the Parliament, what will you do? We have no order to stay you. If you stay my husband, you must stay me also. What, are you willing to go to gaol with your husband? For the cause of Christ I am willing to suffer imprisonment. Then you are resolved yours is the way of Truth. Then said I, for the present I know no truth but this. Well Mr *Claxton*, after a while you will be better informed. Never to turn back again. We are to commit you to custody, that you may seduce no more people.

Sir, I must obey your pleasure, but I shall not deny to be obedient to the Command of Christ. Well, we shall talk with you another time: so they ordered to make my *Mittimus*, and in my presence gave it to Captain *Poe* my Keeper, and said, Mr *Claxton*, you may take notice that the Parliament is favourable unto you and will not send you to the common Gaol, but to a house where none but men of quality are kept in Custody. Then said *Poe*, who was my Gaoler, what shall his wife do? Then said my wife, wherever my husband is, there will I be, then the Committee ordered her with me: so coming thither, there was none but two Papists Knights and a Sea Captain,[1] so after we had supped we were directed to a large Chamber, and pretty good Furniture.

Now under a week I told Captain *Poe* that I was not able to board at half a crown a Meal. Then, said he, you must go to the Common Gaol: thither would I go, for I am not ashamed to sit in the stocks in the Market-place, for the Name of Christ. So he informed the Committee, but they would not remove me, and said, he must agree for the Chamber, and I find myself in Diet: at that *Poe* was vexed, and sent up his handmaid Mistress *Tuck*, to agree with me for the Chamber at four shillings a week, which for the space of half a year I gave her, in which time our people increased, there being *William Muly* and some others of this way in *Bury*.[2] I had oftentimes money from the Army, and the Churches at *London* and *Colchester*, so that I wanted for nothing; and some came to my Chamber, and there I preached unto them, in so much that the Keeper informed the Committee, who that Sunday at night assembled, to consider what to do with me: in conclusion they shut me close prisoner, and kept my wife from me, which was more misery than the rest. Well, against the next Lords-day I appointed our friends to stand before my window on the Angel-hill, that being the way for all the great Ones of the Town to go to their worship, so at the very instant time putting my head forth out of the window, I did boldly exhort the people to beware of the priests, and while it is the time of your health, submit your souls and bodies to the true Baptism, and be no

[1] Captain Whiting was imprisoned at Bury at this time on a charge of piracy. In general, wherever Clarkson's story can be checked from other sources his memory seems remarkably accurate. See *Suffolk and the Great Rebellion*, ed. Alan Everitt, 1961, p. 73.

[2] A William Mulley was presented for absence from church, 8/10/1682. Duncan, *Prosecutions of Nonconformists* (MS), p. 8.

longer deluded to think your infants are commanded to obey, or capable of an Ordinance imposed upon them. Oh for shame, if not for fear, stand still and hear the truth related by this true and lawful Minister, otherwise turn back again: at which a great sort of people gave attention, which did enrage the Priest and Magistrate, yet they knew not what to do with me, but charged me to do so no more. Then said I, take heed how you keep my wife from me: is this to do as you would be done unto? So they forthwith took off the Pad-lock, and let my friends come to me.

After this I had the liberty of the whole house, nay, to sit at the street-door; for he had no prisoners save such as gave in great security for their safe imprisonment; and as for me, and Westrop my fellow prisoner, they feared not our going away, onely they were afraid I should dip some. So a little after, Spring coming on, I got liberty, not being well, to go abroad with a Keeper, and Captain *Gray*, who was called Captain *Drinkwater* was to go with me: now above all the rest, I desired Captain *Gray* to go with me to a Wood a mile distant from me; it having rained over night, the Brook was up, so a man coming with a Pole, I desired him to lay it over, so I went over first, and the Captain followed me, and shaking the Pole, he fell into the middle of the water, and in a trembling condition he was, lest the Committee should hear of it: so to the Wood we went, and there he dried his Hose and Stockings, so after we came to the prison again, the Committee hearing of it, questioned Captain *Gray*, but he told them the truth, at which they laughed.

The support which Clarkson received there confirms the impression which we get from other sources that Bury was an important centre of sectarian activities, certainly important enough to attract leading preachers from other areas. In 1646 Katharine Chidley, one of the women preachers who so shocked the Presbyterians, and her son Samuel, soon to be an outstanding figure in the Leveller movement, were established here and set up a gathered Church. Long after his departure for London Chidley maintained his contact with the church in Bury, as is shown by the dedication of a pamphlet written by him in 1652, which is addressed

To the Church of God (in Edmondsbury) even to the *living Temples*

of the Holy Ghost, Samuel Chidley, *the Servant* of Jesus Christ
sendeth greetings.[1]

But perhaps the most revealing glimpse of sectarian ideas is one
given by Edwards, and it provides a key to the whole of Clarkson's
future development:

> Some of the Sectaries in London do hold, that in Suffolk there is
> a prophet raised up to come and preach the Everlasting Gospel
> to them, and he stayes but for a vocal call from Heaven to send
> him, which is expected daily.[2]

The idea of the Everlasting Gospel is so essential to any understanding
of the advanced sects, as well as Clarkson himself, that it will be
necessary to spend a little time elucidating it, more especially as its
significance for this time seems so far to have been very little appre-
ciated. Edwards himself, I think, did not understand what he was
writing about, but the origins of the doctrine go back to the twelfth-
century mystic, Joachim of Fiore. He taught that the history of the
world fell into three Ages, those of the Father, the Son and the Holy
Ghost. The first was the Age of Fear and Servitude, and ended with the
birth of Christ, the second was the Age of Faith and Filial Obedience,
and the third, which he expected shortly, was to be the Age of Love and
Spiritual Liberty for the Children of God. The scripture of the first Age
was the Old Testament, of the second, the New Testament. In the
coming third Age the full truth of the Everlasting Gospel will be
revealed, not in a new sacred book, but in a completely new understanding of the meaning of the Bible, which will illuminate the hearts
of men.[3]

It will be seen that there are two main strands in Joachite thought:
the conception of the three Ages or Commissions, and the conception
that God had not yet fully revealed himself in the scriptures but will
shortly do so. Both strands are to be found, sometimes separate but more
often together, in the English sects of the seventeenth century, especially
among the Antinomians, Seekers and Ranters, and, as we shall see
later, the Muggletonians, by whom Joachite ideas were carried to their

---

[1] *Thunder From the Throne of God Against the Temples of Idols.* For a short general account
of Chidley see W. Schenk, *The Concern for Social Justice in the Puritan Revolution,* pp.
74–7. For Chidley's activities in Bury, see pp. 32, 41 of this volume.
[2] *Gangraena,* I, p. 35.
[3] The life and ideas of Joachim are discussed in Coulton, *Studies in Medieval Thought,*
pp. 151–62.

logical conclusions. There is plenty of evidence that by about 1645 the Everlasting Gospel was being widely preached. Winstanley, in an early pamphlet, writes that the authority of the Apostles and Prophets

> are to cease, when the Lord himself, who is the everlasting Gospell, doth manifest himself to rule in the flesh of sonnes and daughters.[1]

It is not easy to fill the gap between the Italian Joachim of the twelfth century and the English sectaries of the seventeenth, but it is probable that his ideas reached England by way of Germany and Holland. It was in these years that the works of Hans Drench, Sebastian Franck, and, above all, of Jacob Boehme[2] were appearing in English translations, many of them the work of Seekers and the closely related sect of Familists. Boehme was clearly much influenced by Joachite ideas: his Epistles

> predicted that "the Age of the Lily" was near at hand and that its bloom would soon burst forth, especially in the cold lands of the North, where lilies are not expected. . . . The Nettle was the symbol of the stern dispensation of the Law, the Rose was the blood-red flower that characterised the dispensation of the Son . . . the coming of the Lily meant in symbolic fashion the birth of the Life and Love and Joy of God in the lives of man.[3]

Under such influences the Seekers rejected all forms of a visible Church and contented themselves with waiting for the coming of the higher light promised in the new age:

> We must be content to wait until God shall raise up some such, whose authority in this behalf he shall attest with visible signs of his presence by Gifts of the Holy Ghost.[4]

John Saltmarsh says that they believed,

> That there is a time and fulnes for the Spirit and for the later pure

[1] *Truth Lifting up its Head above Scandals*, 1648, *Works*, ed. G. H. Sabine, p. 122. The phrase is used in works by Ephraim Pagitt, Coppe, Richard Huberthorne and George Fox. No doubt a close search would reveal others: the doctrine for which it stood was more widespread.

[2] Many of Boehme's writings were published by Giles Calvert, the publisher of many Antinomian, Digger, Leveller and Quaker works. Calvert brought Clarkson to the Ranters and published at least one of his pamphlets.

[3] Rufus M. Jones, *Mysticism and Democracy in the English Commonwealth*, p. 105.

[4] William Allen, *A Doubt Resolved*, p. 14.

spiritual dispensations, as there was formerly for the first dispensations. And [they query] whether this shall be while the Angels are pouring out their vials or not, or when Babylon is fallen; and whether there is not as much need for new tongues to reveal the pure original to us, it being conveyed with corruptions and additions in translations, by which the truth may be more purely discovered and the waters of life that now run muddily may flow more clear and crystal-like from the throne of God.[1]

Here, as often, Joachite ideas can be seen in relation to the conception of Babylon and Jerusalem as social symbols; and the belief in the imminent fall of Babylon and the advent of a new Jerusalem is indeed often a special form of the third Age. The connection appears in a sermon preached in 1641 by Hanserd Knollys:

> Babylon's falling is Sion's rising. Babylon's destruction is Jerusalem's salvation. . . . This is the work, that is in hand. As soon as ever this is done, that Antichrist is down, Babylon fall'n, then comes in Jesus Christ reigning gloriously; then comes in this Hallelujah the Lord God Omnipotent reigneth.[2]

In the writings of Knollys, Saltmarsh or Thomas Collier,[3] as well as in those of the Digger Winstanley or the Ranter Salmon, the relation of these ideas to the events of the Civil War, with the overthrow of the royal power, can be clearly seen. The victory in the war was regarded as a clear sign of the imminent coming of the new Age of Liberty. The Levellers carried this a stage further, giving the doctrine of the Everlasting Gospel a secular twist in their theory that the fundamental contract binding society together had been entirely dissolved in the wars and that a completely new society had to be constructed on a democratic basis. *An Agreement of the People* was, in a sense, the Everlasting Gospel translated into the language of practical politics. So it is possible to see the Joachite doctrine developing in two totally different directions, one stressing its mystical side, as among the Fifth Monarchy Men, and, later, the Quakers and Muggletonians, the other its practical and secular side, as in the rationalism of Winstanley, insisting that

[1] *Smoke in the Temple.* Quoted from A. S. P. Woodhouse, *Puritanism and Liberty*, pp. 181–20.
[2] *A Glimpse of Sion's Glory*, Woodhouse, *op. cit.*, p. 233.
[3] *Discovery of the New Creation in a Sermon Preached at the Headquarters* [of the Army] *at Putney, Sept. 29, 1647.* Into this sermon Collier introduces almost the whole Leveller programme.

reason is the voice of God in man, or in Walwyn's infuriating question, "How can you *prove* that the Scriptures are the Word of God?" In Clarkson both tendencies can be found combined in an unusual degree, though, in the end, it was the mystical strand that came uppermost.

Perhaps the most complete expression of the doctrine of the Everlasting Gospel is to be found in the Welsh Seeker William Erbury, who was preaching in Bury in 1644 and again in 1645. He also came under the disapproving eye of Thomas Edwards:

> This man was a chaplain in the Earl of Essex's Army a great while, and did broach there many Antinomian Doctrines, and other dangerous Errors. . . . In July last [1644] he was at *Berry* where he exercised in private, some forty persons being present, he declared himself for general Redemption, that no man was punished for Adam's sin, that Christ died for all. . . . He also said that within a while God would raise up Apostolicall men, and after that should be the fall of *Rome*: he spoke against gathering churches, the Anabaptists Re-baptising, and said that men must wait for the coming of the Spirit as the Apostle did. . . . And then, after the fall of *Rome*, there shall be the new *Jerusalem*, and then the Church shall be one, one street in that city and no more.[1]

Most of the essentials of the doctrine of the Everlasting Gospel can be detected here, but Edwards did not understand it sufficiently to present them in their true form. For this, however, we can turn to Erbury's own writings:

> The Saints in Wales will not onely walk in the same light they formerly did, but in higher discovery of God and of Christ; yea in more holy and righteous ways with men. This is the new Jerusalem, and new Earth wherein dwells righteousness. . . .
>
> This was not fulfilled in the Gospel-dispensation (though in part performed therein), yet that the full accomplishment thereof is referred to a third dispensation in these last days appears by the parallel of Isai. 60, 19, 20, 21, with Rev. 21, 22, 23, 24, 25, this new Jerusalem being the third dispensation differing from Law and Gospel-Churches, yet comprehending both, and above both, as the glory of the Gospel was above that of the Law, and darkened the light thereof, even as the rising Sun doth the Moon.[2]

Sometime in the early summer of 1645, Erbury returned from a

---

[1] *Gangraena*, I, pp. 77–8.   [2] *A Call to the Churches*, pp. 36–7.

preaching mission in Northampton and from his quarters in Ely, to Bury, where Clarkson had been in prison since January 24th. The two men had long discussions, as a result of which Clarkson himself became a Seeker, thus taking his first decisive step in the quest of the Everlasting Gospel which was to occupy the remainder of his life.

> Mr *Sedgwick*[1] and Mr *Erbery* came to visit with me with whom I had a great discourse, and after they were gone I had a great contest in my mind, as touching the succession of Baptism, which I could not see but in the death of the Apostles, there was never since no true Administrator; for I could not read that there was ever any that had the power by imposition of hands, to give the Holy Ghost, and work miracles after they did; so that in the death of these I concluded Baptism to either young or old was ceased. Now observe, I could discern this, but could not by the same tale see that preaching and prayer was to cease: for this I now know, as in the death of the Apostles, and those commissionated by them, the Commission ceased, as unto all their Forms and Worship: So finding I was but still in *Egypt* burning Brick, I was minded to travel into the Wilderness; so seeing the vanity of the Baptists I renounced them and had my freedom.

Edwards, as might be expected, gave a less favourable but not essentially contradictory explanation:

> Now lying in Prison for some months, and seeing he could not get out by all the friends he could make there . . . but must lie in Prison, he then Petitioned the Committee of *Berry* and made a Recantation . . . being thus discharged of his imprisonment, he turned from Anabaptist and Dipper to be a Seeker, and to deny the Scriptures to be the rule of a Christian, or that in Doctrine or Practice half of God's glory was revealed as yet.[2]

Once free, Clarkson went to Ely[3]

---

[1] William ("Doomsday") Sedgwick of Ely. Not to be confused with the Presbyterians Obadiah and John Sedgwick, brothers who were both Ministers at Coggeshall.

[2] *Gangraena*, I, pp. 72–3.

[3] Ely, "that Island of Errors and Sectaries" as Edwards calls it, was at this time a Seeker stronghold. Wood says it was Erbury's "ordinary residence" from 1645 (*Athenae Oxonienses*, II, p. 104). In October 1646 Cromwell wrote his well-known letter to his daughter Bridget Ireton about the conversion of his younger daughter Elizabeth Claypole to the Seeker doctrines. As Elizabeth was then living at Ely, it is reasonable to conclude that she was a convert to the preaching of Erbury and Sedgwick.

to look for *Sedgwick* and *Erbury*, but found them not, only their people were all assembled, with whom I had discourse but found little satisfaction, so after that for *London* I went to find Seekers there.

In London Clarkson published (1646) his first book, *The Pilgrimage of Saints, By Church Cast Out, In Christ Found, Seeking Truth.*

After this I returned to my wife in *Suffolk*, and wholly bent my mind to travel up and down that country, preaching for monies, which I then intended for *London*, so coming to *Colchester*, where I had *John Aplewhit*, *Purkis*, and some other friends, I preached in public; so going for *London*, a mile from *Colchester* I set my Cane upright upon the ground, and which way it fell, that way I would go; so falling towards *Kent*, I was at a stand what I should do there, having no acquaintance, and but little money, yet what-ever hardship I met withal, I was resolved for *Gravesend*, so with much ado I got that night to a town called *Bilrekey*, it being in the height of the summer, and in that town having no friends, and I think but six pence, I lodged in the Church porch all night, so when day appeared I took my journey for Gravesend.

After preaching for some time in Kent he returned to Suffolk on a short visit to his wife and then made a second journey to Kent. Here occurred an episode which he describes with remarkable frankness:

Coming to Canterbury there was some six of this way, amongst whom was a maid of pretty knowledge, who with my Doctrine was affected, and I affected to lye with her, so that night prevailed, and satisfied my lust, and afterwards the mayd was highly in love with me, and as gladly would I have been shut of her, lest some danger had ensued, so not knowing I had a wife she was in hopes to marry me, and so would have me lodge with her again, which fain I would, but durst not, then she was afraid I would deceive her, and would travel with me, but by subtility of reason I perswaded her to have patience, while I went to Suffolk, and settled my occasions, then I would come and marry her, so for the present we parted, and full glad was I that I was from her deliv-ered, so to *Maidstone* I came, and having got some six pounds, returned to my wife, which after a while I went for Kent again, but found none of the people so zealous as formerly, so that my journey was but a small advantage to me, and there I heard the maid had been in those parts to seek me, but not hearing of me, returned home again, and not long after was married to one of that sect, and so there was an end of any further progress in Kent.

He then preached in London and Hertford. Meanwhile, the Leveller agitation was rising to its climax at the time of the Putney debates and it was in 1647 that Clarkson wrote his one directly political pamphlet: *A Generall CHARGE or Impeachment of High Treason, in the name of JUSTICE EQUITY, against the Communality of England . . . by L.C. a friend of the enslaved Communality*.[1] Beginning with the statement that the Parliament is inferior to and derives its power from the people he accuses it of having betrayed its trust and argues that it should be dismissed. In detail, his charges are very similar to those being made by the Levellers at this time. He condemns the imprisonment of many faithful subjects for trying to free the community from insufferable bondage.

Clarkson then went to Lincoln as an Army chaplain, but, meeting with financial difficulties, "I concluded that all was a cheat, yea, preaching itself." For Clarkson such a state of mind was a sure sign that he was ready to embrace a new faith, and on his return to London with his regiment he began to take steps in this direction:

a former friend of mine asked me if I heard not of a people called *My one flesh*? I said no, what was their opinion and how should I speak with them? Then he directed me to Giles Calvert.

Calvert gave him an introduction to one Brush "who told me that if I had come a little sooner I might have seen Mr *Copp*, who then had lately appeared in a most dreadful manner".[2]

The "people called *My one flesh*" were the Ranters and Clarkson soon became one of their leading preachers; in one hostile pamphlet they are actually described as

a sort of people . . . newly sprung up among us, called Ranters *alias* Coppinites, or Clatonians.[3]

They were antinomians of the most uncompromising order, whose views Clarkson explains in a sermon of which he gives a summary:

[1] For a discussion of this pamphlet see Perez Zagorin, *A History of Political Thought in the English Revolution*, pp. 31–2.

[2] The reference to Abiezer Coppe helps to place Clarkson's conversion as probably about the middle of 1649. Earlier in the year Coppe had preached a sensational series of sermons against the rich in the streets of London and this was probably the "appearance" referred to. See p. 100 of this volume.

[3] *The Routing of the Ranters*, p. 1.

I affirmed that there was no sin, but as man esteemed it sin, and therefore none can be free from sin till in purity it be acted as no sin, for I judged that pure to me, which to a dark understanding was impure, for to the pure all things, yea all acts were pure.

These views he elaborated in his pamphlet *A Single Eye all Light No Darkness; or Light and Darkness One*, published by Calvert in October 1650.

On the face of it, this was a further step towards the doctrine of the Everlasting Gospel. The Ranters did not, indeed, claim any more than the Seekers that the third Age was already come, but they did claim for themselves in practice the complete liberty proper to the sons of God in that Age. Yet in fact this was a premature and therefore a false step, which brought Clarkson, as we shall see, no satisfaction but rather a growing disillusion and despair. That lay ahead. In the meantime, he was "Captain of the Rant", preaching in London, returning now and then to his long-suffering wife in Suffolk, who in due time bore him five children, or living at Ilford with Major Rainborough and other members of the sect:[1]

> where was no small pleasure and delight in praising of a God who was an infinite nothing, what great and glorious things the Lord had done, in bringing us out of bondage to the perfect liberty of the sons of God, and yet the very motion of my heart was to all manner of theft, cheat, wrong or iniquity that privately could be acted, though in tongue I professed the contrary.

The presence of so prominent a Leveller as Rainborough among the Ranters is of special interest when taken in conjunction with the way in which Clarkson combined the Ranters' doctrines with social views that were close to those of Winstanley, and the very similar views expressed by Coppe in *A Fiery Flying Roll*:

> the ground of this my judgement was, God made all things good, so nothing evil but as man judged it; for I apprehended there was no such thing as theft, cheat, or a lie, but as man made it so: for if the creature had brought this world into no propriety, as *Mine* and *Thine*, there was no such thing as theft, cheat, or a lie; for the prevention thereof *Everard* and *Gerrard Winstanley* did dig up the Commons, that so all might live of them selves, then there had

---

[1] Major William Rainborough, brother of Col. Thomas Rainborough, and himself a leading Leveller who had taken an active part in the Putney debates.

been no need of defrauding, but unite with one another, not then knowing this was the devil's kingdom, and Reason lord thereof, and that Reason was naturally inclined to love itself above any other, and to gather to itself what riches and honour it could, so that it might bear sway over its fellow creature; for I made it appear to *Gerrard Winstanley* there was self-love and vain-glory nursed in his heart, that if possible, by digging to have gained people to him, by which his name might become great among the poor Commonalty of the Nation, as afterwards in him appeared a most shameful retreat from *Georges-hill* with a spirit of pretended universality, to become a real Tithe-gatherer of propriety;[1] so that by these things in others, and the experience of my own heart, I saw that all men spake or acted, was a lye, and therefore my thought was, I had as good cheat for something among them, and not come under the lash of the Law.

The Ranters were, indeed, a curiously mixed body, in which mysticism rubbed shoulders with a rather primitive rationalism. It was this latter which, in the long run, Clarkson found unpalatable. For a time he was lodged in Rood Lane, "where I had clients many that I was not able to answer all desires. . . . I had most of the principal women come to my quarters", but, "I was still careful for moneys for my Wife, onely my body was given to other women". Soon "it became a trade so common, that all the froth and scum broke forth" and the authorities began to interfere. For a time he avoided trouble by visits to the country, but returned to London again, still convinced,

> that in the grave there was no remembrance of either joy or sorrow after. For this I conceived, as I knew not what I was before I came in being, so for ever after I should know nothing after this my being was dissolved . . . yet notwithstanding this I had sometimes a relenting light in my soul, fearing this should not be so, as indeed it was the contrary; but however, then a cup of Wine would wash away this doubt.
>
> But to return to my Progress, I came for *London* again to visit my old Society; which then *Mary Middleton* of *Chelsford* and Mrs *Star* was deeply in love with me, so having parted with Mrs

---

[1] There is no other evidence for or against this charge. In its absence it is possible rather than probable. Winstanley had attacked the Ranters in, *A Vindication of those whose endeavour is only to make the Earth a Common Treasury . . . Or Some Reasons given against . . . Ranting* (1649).

Middleton, Mrs *Star* and I went up and down the countries as man and wife, spending our time in feasting and drinking, so that Tavernes I called the house of God; and the Drawers, Messengers; and Sack, Divinity; reading in *Solomons* writings it must be so, in that it made glad the heart of God; which before, and at that time, we had several meetings of great company, and that some, no mean ones neither, were there, and at that time, they improved their liberty, where Doctor *Pagets* maid stript herself naked and skipped among them, but being in a Cooks shop, there was no hunger, so that I kept myself to Mrs *Star*.

Presently these activities attracted so much attention that Parliament issued warrants against Clarkson, Rainborough and others, offering a reward of one hundred pounds for Clarkson's capture. This induced one Jones to turn informer and Clarkson was taken to Whitehall and examined before a Parliamentary Committee. He behaved with the same boldness he had shown when before the Committee at Bury, denying all charges and standing on his right to refuse to answer any questions that might incriminate him:

What did you at Mrs *Croes* in *Redriff*? I had conference with the people. As you were preaching you took a pipe of Tobacco, and women came and saluted you, and others above was committing Adultery. This is more than I remember. No, you will not remember anything against you.

A book, probably a copy of *A Single Eye*, was then produced:

Why did not you write this book? That you are to prove. Here is the first two letters of your name. What is that to me? It may serve other names as well as mine. Did not Major *Rainborough* and these men give you monies to print this Book? How should they give me monies to print that which neither I nor they know of. This Book must be yours, for it speaks your language, suitable to your practice. I being a stranger to you, how should you know my language or practice? Though you will confess nothing, yet we have witness to prove it. Let them be examined in my presence.

After a good deal more of this,

they dismissed me to the place from whence I came, and said we shall report it to the House, that so with speed you may have your trial, but I think it was about fourteen weeks before I received the

Sentence of the House, which took up the House a day and a half work, as *John Lilburne* said stood the Nation in a Thousand pounds: And thus they sate, spending the Commonwealths monies, about frivolous things.

Rainborough was banned for life from serving as a Justice of the Peace and Clarkson was sentenced to banishment. This sentence was never carried out and a month later he was released and once more returned to his wife and to Suffolk. This ended his active connection with the Ranters. It seems clear that this was largely due to his growing disillusion with the negative character of his beliefs, but he always combined with his religious absolutism a remarkable vein of hard common sense, and it is not unfair to suppose that the unpleasant results that could follow the attempt to put Ranting principles into practice had some weight with him. This had been demonstrated both by his own imprisonment and the much worse sufferings of his fellow-Ranter, Coppe. In any case he seems never to have had much of the millennial enthusiasm which had motivated Coppe, Salmon and others. He did not as yet adopt a new faith, but contented himself for a time with the combined practice of medicine and somewhat bogus magic in south-west Suffolk and Cambridgeshire:

> I came forth of prison, and then took my journey with my wife to my house in *Stainsfield* and from there my progress into *Cambridgeshire* to the towns of *Foxen* and *Orwel* where I still continued my Ranting principle with a high hand.
>
> Now in the interim I attempted the art of Astrology and Physick, which in a short time I gained, and therewith travelled up and down *Cambridgeshire* and *Essex*, as *Lintin* and *Saffron-walden* and other countrey towns, improving my skill to the ut-most, that I had clients many, yet could not be therewith contented, but aspired to the art of Magick, so finding some of Doctor *Wards* and *Wollerds* Manuscripts, I improved my genius to fetch Goods back that were stolen, yea to raise spirits, and fetch treasure out of the earth, with many such diabolical actions, as a woman in *Sudbury* assisting me, pretending she could do by her witch-craft whatever she pleased; now something was done, but nothing to what I pretended, however monies I gained, and was up and down looked upon as a dangerous man, that the ignorant and religious people was afraid to come near me, yet this I may say, and speak the truth, that I have cured many desperate Diseases,

and one time brought from *Glenford* to a village town wide of *Lanham* to Doctor *Clark*, two women and one man that had bewitched his daughter, who came in a frosty cold night, tormented in what then *Clark* was doing, and so after that his daughter was in perfect health, and many such like things, that it puffed up my spirit, and made many fools believe in me, for at that time I looked upon all was good, and God the author of all, and therefore have several times attempted to raise the devil, that so I might see what he was, but all in vain, so that I judged all was a lie, and there was no devil at all, nor indeed no God, but onely nature, for when I have perused the Scripture I have found so much contradiction as then I conceived, that I had no faith in it at all, no more than a history, though I would talk of it, and speak from it to my own advantage, but if I had really related my thoughts I had neither believed that Adam was the first Creature, but that there was a Creation before him, which world I thought was eternal.

To a man of Clarkson's character and antecedents such an absence of positive faith could not but be intolerable, yet it would be wrong to see in his state of mind a purely individual distress. By this time the splendid hopes of the revolutionary years were fading, as the Protectorate followed the Commonwealth, and it was among the Levellers and the advanced sects, in whom these hopes had been highest, that despair made its greatest inroads. The Army, which ten years before had marched on London from Putney singing:

> The Lord begins to honour us,
> The Saints are marching on;
> The sword is sharp, the arrows swift
> To destroy Babylon,

were carrying on with unbroken discipline but with steadily diminishing enthusiasm the task of policing a largely hostile or indifferent civilian population. The Levellers had ceased to be a popular movement and had become a conspiracy. The sects were disintegrating, the dividing lines were becoming blurred, and many, as the Quakers were beginning to do, were turning away from a world which had so grievously disappointed them. This situation is already revealed in a report from Major General Haynes, Fleetwood's deputy in East Anglia, made to Thurloe in 1656:

Our fifthe monarchy men have many of them turned Anabaptist

. . . others have renounced that and all other ordinances and are turned Seekers, and feared by sober people will soon profess to be Quakers.[1]

Clarkson's state was therefore an extreme expression of feelings that were almost universal. By the beginning of 1658 he was ready for his next and final change. The instrument of this change was the Muggletonian prophet John Reeve, whom he first met in London in February of that year:

> so having some conference with *Reeve* the prophet, and reading his Writings, I was in a trembling condition . . . considering how sadly I had these many years spent my time . . . which after I was fully persuaded that there was to be three Commissions upon this earth, to bear record to the three Titles above, and that this was the last of those three: upon the belief of this I came to the knowledge of the two Seeds, by which I knew the nature and form of the true God and the right devil, which in all my travels through the seven Churches I could never find, in that now I see it was onely from the revelation of this Commission to make it known.
>
> Now being at my Journeys end, as in point of notional worship, I came to see the vast difference of Faith from Reason, which before I conclude you shall hear and how that from Faiths royal prerogative all its seed in *Adam* was saved, and all Reason in the fallen Angel was damned, from whence I came to know my election and pardon of all my former transgressions; after which my revelation growing, moved me to publish to the world, what my Father was, where he livith, and the glory of his house, as is confirmed by my writings now in publick.

In these two central Muggletonian doctrines of the Three Commissions and the Two Seeds Clarkson found a precise and authoritative formulation of ideas which as Anabaptist, Seeker and Ranter he had long held or groped after. Reeve and Muggleton, strongly and directly influenced by the translated writings of Boehme,[2] carried the Joachite gospel to its logical conclusion; for them the Third Age had actually begun with the Commission given to Reeve in 1652. Muggleton

---

[1] Thurloe, V, p. 187.

[2] Augustus Jessop, *The Coming of the Friars*, pp. 323–4. His essay on Muggleton, valuable in many ways, quite misses the point of the doctrines of the Three Commissions and the Two Seeds. See also Alexander Gordon, *The Origin of the Muggletonians*. Lytton Strachey's essay in *Portraits in Miniature* is of very slight value.

explained the doctrine in his posthumously published history of the
Sect. He tells that, being under examination at Derby, he expounded:

> who those Men were and are that have acted the Records of
> Water, Blood and Spirit upon Earth. . . . Now the Water Record
> was to Witness to God the Father, the Blood Record witnessed
> to Christ the Son, and you see they [i.e. Moses and the Apostles]
> were Men like yourselves. . . . So likewise must the Record of
> Spirit upon Earth be acted by Men also.
>
> Now, said I, God chose John Reeve and myself, by Voice of
> Word, to the hearing of the Ear, to be his Two last Prophets
> and Witnesses of the Spirit, and he gave us understanding of his
> Mind and Scripture above all Men in the World at this Day.
>
> Also we being the third Record of the Spirit upon Earth, we use
> no outward visible Form of Worship, but do Worship God in
> Spirit and Truth as Christ said.[1]

Here indeed was Clarkson's "Journeys end", the doctrine of the
Everlasting Gospel not as something in the utopian future but as a
present reality. In the doctrine of the Two Seeds he found another
thought common to many of the sects given a new and, to him, completely satisfactory form. It was currently held by these sects that the
rich, powerful and wicked were descended from Cain and the poor,
oppressed and godly were descended from Abel. Bunyan, among
many others, held this view:

> The Holy Ghost, as Bunyan and every reputable Baptist, Fifth
> Monarchy Man and Quaker knew, had intended Cain and Nimrod
> as the types of all kings and tyrants. . . . "It is the lot of Cain's
> brood to be lords and rulers first, while Abel and his generation
> have their necks under oppression."[2]

The Muggletonians linked this idea with their doctrine of the Fall, in
which Cain was not the son of Adam but of Eve and the devil "whose
nature is pure Reason", and, consequently, the inhabitants of the earth
are divided into the Seed of Adam (through Abel) who are to be saved,
and the Seed of Cain who are not only automatically damned but are
in fact devils, for the "right devil" had indeed no existence except in

---

[1] *The Acts of the Witnesses of the Spirit*, 1699, III, Chs. 11 and 12. Compare John Reeve,
A General Treatise of the Three Records or Dispensations, 1652, and *The Lost Sheep*, pp. 42–3.

[2] William York Tindell, *John Bunyan, Mechanick Preacher*, p. 141. The quotation is
from Bunyan's *Exposition of Genesis*. Compare Coppe's coupling of the blood of "the
righteous Abell" with that of the executed Levellers.

the Seed of Cain. Thus, the power to damn, which Reeve and Muggleton claimed and exercised freely, was really no more than the power to
recognise at sight the Seed of Cain and to pronounce upon it the
sentence of a damnation already existing. It was to the exposition of the
doctrine of the Two Seeds that Clarkson devoted the first book which
he wrote after his conversion.[1]

    The effect of Reeve, "the greatest prophet that ever shall be", upon
Clarkson was clearly overwhelming, but in 1658 Reeve was a dying
man and only survived his meeting with Clarkson by a few months. It
may not be without significance that Reeve was also a former Ranter,
though apparently of the stamp of Robins and Tany rather than
Coppe and Salmon. He was the mystic and prophet of the sect:
Clarkson's reaction to Muggleton was very different. Muggleton was
the practical leader and organiser, a man of great courage and un-
breakable determination, a true hero, though perhaps not a very
attractive one. And Clarkson's character was such that he aspired to be
the leader of any sect of which he became a member. There was always
an element of bombast and self-glorification in him, even when he was
most sincere, and this is well illustrated by an episode which happened
about 1659. The Muggletonians' chief rivals were the Quakers, and
one of Clarkson's contributions to the paper war between them was a
pamphlet called *The Quakers Downfall*. This was answered by the
Quaker John Harwood in *The Lying Prophet Discovered and Reproved*,
in the course of which Harwood described a dispute he had with
Clarkson and Muggleton, during which Clarkson boasted that,

> he had damned the Lord Mayor seven or eight years ago and
> 1000 more within these eight years, and that he had justified forty
> or fifty.

This cannot be true, since Clarkson had only been a Muggletonian
about a year at this date. The facts were that the Lord Mayor *had*
been damned in 1653 by Reeve and Muggleton, and after Reeve's
death Muggleton strongly objected to the exercise of the power of
damnation by any of his followers. He was the last man to tolerate any
attempt to steal his spiritual thunder, as Clarkson was clearly trying to
do.[2]

----

[1] *Look About You, for the Devil that you fear is in You*, 1659. Published by Larner, another
link with the Levellers.
[2] It is, of course, possible that Harwood was lying or mistaken, but the explanation I
have given squares exactly with everything Clarkson tells us about himself.

A conflict was inevitable, and it came with the publication of *The Lost Sheep*, in which Clarkson seemed to place himself on a level with Reeve and did not mention Muggleton at all. Muggleton acted at once to crush this threat to his supremacy:

> For as John Reeve was like unto Elijah, so am I as Elisha, and his place was but as Gehazi, and could stand no longer than my will and pleasure was.[1]

In Vol. III of *The Works of John Reeve and Ludowick Muggleton* (1820) there are letters from Muggleton which give more information about this dispute. On December 25th, 1660, he writes to Clarkson:

> ... You have made use of your beloved Frances and Ananias and Sapphire like, you have consulted with that venomous serpent your wife, and have made her your council in all spiritual matters ... your continual consultation with the Devil your wife, hath enraged your wife against the believers in this Commission, and against me; for which I do pronounce your wife cursed and damned to eternity, though she hath been damned by John Reeve already, therefore I have set to my seal, that John Reeve's damnation shall be true upon her.

Frances, being a Devil, of the Seed of Cain, could be damned. Clarkson himself, having already been justified as of the Seed of Adam, could not, much as Muggleton might have wished it. He could only write:

> you shall be as one of the least of believers of this Commission, and you shall be a reproach to saint and devil.

He could also punish Clarkson by cutting off the salary the latter seems to have been receiving from the church. So on January 2nd, 1661, he writes to Christopher Hill, one of his followers in Maidstone, that payments to Clarkson were to cease:

> let him betake himself to some employment in the world as well as the rest of the believers do; for I do not see fit that he and the serpent his wife should be maintained in idleness and pride.[2]

It is good to see that Frances Clarkson, who was evidently a woman of great spirit, as well as of remarkable loyalty to her erratic husband,

[1] Jessop, *op. cit.*, p. 334.   [2] *Op. cit.*, pp. 16–31.

preserved sufficient independence of mind to resist the pretensions of the Muggletonian prophets.

Clarkson was faced with a dilemma. At any previous stage in his life such treatment would have been enough to set him off on his spiritual travels again, but now he had found a faith which fully satisfied his deepest needs and he could not bear to leave it. He made a half-hearted attempt to oust Muggleton from his leadership, but, when it failed, he submitted. In 1661:

> Laurence Claxton humbled himself to me and acknowledged his Fault, and I forgave him, and took him into my Favour, but ty'd him not to write any more.[1]

It was a cruel sentence for Clarkson, to whom pen and ink were almost as dear as the pulpit, but it was accepted. Clarkson wrote no more, but contented himself for the remaining years of his life with preaching the Everlasting Gospel in humble subordination to Muggleton. It is to Muggleton that we owe our knowledge of the circumstances of his death in 1667. And once again, as so often in his career, it is hardly possible to be sure whether his end was the result of philanthrophy or opportunism, or in what proportions they were intermixed:

> It came to pass, when the Fire destroyed the City of London, he, to get a livlihood, did engage to help persons of Quality to borrow Money, to build their houses again.
>
> But the Persons, that had the Money did run away, and left Claxton in the Lurch; the Debt was one Hundred Pounds.
>
> So he onely was arrested, and put in Ludgate Gaol for this Money: he lay there a whole year and dyed there.
>
> But he gave a very good Testimony of his Faith in the true God, and in this Commission of the Spirit, and of that full assurance of eternal Happiness he should enjoy, to eternity after his Death.
>
> Insomuch that all the Prisoners marvelled, and were sorry they had opposed him so when he was alive.[2]

The circumstances of his end must have been tragic and sordid, but I do not think we should regard him as an object of pity: he died in the full assurance of having found what he had sought so persistently through all the apparent contradictions and inconsistencies of his eventful life, the full and glorious light of the Everlasting Gospel.

---

[1] *Acts of the Witnesses*, III, Ch. 6.   [2] *Ibid.*

6

A Still and Soft Voice

In an age of rhetoric and hyperbole, when men engaged in the fiercest controversy and claimed attention by trying to shout louder than all their neighbours, there was one man who followed exactly the opposite course. He sought and secured attention by lowering his voice so that only the most careful and attentive listener could catch it. One of the most thorough-going revolutionaries in an age of revolution, his main concern was the battle of ideas. As he wrote:

> I never proposed any man for my enemy, but injustice, oppression, innovation, arbitrary power, and cruelty; where I found them, I ever opposed myself against them; but so, as to destroy the evil, but to preserve the person and therefore all the war I have made . . . hath been to get victory over the understandings of men, accounting it a more worthy and profitable a labour to beget friends to the Cause I loved, rather than to molest mens persons, or confiscate mens estates.[1]

Yet William Walwyn, this quiet, reasonable, contemplative man, while no doubt conquering many minds, was perhaps more hated and more vilified than any of his contemporaries. The reason for this is to be found partly in his Socratic method, his questioning and testing of all commonly accepted ideas, which enraged the orthodox because they found it so hard to meet, but still more, perhaps, in the growth of his ideas, which, beginning with the already sufficiently subversive belief in the hope of salvation for all men, the advocacy of religious toleration and the application *in practice* of Christian charity, became progressively secularised, leading not only to a programme of political democracy but to a challenge to the whole social structure. It was as one of the leading group of the Leveller Party that Walwyn was able to develop his ideas to their logical conclusion.

Walwyn was born about 1600, into one of those gentry families

[1] *The Fountain of Slaunder Discovered*, 1649, p. 10.

which, being substantial rather than really rich, tended to put their younger sons into trade. The outline of his early life can conveniently be given in the words of his friend and son-in-law, Humphrey Brooke:

> Mr Walwyn was born at Newland in Worcester-shire of Mr Robert Walwyn Esquire, a man of good Life and Repute in his Country, and of between three and four hundred pounds Annual Estate, that his Mother is still living and was Daughter to Doctor Westphaling, Bishop of Hereford: his Brothers and Sisters are likewise in that Country; but he being a younger Brother, was bound Apprentize in London, and served out his Time with a Silk-man in Pater-noster-Row: a while after, he was made Free of the Merchant Adventurers Company, and hath since traded as Merchant about seventeen or eighteen yeers; during all which time, his aboads have bin known and certain, and his residence in London constant, except two or three journeys into his owne Country, and one or two to the Army, before its first coming to London. That he was never over Sea in any Country whatsoever. That he has from the profits of his Trade, maintained his Family in a middle but contentful condition; having bin much wasted, but never gained one penny by these eight yeers distractions, nor ever desired it.[1]

Brooke adds that he had "almost twenty children".

From the outbreak of the Civil War Walwyn was active in the parliamentary cause, helping to organise the raising of supplies in the City. At this stage the difference between the various sections of the parliamentary party were hardly apparent, yet there were already disquieting signs of Presbyterian intolerance and desire to enforce uniformity. Walwyn's earliest writings, *The Humble Petition of the Brownists* (Nov. 1641) and *Some Considerations tending to the undeceiving those whose judgements are misinformed* (Nov. 1642) both stress the need for unity if victory is to be won and insist that such unity can only be maintained on the basis of freedom and mutual respect for each other's beliefs. Like Walwyn's other early pamphlets these are unsigned, but are generally attributed to him on sound internal evidence. For his authorship of some unsigned pamphlets there is external evidence as well. In the quite narrow world that was concerned with such matters Walwyn's authorship was probably common knowledge at the time.

As the war developed, especially from 1644 onwards, the internal

[1] *The Charity of Church-men*, 1649, pp. 10-11.

differences sharpened. The sects gained confidence from the outstanding role their members played in the Army, the Presbyterians became
increasingly alarmed, and anxious to establish their systems while they
still had power to do so. At the same time the conditions of war were
bringing widespread hardship to the poor and raising new social
problems. All this is reflected in Walwyn's next writings.

In *The Power of Love* (Sept. 1643) he adopted for the first time what
one feels, was a very congenial device. Somewhat in the manner of
Swift, he assumes a mask, a *persona*, from behind which he can speak
with greater freedom, since no one can ever be sure if what he is saying
expresses his own conviction or that of a dramatic personality adopted
for the occasion. In this case he writes as a member of the sect of
Familists, or the Family of Love, a highly suspect group to which was
attributed, with apparently small reason, a variety of peverse doctrines
and unseemly practices. There is no reason to think that Walwyn was
ever a member of this sect, indeed, he specifically denies having been.
Nevertheless his ideas were more in harmony with those of the
Familists, Seekers and other similar groups than with those of the more
respectable Independents.

By this time, especially in London, a sort of dual system of religious
organisation had developed. On the one hand there was the traditional
parochial system, in which each locality had its church serving all who
lived in a neighbourhood. To a great extent this official network was in
Presbyterian hands. On the other, groups with common persuasions
were forming gathered churches, whose members chose their own
minister and might be drawn from a wide area on a voluntary basis.
Walwyn, though from the start he had always defended the right of
such groups to form and worship, tells us that he remained in his own
parochial congregation. This is easily to be understood. Parochial
worship, in its nature, did not involve the same degree of commitment as membership of a gathered church, a commitment which
Walwyn, with his wide-ranging mind and rationalist outlook, would
have found intolerable. There was perhaps a second reason. The
gathered church, especially perhaps in London, soon began to take the
character of a self-constituted elite, social as well as religious. In
1649 Walwyn, replying to sectarian attacks, declared that the Independents "pretend to erect, a holy, pure and undefiled worship", but,

> they as the rest, belyed the Spirit of God (pardon the harshnes
> of the expression, its for Gods cause and must be spoken), they

K

being no more infallibly certain of the truth they raise from the Scriptures than any of those whom they so much condemn; they as the rest, pray, preach, and do all for mony, and without it thay do nothing, taking mony for that which is not bread, but flower, chaffe and sand mixt together; that did not people swallow it whole, without chewing, or examination, it would be as gravell between their teeth, and they would spit it out of their mouths.

An since, they are increased in numbers, and have as it were, scumm'd the Parish Congregations of their most wealthy and zealous members.[1]

The formation of such an elite corresponded closely to the Calvinist doctrine of election, the church members tending to see themselves as the elect also of God, picked out from the unregenerate world doomed to perdition. Such doctrines had always been repugnant to Walwyn, as to many religious radicals of the time. He numbered himself with the Antinomians:

> I, through God's goodnesse, had long before been established in that part of doctrine (called then, Antinomian) of free justification by Christ alone; and so my heart was at much more ease and freedom, than others, who were entangled with those yokes of bondage, unto which Sermons and Doctrines mixt of Law and Gospel, do subject distressed consciences.[2]

and:

> I am not a preacher of the law, but of the gospell; nor are you under the law, but under grace: the law was given by *Moses*, whose minister I am not; but grace and truth came by Jesus Christ, whose minister I am: whose exceeding love hath appeared: and because I would have you fully to see and consider his love, therefore did I shew the woefull condition, from which only by his love you are delivered.[3]

Christ had died for sinners, that is to say for all men, and at the time he wrote *The Power of Love* Walwyn evidently believed that all men would be saved, whether they would or no:

> for yee are all justified freely by his grace through the redemption that is in *Jesus Christ*: your feares, nor sinnes, nor doubtings

---

[1] *The Vanitie of the Present Churches*, 1649, p. 11.   [2] *Walwyns Just Defence*, 1649, p. 8.
[3] *The Power of Love*, p. 20.

cannot alter that condition which Christ hath purchased for
you . . . and nothing shall be able to separate you from his love
then purchased: neither infidelity, nor impenitancie, nor unthank-
fulnesse, nor sinne, nor anything whatsoever can make void his
purchase: no, though with the Jewes you should deny the Lord
that bought you: so powerful was his bloud-shedding, and of so
full value for discharging of all our debts, past, present and to
come.[1]

There is some evidence that this belief was later modified. Humphrey
Brooke, defending him against the charge of denying the actual existence of Hell, wrote:

For his opinion concerning Hell, 'tis clearly thus: Though he
judges every wicked man to have, *intus Gehennam*, a Hell in his
own Conscience; as on the contrary, every good man to have the
Kingdom of God within him; yet upon strict search, which we
have made into the Scripture, we have concluded, that there is
another Hel succeeding judgement. . . . And though it seems
contrary to reason, that a man should be punished everlastingly
for a little sinning in this world, in which sense only he spoke it:
yet have we both submitted our Reasons to Gods Word, the
places fore mentioned being expresse for the same.[2]

However this may be, and the whole question of the credibility of the
evidence for and against Walwyn will have to be considered later, there
is little doubt that for him the door of salvation was indeed widely
open and the gates of Hell correspondingly narrow.

Alongside the doctrine of free justification there was another strand
in Walwyn's religion which was also common among seventeenth-
century radicals—the influence of the Epistle of St. James. This Epistle,
with its stress on the social implications of Christianity and its fierce
denunciations of the rich had disturbed Luther since it seemed to call in
question his key dogma of justification by faith alone, with its implication that the heart of religion lies in works, in good actions. It is in
The Power of Love that we can first see its influence on Walwyn, an
influence which was to grow as he became involved in the political
battle.

The Power of Love opens by contrasting the lot of rich and poor:

[1] *Ibid.*   [2] *The Charity of Church-men*, p. 4.

> looke about you and you will finde in these woefull dayes thous-
> ands of miserable, distressed, starved, imprisoned Christians: see
> how pale and wan they look: how cold and raggedly, and un-
> wholesomely they are clothed; live one weeke with them in their
> poore houses, lodge as they lodge, eate as they eate, and no oftner,
> and bee at the same passe to get that wretched food for a sickly
> wife, and hunger-starved children; (if you dare do this for feare of
> death or diseases) then walk abroad, and observe the general plenty
> of all necessaries, observe the gallant bravery of multitudes of
> men and women abounding in all things that can be imagined:
> observe likewise the innumerable numbers of those that have
> more then sufficeth.[1]

The man who accepts such a situation, is, Walwyn argues, no true
Christian, and the mark of a true Church is in doing works of charity
and mercy, "in feeding the hungry, cloathing the naked, visiting and
comforting the sick". So far he would, no doubt, command general
agreement, at least in theory, but not perhaps when he adds to this
traditional list, "or in freeing a Common wealth from all Tyrants,
oppressors and deceivers".[2]

> The politicians of this world would have religious men to be
> fooles, not to resist, no by no meanes, lest you receive damnation:
> urging Gods holy Word, whilst they proceed in their damnable
> courses; but they will finde that true Christians are of all men the
> most valient defenders of the just liberties of their Countrey,
> and the most zealous preservers of true Religion: vindicating
> the truths of God with their lives, against all ungodlinesse and
> unrighteousnesse of men.[3]

Just as all men are capable of Grace, and through Grace, of right
action, so all are endowed with reason and so capable of right understanding. Walwyn believed that this reasoning power had been ob-
scured by the corruptions of civilisation:

> You know it is said, that God made man righteous, but he sought
> out many inventions: that is, he made him naturally a rationall
> creature, judging rightly of all things, and desiring only what was
> necessary, and so being exempt from all labour, and care of ob-
> taining things superfluous, he passed his dayes with aboundance
> of delight and contentment: until he sought out unto himself

[1] P. 4.   [2] *The Vanitie of the Present Churches*, p. 43.   [3] *Ibid.*, p. 41.

many inventions: inventions of superfluous subtilities and arti-
ficiall things, which have been multiplied with the ages of the
world, every age still producing new: now in these later times we
see nothing but mens inventions in esteeme, and the newer the
more precious.[1]

This rather romantic primitivism, with its implications of a golden
age and of the possibility of recapturing it, was by no means uncommon
in the seventeenth century—we meet it in Winstanley and in the
popular anti-Normanism. But Walwyn, like Winstanley, developed
it in a new and revolutionary direction. As all men are capable of
Grace so all are capable of right understanding once the causes of
corruption have been removed:

> as it is in naturall things, so holds it in spirituall: God hath dealt
> abundantly well with us; there being nothing that is necessary
> either for the enlightening of our understandings, or the peace of
> our mindes, but what hee hath plainely declared and manifestly
> set forth in his Word: so plainly, that the meanest capacity is fully
> capable of a right understanding thereof, and need not to doubt
> but that he is so.[2]

To this democratic conviction of the ability of the common man,
given the necessary conditions, to understand whatever is necessary
for his happiness and well-being, Walwyn adds the belief that truth is
a liberating force and can best be discovered by free discussion. The
concluding pages of the Introduction to *The Power of Love* anticipate
by more than a year the most famous passage in Milton's *Areo-
pagitica*:

> Let brotherly love continue, and let every one freely speake
> his minde without molestation: and so there may be hope that
> truth may come to light, that otherwise may be obscured for
> particular ends: plaine truth will prove all, sufficient for vanquish-
> ing of the most artificiall, sophisticall error that ever was in the
> world; give her but due and patient audience, and her perswasions
> are ten thousand times more powerfull to worke upon the most
> dull refractory mindes, then all the adulterate alurements and
> deceivings of art.[3]

Many of the ideas of *The Power of Love* reappear, but in a sharper,

---

[1] *The Power of Love*, pp. 2–3.   [2] *Ibid.*, pp. 6–7.   [3] *Ibid.*, pp. A 7–8.

more polemical form in *The Compassionate Samaritaine*, published in
the summer of 1644. By this time the attempts to impose Presbyterianism on the whole nation were taking shape in actual ordinances and the
Independents and sects were thoroughly alarmed. Scottish ministers
in the Westminster Assembly were trying to force the pace, with
demands for the suppression and burning of heretical and tolerationist
books. It was to meet this situation, to reaffirm the principle of religious
liberty in the face of increasing attacks, that *The Compassionate Samaritaine* was written. That it was felt relevant may be deduced from the
fact that a second edition was needed by January 1645, perhaps even
earlier.

It was aimed, first at persecution and second at the pretensions of the
clergy to be men apart, different in kind from their congregations. The
Presbyterians, Walwyn argues, are now continuing the work of
the Bishops from whom they once suffered, and look like being even
more oppressive:

> I cannot thinke that the Bishops in their times used so many
> stratagems of vexation and cruelty against good people . . . some
> say the tyrannie over conscience that was exercised by the Bishops,
> is like to be continued by the Presbiters: that the oppressours
> are only changed, but the oppression not likely to be removed. . . .
> But the Presbiters, as it is conceived, will be more violent, as
> slaves usually are when they become masters.[1]

Similarly, having taken the place and enjoying the revenues of the
former clergy, it is even more necessary for the new ministers, being
parvenus, to set themselves apart:

> They would not have us thinke that a Minister comes to be so as
> an other man comes to be a Merchant, Bookseller, Taylor &c.,
> either by disposall of him by his friends in his education, or by
> his owne making choyce to be of such a Trade: no, there must be
> something spirituall in the businesse, a *Iure Divino* must be brought
> in. . . . Because otherwise, if the people did not beleive so, they
> would examine all that was said, and not take things upon trust
> from the Ministers, as if whatsoever they spake, God spake in
> them: they would then try all things. They would then handle
> their ministers familiarly, as they doe one an other, shaking off
> that timorousnesse and awe which they have of the Divines,

[1] *The Compassionate Samaritaine*, pp. 15–17.

with which they are ignorantly brought up. He that bade us try
all things, and hold fast that which was good, did suppose that
men have faculties and abilities wherewithall to try all things, or
else the counsell had beene given in vain.[1]

Meanwhile the situation was changing. Towards the end of 1644
dissatisfaction at the half-hearted and incompetent conduct of the war
led to the debates around the Self Denying Ordinance and the formation of the New Model Army. Lilburne was among those actively
agitating for these measures, as, apparently, was Walwyn at the head
of a group of citizens meeting at Salters' Hall. In January 1645 William
Prynne published his *Truth Triumphing Over Falsehood*, an attack on
all those opposed to Presbyterianism and the Presbyterian majority
in the House of Commons. Lilburne, once Prynne's admiring disciple,
replied immediately and in February Walwyn entered the controversy
with *A Helpe to the right understanding of a Discourse Concerning Independency*. Overton soon followed. Walwyn certainly and Overton
probably were still acting independently of Lilburne, but already we
can see the future leaders of the Leveller Party being drawn together
by the pressure of events and around an issue in which religion and
politics were closely related. 1645 was to see their co-operation firmly
established.

In June, after the news of Rupert's capture of Leicester reached
London, Lilburne was chairman at a meeting at the Windmill Tavern
to demand the more efficient conduct of the war. Walwyn also attended
with his Salters' Hall associates and the two men may have met.
However, they are recorded as meeting at Westminster on July 19th,
when Walwyn was leading a deputation to bring charges of corruption
against the Speaker, Lentall. Lilburne was present at the same time on
business of his own.

Walwyn's appearance and following are described in lively if
unflattering terms by John Bastwick:

> ... the complexion also of many of them being like the bellie of
> a toad; and to speake the truth, *Worley* was one of the properest
> gentlemen amongst them all, as he was the most remarkable and
> taken notice of, by reason of his habit and busie diligence; he
> went that day in a great white and browne basket-hilted beard,
> and with a set of teeth in his head, much like a Pot-fish, all
> staring and standing some distance from one another, as if they

[1] *Ibid.*, pp. 23–5.

had not been good friends; it may be conjectured, he picks them twice a day with a bed-staffe, they looke so white and cleare; he was mighty diligent about the Common-wealth that day, and the Privileges of the Subject, and all the fraternity came flocking about him upon all occasions, as a company of Turkyes doe about a Frogge, wondering at him as at a strange sight: Without doubt when the Parliament comes to be recruited, the Independents will make him a Member; and I am confident he will prove a rotten one, for he looks as if he had gotten a blow with a French colt-staffe, and it is notorious he is bankrupt of all goodnesse, and whatsoever show he makes now of Independence, Anabaptisme, or any of the new wayes, both he and Saint Sprat their Soliciter, have been knaves from their mothers womb; and therefore Master *Vicars*, if you have any hand in chosing new Members, let him not have your voyce.[1]

Bastwick says that Worley, as he calls Walwyn, was already an associate of Lilburne, but this may be an exaggeration or an anticipation. Curiously, Lilburne at this time also calls Walwyn Worley, in *The Copy of a Letter From . . . Lilburne to a Friend*, published in July, and again in *Innocency and Truth Justified* in December, which must indicate that their relations cannot yet have been very close. It must be remembered, however, that Lilburne was arrested soon after the meeting of July 19th.

In October Walwyn wrote his first overtly political pamphlet, *Englands Lamentable Slaverie*, "A private Letter of publique use, to the constant maintainer of the Just Liberties of the People of England, Lieuten. Coll. *John Lilburn* Prisoner in Newgate by command of Parliament." Though political it was not programmatic: the Leveller programme, and, indeed, the Leveller party were still some way in the future. But the conditions for a democratic party were already developing. Naseby had been won in June. By October the war was virtually over and now the question was being asked, where is the freedom for which it was allegedly fought? It is this question that Walwyn considers in principle, with the illegal imprisonment of Lilburne as the immediate case in point:

All the Art and Sophisterie in the world, will not availe to persuade you, that you are not in Newgate, much lesse that you are at libertie.[2]

[1] *A Just Defence of John Bastwick*, p. 17.   [2] *Englands Lamentable Slaverie*, p. 6.

But Lilburne is in Newgate by order of Parliament, and, now that King and Lords had virtually ceased to count, claims were being made that the House of Commons had become in fact sovereign, with unbounded power. Walwyn, though more than ready to admit that the Commons were now the supreme authority, examined and rejected this theory:

> Others there are [and clearly he is one of them] who affirme, that a Parliamentary authority is a power intrusted by the people (that chose them) for their good, saftie and freedome; and therefore that a Parliament cannot justlie do anything, to make the people lesse safe or lesse free then they found them.[1]

It is the people, "the whole Nation" who are sovereign and Parliament can only act on their behalf within limits that need to be carefully defined:

> For the Parliament is ever at libertie to make the People more free from the burthens and oppressions of any nature, but in things appertaining to the universall Rules of common equitie and justice, all men and all Authoritie in the world are bound.[2]

Walwyn conceded that much had been done in the putting down of the Bishops and the abolition of the Prerogative Courts, but more remained to be done:

> But if the people be not totally freed from oppression of the same nature they have a very small benefit of the taking downe of those oppressing Courts. Seeming goodnesse is more dangerous than open wickednesse. . . .
> And what became of that threed-bare doctrine that Kings were accountable only to God, what good effects did it produce? No, they are but corrupt and dangerous flatterers that maintaine any such fond opinions concerning either Kings or Parliaments.[3]

Walwyn bases his argument, as is usual with him, upon reason and natural law, rather than, like Lilburne, on precedent. In an interesting section of his pamphlet he explains why he does not share Lilburne's high regard for *Magna Carta*, which "is but a part of the peoples rights and liberties", and, "so little as lesse could not be granted with any pretence of freedom".

If a new political struggle was developing this did not mean that the

---

[1] *Ibid.*, p. 3.   [2] *Ibid.*, p. 6.   [3] *Ibid.*, p. 6.

religious struggle was any less bitter; rather that the political and religious struggles tended to overlap and merge and the most consistent fighters for toleration and the rights of the man in the pew against the pretensions of the man in the pulpit proved themselves also the best champions of political democracy. This was to be shown in a striking way in 1646 with the publication of the three parts of Thomas Edwards' *Gangraena*. These, appearing in February, May and December, were huge shapeless compilations of "the Errours, Heresies, Blasphemies and Pernicious Practices of the Sectaries of this time", and it is significant that Edwards, starting from the specifically religious errors, concentrated increasingly, as the year went on, upon the politically subversive ideas to which these errors gave birth. *Gangraena* grew alongside the growth of the Leveller Party as an organised political force, and its leaders claimed an increasing share of his attention.[1]

Gangraena became the focus of one of the bitterest controversies of the age, and of all Edwards' opponents Walwyn was perhaps the most effective. In the February *Gangraena* he was only mentioned in passing as "a dangerous man, a Seeker and a strong head". In his reply, *A Whisper in the Eare of Mr Thomas Edwards*, he took the opportunity of defending his character and in doing so of defending the principles for which he stood:

> I am one that do truly and heartily love all mankind, it being the unfeigned desire of my soul, that all men might be saved, and come to the knowledge of the truth, it is my extream grief that any man is afflicted, molested or punished, and cannot but most earnestly wish, that all occasion were taken away: there is no man weake, but I would strengthen; nor ignorant, but I would informe: nor erronious but I would rectifie, nor vicious but I would reclaim, nor cruel, but I would moderate and reduce to clemency . . . and however I am mistaken, it is from this disposition in me, that I have engaged my self in any publick affairs and from no other.[2]

He then outlines his political activities, beginning in his own parish, after which:

---

[1] A general account of Edwards and the *Gangraena* controversy is given in *John Lanseter*, pp. 20–6 in this volume.

[2] *A Whisper in the Eare*, pp. 2–3.

our next indeavours were for the whole ward, wherin after much labour, we so prevailed, that the well affected carryd the choice of Alderman and common councell men, and all other officers in the Ward: my next publike businesse was with many others, in a remonstrance to the Common Councell, to move Parliament to confirm certain maximes of free Government: wherein the power of Parliament was plainly distinguished from the Kings Office, so plainly, that had it taken effect: few men after due consideration thereof would through error of judgement have taken part against the Parliament or have befriended arbitrary power, as too many did for want of light; but it was stifled in the birth. I was also interrested in all the proceedings of *Salters Hall*, whence much good issued to the whole City and Kingdom; where I beleeve it will be testified by all, I was never heard or observed to propose or second a bad motion, nor far short of any in prosecution of anything that was good. . . . I ever associated my self with persons of known good affections to Parliament and Commonwealth: that it is my extream wonder that any well-affected person should affirm me to be a man dangerous.[1]

Denying that he was a Seeker he explained that his only desire was to find the element of truth in all religious creeds:

I a seeker, good now; whose your author? Am I one because I know many, and have been amongst them often, that I might know them fully; so have I been with all other judgements, but I carry with mee in all places a Touch-stone that tryeth all things, and labours to hold nothing but what upon plain grounds appeareth good and usefull: I abandon all niceties and uselesse things: my manner is in all disputes reasonings and discourses, to enquire what is the use: and if I find it not very materiall, I abandon it, there are plain usefull doctrines sufficient to give peace to my mind . . . hence it is that some have said I am a great Anabaptist, others (upon as good ground) a great Antinomian. . . . I conceive I should sinne if I should do more than in a loving way offer my argument, and gently perswade to what I conceive is both evidently true, and really usefull.[2]

In March, in *A Word More to Mr Thomas Edwards*, Walwyn defended

---

[1] *Ibid.*, pp. 4–5.
[2] *Ibid.*, pp. 6–7. Actually 10–11, the pagination is completely confused.

himself against the charge of having taken and then broken the Covenant. In his understanding of its sense he was pledged to defend the reformed religion *according to the word of God*. This he had always tried to do. The extirpation of heresy and schism does not mean the persecution of heretics and schismatics, but the attempt to persuade them of the errors of their views.

Walwyn's soft answers seldom had the effect of turning away wrath, and in the Second Part of *Gangraena*, published in May, Edwards devoted much more space to attacking him, and his charges were in the main those which pursued him through the rest of his political life.

> I shall lay him open to the world, and prove him to be a dangerous man, a Seeker and Libertine, a man of all Religions, pleading for all; and yet what Religion he is of no man can tell; A man of an equivocating Jesuistical spirit, being full of mentall reservations and equivocations, as appears by the sense he hath put upon the National Covenant.[1]

Edwards goes on to quote from a letter received from a Mr. T. C.:

> That Master *Walwyn* did say it was a sinne to pray for the King, and that it would be a sinne upon the Priests so to delude the people; and that he did admire at our Priests that they should stand bauling and praying for the King, that God would turn his heart and say of him that he was annoynted of God. And he said they were glad to do it (namely the Ministers) because if the King maintaine them in this way they would cry him up to the people. . . . And he further said that he did much admire at the simplicity that was in the hearts of the people, that they should suffer themselves to be governed by a King, and that under such a government the Kingdome could not be safe. He being asked what he thought of M. Marshall, M. Calamy, M. Sedgwick, and other godly Ministers; he answered and said they were a company of Mountebancks, and thet they kept the people in ignorance and blindnesse, and that they preached nothing but what we know already, and that he knew no Scriptures for them to be Preachers more than other men, as he named Shoemakers, Coblers, Weavers or Sopeboylers and the like . . . and that if their tythes were taken from them, they would soon leave their trade; and said that the

---

[1] *Gangraena*, II, p. 26.

Apostles were tradesmen and were not chargeable to the brethren.
. . . I asked him who should preach to the people and how they
should be maintained, if they would have them have nothing, he
answered he knew no Ministers that ought to be maintained, but
that every man that had gifts might be a Minister, and use the
liberty of his Conscience; and he spake on behalf of *Paul Best*
for his Blasphemy; saying, that if we could not convince his
Conscience, we ought not to punish his body. Touching the
Rebellion in *Ireland,* Master *Walwyn* said, the Irish did no more
but what we would have done ourselves, if it had been our case;
and said, What had the English to do in this Kingdome? And
that they were a better natured people than we, and said, why
should not they enjoy the liberty of their Consciences?[1]

There is also an anecdote of the kind that makes *Gangraena* so valuable
a mirror of the time, which Edwards claimed was told to him by a
Common-Councilman of the City:

There being a meeting at a Tavern of some wel-affected Citizens
to consider of some things in reference to the publique, as they
were sitting by the fire (before they began to fall on the businesse
thay met for) M. *Walwyn* spake of the Trinity in such strange
manner, and so slightly, that al the company was troubled at it
and they brake off and departed without doing anything of what
they came for.[2]

Edwards suggests that Walwyn stressed liberty of conscience to
ingratiate himself with the Independents so as to be brought in to
Parliament, perhaps for Cornwall. He adds that Walwyn and Lilburne had tried to secure election for Southwark, but had failed. Taken
with Bastwick's remark already quoted this suggests that Walwyn was
suspected at this time of Parliamentary ambitions. While this may have
been so, there is nothing whatever in his writings to suggest it, and
such ambitions hardly seem in keeping with what we know of his life
and habits. What can be said is that his way of advocating toleration
was so far from ingratiating him with the Independents that they were
already becoming suspicious of this too outspoken ally and that he
must have been aware of this.

John Vicars, another leading Presbyterian, writing in support of
Edwards, finds Walwyn's manner distasteful:

[1] *Ibid.*, pp. 26–7.   [2] *Ibid.*, p. 28.

> we have also one M. *Walwyn*, a most egrediously *Pharasaicall Whisperer*, Pharasaicall, I say; For in his frothy *Whisper* in M. *Edwards* his Eare, he takes occasion . . . to Magnifie himself, not whispering (now) but *blowing a Trumpet* of his own high prayses, with a *long-breath*, and a *lowd-Stentorial-voice*, about two pages long in quarto, and all to paint out his own person to be such a *Seraphicall* and *Angelicall-saint*, yea, as it were of such an *immaculate* and *sublimely refined* nature and *celestiall-temper*, as if there were *Nihil humani* in the man; in so much so, that truly for my part, I professe I never read or heard of such a notorious *Self-flatterer* in all my life.[1]

Edwards and Vicars were scurrilous writers who would stop at little to blacken anyone with whom they were at odds, yet these passages do reflect a widespread feeling about Walwyn which perhaps still troubles us. His piety, his universal benevolence and the unself-consciousness with which he proclaims them, are they not just too good to be entirely true? Is not this apparent candour a mask behind which something more may be concealed? "A man of all Religions, and yet what Religion he is of no man can tell." Is there not, at the least, a certain smugness, or, as Vicars puts it, self-flattery here?

Many of the charges made against him, as we shall see when discussing *Walwins Wiles*, are manifestly absurd. But can we accept his denials in all cases and without reservation? Perhaps we do not have, nor ever can have, the materials for a complete answer to such questions, but between his own statements and those of his enemies a provisional picture of the vernacular humanist begins to emerge.

Walwyn was by now 45, a comfortable though not rich merchant, with a house and garden and, for the time, a varied and well-read library. He was charitable, politically active, with a large circle of friends whom he liked to entertain and with whom he would discuss freely. It was alleged, and he did not deny it, that he used to go with them from one church to another, hearing sermons and afterwards discussing them—a gross presumption in the eyes of the Ministers. In any case he had a low opinion of preaching. Truth could better be attained:

> not by preaching or long set speeches: which are apt to deceive; but by conferences, and mutuall debates one with another, (the best way for attaining a right understanding) far excelling that

[1] *The Schismatick Sifted*, p. 23.

which is called preaching. But then, how shall Demetrius and the Craftsmen live?[1]

He had, he insists, a high regard for the Scriptures, but interpreted them liberally and took from them what he felt to be important—the love of God, his goodness to man and the social duties of Christian people:

> The truth is, and upon experience it will be found a truth: that once exceed these plain indisputable Doctrines, and you will be ever to seeke.[2]

Since the essentials were plain and simple there was little need for Ministers, "that pretend to expound the Scriptures, when they raise nothing but doubts, and darken them".[3] And he would goad the pious to fury by such questions as, "How can you *prove* the Scriptures to be the word of God?"

But as well as the Bible and theological writings he read and liked to discuss "humane" books. Plutarch, Seneca and Lucian are among those he mentions, as well as Montaigne whom he quotes more than once with evident admiration. All these he read in English translations: "Such a wise Jesuit I am, that with all my skill I cannot construe three lines of any Latin author."[4]

It is not surprising that his more orthodox companions felt some alarm and discomfort with this quiet, well-read man in whom the mystic and the sceptic seemed to merge—there is indeed a sense in which, among all the antinomian radicals of the seventeenth century, mysticism and materialism appear as the two sides of the same coin. Nor was he only disliked by his open, Presbyterian enemies, by Edwards, Vicars or Bastwick. The Independents, still nominally his allies, were hardly more happy. No doubt they welcomed his help against such attacks as that of *Gangraena*, but they also saw that his reasons for opposing Presbyterianism were very different from their own. Thus we find that when Walwyn's *A Word in Season*, calling for unity in face of a Presbyterian attempt to suppress heresy, come to an agreement with the Scots and a settlement with the King, was published in May 1646, the congregation of John Goodwin subscribed 50s. to have 10,000 copies printed and distributed. Yet at this very time:

---

[1] *The Vanitie of the Present Churches*, p. 22.   [2] *Ibid.*, p. 32.   [3] *Ibid.*, p. 36.
[4] *Walwyns Just Defence*, p. 9.

some leading people of master John Goodwins, set themselves down as a Committee, calling before them, all they could finde had ever conversed with me, to inform whatsoever I had said that might tend to my disparagement. . . . Which I had continual notice of as they came in, and who did inform: and who would not . . . me thoughts it was a strange work, for a people who called themselves the people of God: but so they did; and at length had possest divers, who formerly had well respected me, that I was a dangerous man and not fit for society.[1]

This information was not used at the time, but put into cold storage to form the bulk of the charges made three years later in *Walwins Wiles*. In the meantime Master Goodwin's people continued for some time an uneasy co-operation with the Levellers, who were now increasingly coming to act as an organised political party. In June, Lilburne, after an interval of liberty, was sent back to prison by order of the House of Lords, and Walwyn came to his defence with *A Pearle in a Dounghill*. After praising Lilburne's faithfulness to the cause of the people Walwyn came to his real point, an attack on the authority of the House of Lords. The Commons, as the representatives of the people, were alone qualified to exercise the sovereign powers of Parliament, and this only so long as they remained truly representative. It was their duty to deliver the people from all oppression, "otherwise they will abominate them, because for a People to be made slaves by or in time of Parliament is like as for a man to be betrayed or murthered by his own father".[2]

A month later Overton joined the battle with *A Remonstrance of Many Thousand Citizens*, which set out the basic political programme of the new party and expounded the doctrine of popular sovereignty in more aggressive language:

> Wee are well assured, yet cannot forget, that the cause of our choosing you to be *Parliament-men*, was to deliver us from all kind of Bondage, and to preserve the Common-wealth in Peace and Happinesse: For effecting whereof, we possessed you with the same Power that was in our selves, to have done the same: For wee might justly have done it our selves without you, if we had thought it convenient; choosing you (as Persons whom wee thought fitly qualified, and Faithfull,) for avoiding some inconveniences.[3]

[1] *Walwyns Just Defence*, p. 3.   [2] *Pearle*, p. 4.   [3] *Remonstrance*, p. 1.

It will be noted how far this departs from the orthodox Calvinist view that rebellion even against a tyrannical ruler can only be justified if it is carried out under the leadership of authorised magistrates. Overton's *Remonstrance*, perhaps, marks the real beginning of the Leveller Party, in which Walwyn was now to be increasingly involved both as organiser and as theoretician.

This did not hamper the continuation of his attack on Thomas Edwards. Early in June he published *An Antidote Against Master Edwards His Old and New Poyson*, which contains a brilliant and still topical analysis of the technique of the witch-hunt:

> If you observe any man to be of a publique and active spirit, (though he be no Independent or Separatist) he can never be friend to you in your work, and therefore you are to give him out, to be strongly suspected of whoredome, or drunkennesse, or an irreligious person, or an Atheist, and that by godly and religious persons, he was seen and heard blaspheming the holy Scriptures, and making a mock of the Ordinances of Christ, or say he is suspected to hold intelligence with Oxford, or anything no matter what, somewhat will be believed, you cannot be ignorant how much this hath prevailed against divers able persons.
>
> If you see any such man but once talking with a Papist, or (though not) you may give out that very honest men suspect him to be a Jesuit: if any one but demand of any others, how you know the Scriptures to be the word of God, give it out for certain he denieth them, or if any put questions concerning *God* or *Christ* or the *Trinity*, you have more than enough to lay accusations upon them, that shall stick by them as long as they live, if you follow this my counsell thoroughly saith Machiavell (as in part you have done) you cannot fail of your end, you shall never want matter, you shall (amongst those you deceive) be taken for a most zealous, holy, and religious man, you may write book upon book, great and large ones, and make a good profit (or great renowne) by them, and in after days be recorded as a famous author.[1]

In August came *A Prediction of M. Edwards his Conversion and Recantation* which declared ironically that his state of mind being now like that of Saul on the road to Damascus, his conversion may shortly be expected and then he will look for and embrace what is true and good in all creeds.

[1] *An Antidote*, pp. 8–9.

L

Finally, in October, came *A Parable or Consultation of Physitians upon Master Edwards*, in which four doctors, Love, Justice, Patience and Truth, set themselves to the case of Edwards. Cast in dialogue form, it differs markedly from Walwyn's other writings and somewhat resembles Overton's *The Araignement of Mr Persecution*, though it is less vigorous and more ironic. The choice of this form may, perhaps, be an indication of a growing personal friendship and mutual influence between Walwyn and Overton, now both established among the Leveller leadership. The two men were evidently very different in tastes and temperament, but they shared a strongly theoretical bent— for both activity grew out of basic principle, unlike Lilburne whose principles were often a consequence of activity.

The *Gangraena* controversy hardly survived 1646, and, with the self-exile of Edwards in January and his death in August, came to an end. In April 1647 Walwyn published his last tolerationist tract, *A Still and Soft Voice from the Scriptures, Witnessing them to be the Word of God*. Despite its title, this is essentially a defence of the right to try and examine all things, and of Walwyn's methods of enquiry. The title may, indeed, be deliberately misleading—a means of persuading some to read it who would not open an avowedly tolerationist book. It is, in part, a denial of the charge of Atheism:

> If . . . you demand how they come to know there is a God, or that the Scriptures are the word of God: their common answer is, *doe you deny them: it seems you doe? otherwise why doe you aske such questions?* if they offer to proove by some common received argument: and you shew the weaknesse thereof: they'le go nigh to tell you to your face, and report for certaine behind your back, to all they know, or can know, that you are an Atheist and deny the Scriptures to be the word of God: nor do they hate any sort of men so much, as those who are inquisitive after knowledge.[1]

Walwyn distinguishes between the superstitious and the religious man. The former

> will course his poor neighbour out of all he hath, yea out of the Nation, if he cannot course him *into his opinion*: and all upon pretence of doing God service and for the good of his soule.
>
> As for his body, or estate, thats no part of his care . . . he may goe into what prison he will, and ly and rott and starve there: and

[1] *A Still and Soft Voice*, pp. 4–5.

these kind of Religious people are not halfe so much moved at it
as if he goe to another Church or congregation than what they
approve.[1]

To the truly religious man, as to Walwyn himself, civil and religious
liberties are indivisible:

> The liberty of my native Country, and the freedome of all
> conscientious people hath been, and still is pretious in my esteeme:
> nor shall I be discouraged (by any unworthy slanders cast upon me)
> from a just and due prosecution of both, according to my place
> and calling.[2]

In practice, by this time, native liberties had come to take first place in
his activities, and Joseph Frank is probably correct in assigning to him
"the guiding hand in the organisation of radical propaganda".

He never shared Lilburne's passion for martyrdom, or Overton's
warm pugnacity, but he had had a long experience in managing
committees, drafting petitions and presenting them with the maximum
effect. There is no doubt that he had a hand in drafting the many
programmatic statements of the years 1647 to 1649, and for the first of
these, the *Petition* of March 1647, he implicitly claims rather more than
this:

> The Petition is yet to be seen, and is fraught with abundance of
> good things, such as I really desired the House would have
> granted.[3]

Drafted in language of studied moderation and reasonableness, such
as Walwyn well knew how to use, its very opening implies a revolutionary change, being directed to "The right honourable and Supreme
authority of this Nation, the Commons in PARLIAMENT assembled".
This challenged, as we have already noted Walwyn doing, the traditional sovereignty of the King in Parliament, which the majority in
the Commons were still planning to restore. After a number of
positive achievements of Parliament had been "most thankfully
acknowledged", the *Petition* set out a whole programme of reforms in
which nearly all the main Leveller demands were contained.

Presented early in March and circulated for signatures, the *Petition*
came into the hands of the Commons, was rejected, and Nicholas Tue
and Major Tulidah, who had been active in promoting it, were

---

[1] *Ibid.*, p. 8.   [2] *Ibid.*, p. 14.   [3] *Just Defence*, p. 4.

arrested. A petition of protest against these arrests was rejected, as was a third petition on May 20th, which was ordered to be burnt by the Commons hangman. In all, six appeals were made to the Commons between March and June, all unsuccessful. Lilburne gave a detailed account of the struggle in *Rash Oaths*, and Walwyn described it more briefly and analytically in *The Poore Wise-Mans Admonition unto all the plaine People of London* (June 10th) and *Gold Tried in the fire* (June 14th).

The first of these has a detailed class-analysis of the forces opposed to these petitions. They are the secret enemies of the Commonwealth and the men who have done well out of the war:

> Divers men by corruption are growne rich, from small estates or nothing, to be very wealthy; and finding that this Army and such as love them, because they love their country, are inquisitive and unwilling to see the State abused, and the people defrauded, fearing that the mountaines of wealth they have raised, may yet be returned to the right owners, or the common stock, and that their unjust actions may undergo scrutiny and tryall, have for prevention thereof, desperately resolved to embroyle us in a new warre, and bring all to the former confusion, if not utter desolation, finding by experience, that they can best fish in troubled waters, and escape best in the presse; that corruption is no otherwise maintainable, but by might and force, and for that very end and purpose have contrived to engage you against the Army and those that wish them well, by which policie they suppose all your thoughts will be diverted from thinking upon them and their corruption. . . .
>
> The heads of this design are the corrupt men in the House of Commons, even such as have been formerly of the enemies party abroad, and done him services here at home, by discovering our counsels (as apparently by interception of some of their letters) partaking with the Conspirators in the City (as in Wallers plot) opposing the raising of this Army (by which the worke hath been so speedily ended) appearing crosse in all debates of the House for redresse of grievances, or relief of the oppressed and much abused people, constantly manifesting, That they have proposed other ends to themselves, than the common good of the Nation.
>
> Assistant to these is the Mayor of London . . . a man favouring the enemy, and never manifesting any affection to the Parliament, in their undertaking to make us a free people; also many of the

Aldermen and great men of the Citie whose interests depends upon Prerogative; and is supported by the subjection of the plaine people.[1]

Gold Tried in the fire, after a short summary of events, attacks the existing House of Commons in language sharper than any Walwyn had used before. The reader:

> may judge whether their Petitions, or the Petitions burnt, vilified, and disgraced, deserve most thanks, or tend most to the saftie of the Parliament and the Common-wealth.
>
> And will henceforth conclude, that as there is little good to be hoped for from such Parliaments as need to be Petitioned; so there is none at all to be expected from those that burn such Petitions as these.[2]

After this setback, as is foreshadowed in the passages just quoted, there was a shift in Leveller tactics. While undoubtedly political activity in London continued, they began to concentrate their main effort on the Army, where military grievances made the rank and file, and even many officers, ready to listen with sympathy to their policies. We have no means of knowing what part Walwyn took in this, though it must have been at this time that his "one or two" journeys to the Army of which Brooke spoke, were made. In fact, little is known about his activities during the year following June 1647. With the possible, and in any case unimportant, exception of *Englands Weeping Spectacle* (June 1648) he does not appear to have written anything till *The Bloody Project* (August 1648). But, equally, there is no evidence for any discontinuance or slackening of his political activities. He probably had a share in drafting such documents as *An Agreement of the People*— at least his proposed inclusion on the committees set up in November 1648 to prepare a new and agreed version would suggest that he had some responsibility for the earlier one. After the defeat at the rendez- vous at Corkbush Field (November 15th, 1647) had destroyed any immediate prospect of success in the Army, the Levellers once more concentrated on London and the surrounding towns.

A regular party organisation was established, with a central com- mittee, local committees and a membership paying regular weekly contributions. A stream of pamphlets and petitions poured out. It is impossible not to suppose that Walwyn was at the centre of such

---

[1] *Admonition*, pp. 2–4.   [2] *Gold Tried*, p. 4.

activities, at which he was so expert. Yet he remained in the background: his name appears nowhere, for example, in *A Declaration of some Proceedings of Lt Col. John Lilburne and his Associates* (Feb. 1648), though on page 5 it rather ingeniously turns against the Levellers the parable of the sheep, wolves and dogs which Walwyn had included in *An Antidote*. All this, however, need mean little or nothing in view of his evident dislike of publicity.

His personal situation continued to grow more difficult. So long as there was a serious danger that the Presbyterians could impose a persecuting orthodoxy on the nation the Independents, Baptists and other minority groups were ready to welcome the support of such brilliant, if theologically suspect, polemicists as Overton and Walwyn. After 1646 this danger receded as the Independents grew in strength, and as the Army, under Independent leadership, became a major, and finally the major, political force. To the extent that it freed the Independents from the need to seek allies to the left, this in time weakened their alliance with the Levellers as a whole, but it operated with peculiar force against Walwyn. Lilburne, politics apart, remained in the main stream of Puritan belief and could be regarded as an erring brother:

> As for L. C. Jo. Lilburn, I am very apt to beleeve, and hope, that there are yet some seeds of God remaining in him which . . . will . . . at last break forth in beauty and strength, in much sorrow, repentance and humiliation, in much humility, meekness and sweetness of spirit &c, &c.[1]

No such hopes could be entertained for Walwyn, the anti-clerical and sceptical mystic.

The renewal of war in May 1648 led to a temporary suspension of Leveller agitation, as all parties came together in face of the common enemy. Lilburne, out of prison again, wrote to Cromwell pledging his support and no Leveller pamphlets of importance appeared between May and August. On August 17th Cromwell defeated the Scots at Preston; a few days later Colchester fell to Fairfax. Not only was the war over, but it must have been obvious that, after years of indecision, a definite settlement must soon be reached. The speed with which the Levellers launched the *Petition* of September 11th shows that they had anticipated and prepared for this situation.

Their new campaign opened with the publication about August 21st

[1] *Walwins Wiles*, p. 22.

of one of Walwyn's best and most characteristic tracts, *The Bloody Project*. While advancing Leveller policy it reflects to a greater extent than any of his other writings his hatred of war, at points approaching pacifism. In it he expressed his personal distress at the renewal of the war and the human suffering involved, and its tone suggests that most of it was written while the war was actually at its height.

It opens by stressing the necessity for any individual to satisfy himself that the war in which he is engaged is a just war, fought for a good and sufficient cause. It examines the claims made by the opposing parties and especially those of Parliament. They, it implies, have been so general as to be practically meaningless:

> Or was it sufficient thinke you now, that the Parliament invited you at first upon generall termes, to fight for the maintenance of the true Protestant Religion, the Libertyes of the People, and Priviledges of Parliament; when neither themselves knew, for ought is yet seen, nor you, nor any body else, what they meant by the true Protestant Religion, or what the Liberties of the People were, or what those Priviledges of Parliament were, for which yet neverthelesse thousands of men have been slain, and thousands of Familyes destroyed?[1]

In practice, the victors had betrayed the cause for which they claimed to fight and the people whose help they had enlisted:

> And no doubt many of you understood by the Liberties of the People, that they intended to free the Commons in Parliament the peoples Representative, from a Negative voyce, in King or Lords, and would have declared themselves the highest Authority, and so would have proceeded to have removed the grievances of the Common-wealth: And when you had seen Patents, Projects and Shipmoney taken away, the High Commission, and Starchamber abolished, did you ever imagine to have seen men and women examined upon Interrogatories, and questions against themselves, and imprisoned for refusing to answer? Or to have seen Commoners frequently sentenced and imprisoned by the Lords? Did you ever dream that the oppressions of Committees would have exceeded those of the Councel-table; or that in place of Pattents and Projects, you should have seen an Excise established, ten fold surpassing all those, and Shipmoney together? You thought rather

[1] *Bloody Project*, p. 4.

that Tythes would have been esteem'd an oppression, and that Trade would have been made perfectly free, and that Customs if continued, would have been abated, and not raysed, for the support of domineering factions, and enrichment of foure or five great men, as they have been in these late times, to the sorrow and astonishment of all honest men and the great prejudice of the Trade of the Nation.[1]

The rich make war because it is to their advantage—only the poor suffer by it:

> your great ones, whether the King, Lords, Parliament men, rich Citizens &c. feel not the miserable effects thereof, and so cannot be sensible; but you and your poor friends that depend on Farmes, Trades, and small pay, have many an aking heart when these live in all pleasure and deliciousness: The accursed thing is accepted by them, wealth and honor, and both comes by the bleeding miserable distractions of the Common-wealth, and they fear an end of trouble would put an end to their glory and greatness.[2]

Since the people have been deceived and betrayed they must now be ready to defend their liberties against a Parliament just as formerly they did against a King:

> The King, Parliament, great men in the City and Army, have made you but the stairs by which they have mounted to Honor, Wealth and Power. The only Quarrel that hath been, and at present is but this, namely, whose slaves the people shall be . . . and if a people must not be left without a means to preserve it self against the King, by the same rule they may preserve themselves against the Parliament and Army too; if they pervert the end for which they received their power, to wit the Nations safety.[3]

Like the *Large Petition* of March 1647, the *Petition* of September 11th was a party manifesto, expressing the collective views of the whole leadership, but, equally, its style and tone suggests that Walwyn again had a big share in its drafting. Once again we have the familiar combination of conciliatory language with clear and far-reaching demands. The situation appeared more promising than for some time. The Grandees, the dominant group of officers around Cromwell and Ireton,

---

[1] *Bloody Project*, p. 5.   [2] *Ibid.*, p. 14.   [3] *Ibid.*, pp. 14–15.

had at last decided to put the King on trial as a war criminal, to abolish the Lords and to set up a Republic. To carry through this programme they needed the support of the left, or, at the least, its temporary neutralisation. The first step was to deal with the Presbyterians in the House of Commons, upon whom the Grandees were happy enough to see the Levellers putting pressure. The Levellers in turn were per-suaded that the Grandees were moving in their direction and did not at all realise the immense gap which still separated them.

Many of the demands contained in the March *Petition* and other Leveller manifestoes were now repeated, but there were some im-portant new ones—the abolition of excise and "all kind of taxes, except subsidies, the onely and just way of England", the laying open of "all late enclosures of Fens and other Commons, or have enclosed them onely or chiefly to the benefit of the poor", and the execution of "Justice upon the Capitall Authors and Promoters of the former or late Wars", that is, primarily upon the King. One other demand, "That you would have ordered some effectual course to keep people from begging and beggery, *in so fruitful a Nation as through Gods blessing this is*", contains a rather unusual phrase, italicised here, which recurs in Walwyn's *Just Defence*.

When presented to the Commons on September 11th, only a few days after being printed, the *Petition* was claimed to have already 40,000 signatures. Two days later it was supported by a mass lobby at West-minster, demanding its immediate consideration. While the pressure on Parliament was being maintained, the Levellers were to adopt a different and parallel plan to realise their programme. The details of the complex moves involved are mainly known to us from Lilburne's account in *Legall Fundamental Liberties*.

Towards the end of October he had a meeting with Cromwell, who seems to have indicated that he had come to a position close to that of the Levellers. Lilburne was sceptical. At a later meeting in London he and Wildman were told:

> The chief things first to be done by the Army, was first To cut off the King's Head &c. and force and thoroughly purge, if not dissolve the Parliament: All of which we were against, and press'd to know the bottom of their center, and in what they would absolutely rest for a future Settlement.[1]

Lilburne explained that,

[1] *Legall Fundamental Liberties*, p. 29.

there being no other balancing power in the Kingdome against the Army, but the King and Parliament, it was our interest to keep up one Tyrant to balance another, till we certainly knew what that Tyrant that pretended fairest would give us as our Freedoms . . . and therefore I pressed very hard for an Agreement amongst the People first, utterly disclaiming the thoughts of the other, till this was done. And this (I told them) was not onely my opinion, but I beleeve it to be the unanimous opinion of all my friends with whom I most constantly conversed.[1]

The "gentlemen Independents" were furious, but seeing no other way of securing Leveller backing agreed to a committee of eight— four on each side—to prepare a draft *Agreement of the People*. Walwyn was chosen as one of four Leveller representatives:

But John Price sent some of the company to tell us (after we were parted, and some of us drinking a cup of wine below) he would not make one, if Mr Walwyn was one, for he had a prejudice against him. Unto which I replyed, M. Walwyn had more honesty and integrity in his little finger, than John Price had in all his body; and therefore No meeting for me, seeing John Price was so base, unlesse Mr Walwyn was one, though we had but two of a side; but the business being much debated and expostulated, Mr. Walwin and John Price both (for peace sake) were at present laid aside.[2]

This John Price was soon to be the principal author of *Walwins Wiles*, and it may be assumed that his objection was not the result of mere personal prejudice, but reflects the growing opposition to Walwyn in clerical circles. The remaining six members of the Committee met at the Nag's Head in London, on November 15th, when it was agreed that a broader and more representative committee should be formed, with four delegates each from the Levellers, the Grandees, the House of Commons and the Churches. To this committee Walwyn was again chosen with Lilburne, Wildman and Maximilian Petty, "by unanimous consent of the Agents from our friends in and about London, at a very large meeting".[3] This time no objection seems to have been made against him. It met at Windsor, but its proceedings were immediately interrupted by the decision of the Army chiefs to march

[1] *Legall Fundamental Liberties*, pp. 29-30. Lilburne, in effect, explains that he was expressing a Party decision.
[2] *Ibid.*, p. 30.   [3] *Ibid.*, p. 33.

on London, which was reached on December 2nd. Pride's purge of the Presbyterian Members of Parliament followed on December 6th. "Which journey", Lilburne writes, "was very much opposed by Mr. Walwyn, and many reasons he gave against the march to London at all."[1]

The four Levellers, with Henry Marten, drafted a new version of the *Agreement*, and discussions around it were resumed in London. These discussions and their outcome are described elsewhere,[2] and here it need only be said that the Levellers were deceived and out-manœuvred by Ireton and Cromwell, who made no attempt to put the *Agreement* into effect once they had won the time they needed to try and execute Charles and establish their Council of State as the effective ruling power in the nation.

Not long after this Walwyn appears to have ceased for a time to play any active part in Leveller affairs. When he, with Lilburne, Overton and Thomas Prince, was arrested on March 28th on a charge of publishing *The Second Part of England's New-Chaines Discovered*, Lilburne was surprised, since he had had no part in its preparation:

> We could not but wonder at the apprehending of M. Walwin about that, he having for some months past (that ever I could see, or hear of) never bin at any of our meetings, where any such things were managed.[3]

The reason for this temporary inactivity is obscure: it does not seem to have been due to any change of principle, on the evidence of his subsequent conduct or writings, and it may, of course, have been for purely personal and private reasons of which we can know nothing. Two other possibilities, however, suggest themselves. It may have been due to a feeling that while he was under such strong attack from the clerical faction, with whom it was important for the Levellers to maintain as good relations as possible, his presence in the leadership could be an embarrassment to his colleagues. On the other hand there is a hint of a tactical difference between the estimates that Lilburne and Walwyn made of the modified version of the *Agreement* presented by the Army officers to Parliament on January 20th. Lilburne, speaking, presumably, for a majority of the leadership, had criticised it very severely in *Englands New Chains Discovered*, while Walwyn, if we can take *A*

---

[1] *Ibid.*, p. 34.   [2] See *Leveller Democracy*, pp. 210–12 in this volume.
[3] *The Picture of the Councell of State*, p. 2.

Manifestation as representing his viewpoint, seems to have thought that it should have been welcomed as a first step:

> ... although in many things short ... And although it hath some things of much hazard to the Publick—yet, had it been put in execution, we should scarcely have interrupted the proceedings thereof, since therein is contained many things of great and important concernment to the Common-wealth.[1]

He may well have thought that the savage attack on the new regime in the two parts of *Englands New Chains* was impolitic or at the least premature.

If any such difference existed it would have lost its practical importance after it had become clear that even this watered-down *Agreement* was to be quietly jettisoned, and still more after the arrests of March 28th. In any case a strange and perhaps fatal paralysis seems to have come over the Leveller movement around the turn of the year. Lilburne went north on private business (he had refused a seat on the Court which tried Charles) and after his return to London, as he wrote, "I fixed up my resolution wholly to devote my self to provide for the future well-being of my wife and children, and not without the extraordinariest necessity engage in any publick contests again."[2] Without his driving personality the whole movement tended to grind to a halt, and one can only conclude that there was an over-confidence in the good faith of the Grandees. The shock of the disillusion can be judged from the tone of *Englands New Chains* and Overton's *Hunting of the Foxes*—perhaps the angriest of all the Leveller writings.

If Walwyn had withdrawn from the Leveller leadership he had not been idle: his bonus of leisure must have been employed in writing *The Vanitie of the Present Churches* which appeared early in March.[3] If this is a continuation of his tolerationist pamphleteering, it is also a new development, marking a stage in the Leveller progress from religion-based to secular and political protest. Always, previously, Walwyn had written from the side of the Churches, defending their right to grow in their own way, urging co-existence and unity upon those essential beliefs which they held in common. When he criticised it was, as it were, from within the family. Now he condemns them all as falling short of true Christianity, and the weight of his attack falls

---

[1] *A Manifestation*, p. 7.   [2] *Legall Fundamental Liberties*, p. 42.
[3] Like many of Walwyn's tracts this is unsigned, but both style and sentiments are his and in his *Just Defence*, p. 23, he refers to it in a way that virtually admits authorship.

not on his old enemies the Presbyterians but upon the Independents and the sects of the left who had formerly been his allies.

He traces the process by which the persecuted, so soon as they had the power and opportunity, became persecutors:

> Do they not freely discover a serpentine disposition hankering after persecution? Do they not dayly spet their venom privatly and publickly, against any that either seperate from them, or joyne not with them, and that in as foul aspertions, as ever the Pope uttered against Luther, the Bishops against the Puritan, or the Presbyter against the Independents, are they not high and skillfull in rayling? making whom they please Atheists, Anti-scripturists, Antinomians, Anti-magistrats, Polligamists, Seekers, or what they will: and can these proceed from the true Spirit of God, or from the Spirit of Antichrist?[1]

He condemns their narrowness, their bigotry, their lack of Christian charity and social concern, and, an old complaint with him, the pedantry and intellectual pretensions of the ministers, that "iniquity of learning" which confuses the simple and obscures the light of the gospel, so that:

> all their preachings and prayings are only for mony, and that their greatest skill and labour, is to hold men ever in suspence; and upon pretence of truth, to give them a bastard Scholastik know-ledge, which only serves to make men proud, wrangling Sophis-ters, and Disputers, vain boasters, talkers, busie-bodies, censurers, Pharisees, wise in their own eyes, and despising others, void of all true piety or reall Christian vertue.[2]

Nor did he spare the sects of the extreme left. Antinomian though he was, he could not accept the extremists of antinomianism, like the Ranters, who:

> maintaine there is no sin, no evill, no difference of things, that all things are good, are one; and that all things are God, and that to see or judge any otherwise, is for want to the teaching of the Spirit.[3]

Yet it was not with these, but with the established and prosperous, "these proud boasting Churches", that he was principally concerned:

[1] *Vanitie*, p. 11.   [2] *Ibid.*, p. 22.   [3] *Ibid.*, p. 14.

view them well in their apparell . . . their fine and delicate linnen, their Laces, Beavers, Plushes; their Fancies, Plate, Rings and Jewells; do [they] not demonstrate from what roote they are, that they are meere worldlings indeed, and Christians only in name and tongue, and not that neither, if they are well observed.[1]

The Vanitie of the Present Churches was less a declaration of war than a recognition that war already existed. Behind a façade of friendship the Independent Churches were preparing to rally behind the Grandees and dissociate themselves from the Levellers as the disturbers of a now satisfactory *status quo*. Walwyn, upon whom this hostility had been concentrated, was well aware of the growing intrigue and the campaign of slander which was being organised against him. He condemned it in a manner that anticipated that employed again in his *Just Defence*:

> For there are many amongst them, for slandering and back-biting; for circumvention and an hipocriticall carriage, shall vie and compare with any sort of men in the world; they can play the part of Spies, Intelligencers, plot and betray upon pretence of intimacy, of endeared friendship and familiarity, eat, drink, be merry with you, day after day, week after week, for months, yea for many years and after al: professe boldly, openly, confidently, before their Church, to Neighbors, friends, or strangers, that all this intimacy, friendship, familiarity, was only and meerly to deceive, and to discover what might be, to mischief the parties with whom they held it: shall we aske which of the Apostles was a slanderer, a spy, an Intelligencer, a betrayer; certainly none but Judas and the followers of Judas.[2]

The Churches could no longer be regarded as a means of social change:

> So that it were much better for the Common-wealth, that all mens mindes were set at Liberty, from these entanglements, that so there might be an end of wrangling about shaddows; for if men were once free from this Church-bondage . . . it would enlarge their hearts toward all men, making them like our heavenly Father, who causeth his Sun to shine on the just, and unjust: that giveth to all men liberally, and upbraideth no man.[3]

What Walwyn seems to be saying here is that freedom is not only for the Saints, for the justified minority, but for all citizens, saints and

[1] *Vanitie*, p. 25.   [2] *Ibid.*, p. 26.   [3] *Ibid.*, pp. 42–3.

sinners alike. This development was perhaps initiated by Walwyn and Overton, but it was endorsed by the more orthodox Lilburne in a passage that also provides evidence of the fury Walwyn's tract aroused among the Churches:

> I have bin lately told, some of the Congregationall Preachers are very mad, at a late published and licensed booke sold in Popes head Alley and Cornhill, intituled *The vanity of the present Churches*; supposing it to be the Pen of some of our friends, and therefore out of revenge might Petition against us; I confesse I have within a few houres seen and read the booke, and must ingenuously confesse, it is one of the shrewdest bookes that ever I read in my life, and do believe it may be possible they may be netled to the purpose at it; but I wish every honest unbyassed man in England should seriously read it over.[1]

Lilburne dated this from the Tower on April 4th. On March 24th he had presented to the House of Commons *The Second Part of Englands New-Chaines Discovered*. At first light on March 28th detachments of soldiers arrested him, with Overton, Walwyn and Thomas Prince, and carried them before the Council of State. Walwyn in *The Fountain of Slaunder* and the other three in *The Picture of the Councell of State*, described these events in vivid language which reveals a great deal about their respective characters. Lilburne described his arrest with a high-riding indignation at the affront to the liberties of a free-born Englishman. Overton was indignant too, but his indignation was tempered with something like delight at a challenge to be met, and he was even able to extract some amusement from the situation, which comes out, for example, in his reflections upon his captor Col. Axtel:

> Surely the Lieutenant Collonel at that instant had forgot the Bugget from whence he dropt, I presume when he was a pedler in Harford-shire he had not so lofty an esteem of himself, but now the case is altered, the Gentleman is become one of the Grandees of the Royall palace: one of the (mock-) Saints in season, now judgeing the Earth, inspired with providences and opportunities at pleasure of their own invention as quick and nimble as an Hocas Spocas, or a Fiend in a Juglers Box. . . .[2]

and so on for a couple of close printed pages. Prince told his story briefly, with a quiet dignity:

<hr>

[1] *The Picture of the Councell of State*, p. 24.   [2] *Ibid.*, p. 29.

The Lieutenant Colonel asked me if I missed anything, wished me to search the Souldiers.

I looked upon the Souldiers, and told them, By their faces they seemed to me to be no such men: I told them I had better thoughts of them; I, for my part, have done the Souldiers no wrong:

And I doubt not but these men and their fellow-Souldiers will stand for their own and the Peoples just Liberties against all Tyranny in whom soever.[1]

Lilburne and Overton were experienced agitators to whom arrest and imprisonment were familiar experiences. Prince had served in the war for at least one campaign. Walwyn was older than the others. He had always lived a quiet, settled and apparently comfortable life with his family. Nothing of this kind had ever happened to him before, and his account makes it plain that the whole affair was a deep shock, though he met it calmly enough. Adjutant-General Stubber, with a strong party of horse and foot,

> Knockt violently at my garden gate, between four and five in the morning; which being opened by my maid, the Adjutant Generall, with many souldiers, entered and immediately dispersed them-selves about my garden, and in my house, to the great terror of my Family; my poor maid comming up to me, crying and shivering, with news that Souldiers were come for me, in such a sad dis-tempered manner (for she could hardly speak) as was sufficient to have daunted one that had been used to such sudden surprisals; much more my wife, who for two and twenty years we have lived together, never had known me under a minutes restraint by any Authority; she being also so weakly a woman, as in all that time I cannot say she hath enjoyed a week together in good health; and certainly had been much more affrighted, but for her confidence in my innocence; which fright hath likewise made too deep an impression upon my eldest Daughter, who hath con-tinued sick ever since, my Children and I having been very tender one of another: nor were my neighbours lesse troubled for me, to whose love I am very much obliged.[2]

After being detained all day the prisoners were brought before the Council of State at Derby House and each was asked separately if he had "any hand in making or compiling" *The Second Part of Englands*

---

[1] *The Picture of the Councell of State*, p. 50.   [2] *Fountain of Slaunder*, p. 11.

New-Chaines. Each in turn declined to answer because this was a demand that they should inculpate themselves. They also disputed the legal authority of the Council. Walwyn said:

> That I could not but very much wonder to be asked such a question; however, that it was very much against my judgement and conscience, to answer to questions of that nature which concern'd my self; that if I should answer it, I should not only betray my own liberty but the liberties of all English-men, which I could not do with a good conscience. . . .
> Then the President [Bradshaw] said, I was to answer the question; and that they did not ask it, as in way of triall, so as to proceed in judgement thereupon, but to report it to the House: to which I said, that I had answered it so as I could with a good conscience, and could make no other answer; so I was put forth in a back way, as Mr Lilburn had been, and where he was.[1]

Walwyn also protested, as he had done at the time of his arrest, at having been sent for "with a party of horse and foot, to the affright of my family, and ruine of my credit".

The four Levellers were then committed to the Tower on suspicion of treason. Immediately, the clerical vultures began to gather. Independent ministers visited the prisoners urging them to come to terms with Cromwell—in effect to cease their opposition. Only five days after the arrests Lilburne's old friend William Kiffin presented to Parliament *The Humble Petition and Representation of Several Churches of God in London, commonly (though falsely) called Anabaptists*, signed by himself and a number of other leading Baptists. This was an unqualified attack and made it clear that the Levellers could expect no help from a quarter hitherto regarded as sympathetic. Lilburne characterised it as "a lye and a falsehood" and its authors as "a pack of fauning daubing knaves".[2]

The Levellers, in their turn, resisted with the weapons in whose use they had become so skilful—the mass petition and the agitational pamphlet. They were encouraged by the growing unrest in the Army, whose opposition to the proposed campaign in Ireland reinforced their political dissatisfactions. Only four days after the arrests a petition of protest was presented to Parliament with 10,000 signatures. A fortnight later it was followed by a second, and, perhaps even more remarkable, a week later again by a *Petition of divers wel-affected Women*.

[1] *Ibid.*, p. 13.   [2] *The Picture of the Councell of State*, p. 24.

M

Walwyn had not joined the rest in issuing *The Picture of the Councel of State*, preferring, for tactical reasons, to reserve his account of his arrest for a later date. On April 14th, all four joined to issue *A Manifestation . . . Intended for their Full Vindication From The Many aspersions cast upon them, to render them odious to the World, and unserviceable to the Common-wealth*. This, though in form a joint political manifesto, has commonly been regarded as essentially Walwyn's work. Such was the opinion of the authors of *Walwins Wiles*, in a passage which throws an interesting light on the way the Leveller leaders were regarded by their opponents.

> Behold a fresh appearance of these subscribers in a new dress of later date, as if that spirit would shew his master peece in his crafty translation of himself into the form of an Angel of Light, calling itself by the name of a *Manifestation* . . . whose devout, specious, meek, self-denying, soft and pleasant lips favours much of the sligh, cunning and close subtlety of that additional Subscriber, Mr William Walwyn, who (as the Serpant that deceived our first Parents was more subtle than any beast of the field that the Lord God made) is much more crafty than the rest of his brethren, of whose curious spinning we have several reasons to presume this piece, for here is not the licentious provoking daringness of L. Col. Lilburnes pen, nor yet the notorious profanness of Mr Richard Overtons pen; as for Mr Prince, he is a younger brother lately drawn in, and no further accomplished in his brethrens art then in the lesson of Conformity unto their proceedings and conscription unto their Expresses. Again, he that shall compare this *Manifestation*, subscribed by Mr Walwyn, with *Englands new Chains*, the first and second part, the *Hunting of the Foxes*, and other scandalous pamphlets, subscribed only by the rest, may easily perceive the well known subtlety and craftinesse, phrase and stile of this new Subscriber above his Fellows, who of themselves are no more able to alter the complexion of their pen, then the Leopard his spots, or the Blackamoor his skin; these being Wolves in their own, but the other a Wolf in Sheeps clothing.[1]

Walwyn, as, indeed, he was almost forced to do, disavowed sole authorship:

> In which Manifestation, is to be seen all our very hearts, and

---

[1] *Walwins Wiles*, pp. 2–3.

wherein all our four heads, and hands were nigh equally employed, though this captious author (Mr. John Price, its said) be pleased to suppose me to be all in all therein; yet I must, and truly professe the contrary.[1]

In spite of this it must be admitted that *A Manifestation* resembles the style and temper of Walwyn's other writings as markedly as it differs from those of Lilburne or Overton. It combines the most conciliatory language with a firm restatement of political principle. Its first concern was to correct the many false notions which had gained currency:

> they that know us not are made believe any strange conceit of us, that we would Levell all mans estates, that we would have no distinction of Orders and Dignities amongst men, that we are indeed for no government, but a Popular confusion; and then againe that we have bin Agents for the King, and now for the Queen; that we are Atheists, Antiscripturists, Jesuites and indeed any thing, that is hatefull and of evill repute amongst men.[2]

It denies any intention of interfering with property rights:

> We profess therefore that we never had it in our thoughts to Level mans estates, it being the utmost of our aime that the Commonwealth be reduced to such a passe that every man may with as much security as may be enjoy his propriety.[3]

This, indeed, is no more than the truth. Whatever utopian views Walwyn may have cherished in private, the Levellers as a party (and they constantly referred to themselves as *Levellers falsely so called*) always envisaged a society of secure and independent small producers whose property needed protection from the great owners and rich trading monopolies.

Similarly, they were "for Government and against Popular Confusion. . . . Tis somewhat a strange consequence to infer that because we have laboured so constantly for a good Government, therefore we would have none."[4] Good government requires something more than good intentions, and:

> We confess indeed, that the experimentall defections of so many men as have succeeded in Authority, and the exceeding difference we have hitherto found in the same men in a low, and in an

[1] *Just Defence*, p. 14.   [2] *Manifestation*, p. 4.   [3] *Ibid.*, p. 5.
[4] *Ibid.*, p. 5.

exalted condition, makes us even distrust our own hearts, and hardly beleeve our own Resolutions to the contrary.[1]

The way to overcome this human fallibility was by a constitution which should so bind any government as to make tyranny impossible. This was the purpose of *An Agreement of the People* by which the powers of representative bodies shall be strictly limited, and the Signatories of *A Manifestation* had been occupying their time in prison by drafting a new, and they hoped, final, form of such an *Agreement*:

> We have, with the best care and abilities God hath afforded us, cast the same into a Modell and Platform, which we shall speedily present unto the view and consideration of all, as the Standard and ultimate scope of our Designes, that so [in case of approvall] it may be subscribed and returned as agreed upon by the People . . . to settle the Common-wealth upon the fairest probabilities of a lasting Peace and contentfull Establishment.[2]

The result of these labours was the new version of *An Agreement* which was published on May 1st, 1649.

For all its moderate tone *A Manifestation* did nothing to protect the Levellers from fresh attacks. Only a week later appeared *Walwins Wiles*, the most savage and unprincipled of all the anti-Leveller tracts. It was signed by seven Independent and Baptist ministers, of whom two, William Kiffin and Edmund Rosier, were former friends of Lilburne. A third, John Price, whom we have already seen to be an enemy of Walwyn, was regarded, both by him and by Brooke, as the tract's actual author. Much of the material it contained had been gathered some years earlier, and the bulk of the writing must have been done before *A Manifestation* appeared—a book of such length and detail could not have been composed in the short time separating the two publications. The structure of *Walwins Wiles* suggests that an introductory section, in which the Levellers were attacked as a political group, and some short interpolations here and there, were hurriedly added to an already prepared personal attack on Walwyn. It was against Walwyn that the main attack was directed, and rather clumsy attempts were made to divide him from Lilburne and Prince. Less was said about Overton, who was obviously regarded as beyond hope of recovery.

Humphrey Brooke replied in *The Charity of Church-men* which

---

[1] *Manifestation*, p. 7.   [2] *Ibid.*, p. 7.

appeared about May 28th, and Walwyn himself, briefly, in *The Fountain of Slaunder,* also at the end of May, but at much greater length in *Walwyn's Just Defence,* apparently sometime in June.

Many of the charges in *Walwins Wiles* retread familiar ground—his alleged atheism, his contempt for the Scriptures, his blasphemous levity, his addiction to "profane" authors. Others are evidently absurd, like the accusation that he had encouraged a woman friend to commit suicide or had been involved in a plot to murder Cromwell. Walwyn replied to them in detail and they hardly merit further discussion. There remain a group of charges which do throw light on his character and outlook and call for more detailed consideration. These are: his methods of argument and persuasion, his social ideas and his views on the question of Ireland. This last involves the whole issue of the Leveller attitude to the Irish question, an issue which even today has some practical importance.

After a general opening comes a long section which describes how craftily Walwyn adapted his arguments to suit what he judged to be the character of his hearers:

> His game hath always been the unhappy perversion of honest men generally observed to be forward on the Parliaments behalf against the King and the Royal party, for the effecting whereof his custom was to frame his Endeavours.
>
> First, To discern and feel their temper, genius, natural constitution, and complexion, whether of meek, quiet and peacable, or rash, hasty, and violent spirits; whether of quick, capacious and nimble, or of dull, injudicious and low apprehensions; whether of a more pure, heavenly and spiritual, or more gross, light and vain discourse; whether of a retentive, close and tenacious capacity in keeping secrets, or a more open, free and liberal aptness in discovering; whether of a richer, or mean condition; whether popular, or how intressed in the Parliament, Army, City, or Country.[1]

Then, to men who are "solid, wise, moderate, judicious" he will pose as "an excellent Common-wealths man, full of publique spirit". Having thus won their good opinion he "attempts the undermining of their religion" and persuades them that "there is no other Religion but that which the Apostle James speaks of", or that on Sunday it was better "to meet together, and spend our time in considering what is good for the Common-wealth, read some good moral things, as

[1] *Walwins Wiles,* p. 3.

Plutarchs *Morals*, Ciceroes *Orations*, than reading the Scriptures, and hearing Sermons".[1]

With those of "a low, needy, indigent and wanty condition" he would speak of the lack of charity among the clergy, "the unworthinesse of our times, in making riches, and estates, the great badge of distinction between man and man", then of the evils of social inequality, and finally of the advantages of a community of goods.[2]

With those "whom he apprehends of passionate, cholerike, froward and peevish dispositions, of putting forth bold and daring language, and withall weak, shallow, and injudicious, and yet men that are honest-hearted in the maine, true to the interest of the Commonwealth, and zealous against tyranny and oppression", he would adopt yet a third approach.[3] With these he spoke of the burden of taxation and the failure of Parliament to fulfil its promises, the way its leading men, while betraying the people, "do nothing but vote one another places of power and profit".[4] In this way the confidence of the ordinary citizen in his leaders, from Pym and Hampden at the beginning of the war to Cromwell and Ireton in 1649, had been undermined. Petitions were prepared of a kind which their originators knew could not be granted, and reasonable progress prevented by the continual formation of factions.

No doubt many of the details with which this picture of Walwyn the agitator was presented were false, and a great deal of malice and prejudice went into its making. Yet, when due allowance has been made for all this, the picture carries a certain measure of conviction—there is a sense of a real man promoting his cause with conviction and some subtlety.

Walwyn in his reply presents himself as direct to the point of simplicity:

> These are the plainnesses wherein I have ever delighted; so far am I from that politique, crafty, subtil and hidden reservednesse, which this Author would perswade the world I abound withall; exercising his wit so exquisitly in decyphering me out to be a man of so large capacity and ability, as for my part I do not believe there is any man in the world so; much lesse my self, who setting aside a little consideration and experience, united to an upright conscience, have nothing to please my self withall: Nor do I much desire those extraordinary parts, which are seldom employed to their

---

[1] *Walwins Wiles*, pp. 7–8.   [2] *Ibid.*, p. 10.   [3] *Ibid.*, p. 12.   [4] *Ibid.*, p. 16.

right end, being commonly tempted, to serve some Politicians ends, as may be seen rather in the abilities and application of them, as in this Author; for he hath drawn such a picture of mans ability, as shews only his own parts in so doing; and applyes them to me, that have no part of them, of purpose to make me vile, lifts me up to the top of the pinacle, that he may cast me down to my greater ruine.

Truly, I never thought a good cause ever needed such workings as he exalts himself (not me) withall: and I dare appeal to those many of my Friends, that I daily and hourly converst withall for some years now in publique businesses, whether ever they saw more plainnesse and openheartednesse in man.[1]

Walwyn's integrity and his conviction of the justice and truth of his cause hardly need demonstration. Yet one finds it difficult to believe that the author of the books one knows to be his, or the politician whose activities were so effective, can have been quite so guileless as he suggests here. In any case there is nothing discreditable in using arguments most suited to a particular audience when those arguments are used, as he convinces us they were, for the good of the Commonwealth.

On the question of Walwyn's social ideas, his opponents were trying to do two things—to show that he personally was in favour of equality of condition and confiscation of property, of "Levelling" as the term was then understood, and to infer that these were also the views of the Party as a whole. On the second count Walwyn is quite unequivocal: he refers to the recently issued *Agreement*, which contained "the utmost of my desire concerning this Common-wealth",[2] adding that all his actions and the *Agreement*,

> do sufficiently evince, and doth indeed so fully answer all your remaining rambling scandals, that I shall pray the courteous Reader hereof to read it, and apply it, and then shall not doubt my full and clear vindication: so far as that is, am I for plucking up of all the pales and hedges in the Nation; so far, for all things common.[3]

It will be remembered that Article XXX of the *Agreement* had declared:

That it shall not be in the power of the Representative in any wise,

[1] *Just Defence*, p. 12.　　[2] *Ibid.*, p. 23.　　[3] *Ibid.*, pp. 23–4.

to render up, or give, or take away any part of the Agreement, nor level mens estates, destroy Propriety, or make all things Common.

When we come to Walwyn's personal convictions we are on less certain ground. *Walwins Wiles* gives an account, biassed no doubt, but with explicit detail and worth quoting at some length because they do at the least tell us what ideas were commonly attributed to him, and, more broadly, what ideas were thought likely to be held by a popular leader. How far they are an accurate reflection we can never be sure; all we can do is to draw what deductions we can from a comparison between them and his reply.

Walwyn, it is alleged, insisted,

> that it will not be well, untill such time as men shall be eligible into places of trust, that are vertuous and able, though poor and low in this world; and that Butchers and Cobblers be chosen into the places of Magistracy and Government, as well as others that are rich in this world.[1]

The Butchers and Cobblers, of course, are a standard part of the contemporary rhetoric of reaction, but Walwyn accepts the example and discusses the principle with a damaging irony:

> He upbraids me, that I find fault, that riches, and estates, and the things of this world, should prefer men to offices, and places of trust: but say that virtue, though in poor men, should be more regarded, as in Butchers, or Coblers: and truly I know some Butchers, though not many, as fit as some in your Congregations; and I think you do not exclude for that trade: And as for Coblers, there are trades more in credit, hardly so usefull, and Mr Price knows it well; and were he as busy in self examination, as he is in reproaching others, he would have little time to trouble himself about others motes: he who thought it no robbery to be equall with God, and yet despised not to be esteemed the Son of a Carpenter, and chose simple herdsmen for his Prophets and poor fishermen for his Apostles, did certainly judge otherwise than these Churchmen judge.[2]

Next:

> He is very frequent and diligent, in fomenting the consideration of the disproportion and inequality of the things of this life.

[1] *Walwins Wiles*, p. 11.   [2] *Just Defence*, p. 24.

What an inequitable thing it is for one man to have thousands, & another want bread, & that the pleasure of God is, that all men should have enough, and not that one man should abound in this worlds goods, spending it upon his lusts, and another man of far better deserts, not to be worth two pence, and it is no such difficulty as men make it to be, to alter the course of the world in this thing, and that a few diligent and valient spirits may turn the world upside down, if they observe their seasons and shall with life and courage ingage accordingly.[1]

Walwyn does not really deny this, though he does deny that it implies turning the world upside down. One might rather say that he proclaims an intention of turning the world the right side up:

And as for Riches, Saint James, whom I am exceeding in love with, had no great good opinion thereof. . . . I hope you will say no more, that by these truths I shall destroy what is called Religion amongst you, for this is a part of pure and undefiled Religion. . . .

And where you charge me, that I find fault that some abound, whil'st others want bread; truly, I think it is a sad thing, in so fruitful a land as, by Gods blessing, this is; and I do think it one main end of Government, to provide, that those that refuse not labour, should eat comfortably: and if you think otherwise, I think it your errour and your unhappinesse.[2]

The passage on communism, though perhaps the best known in *Walwins Wiles*, must still be quoted in full on account of its importance:

This Mr. Walwyn, to work upon the indigent and poorer sort of the people, and to raise up their spirits in discontents and clamours, &c. did one time professe, he could wish with all his heart that there was neither Pale, Hedge nor Ditch in the whole Nation, and that it was an unconscionable thing that one man should have ten thousand pounds, and another more deserving and usefull to the Commonwealth, should not be worth two pence, or to that purpose.

At another time discoursing of the inequality and disproportion of the estates and conditions of men in the world, had words to this purpose, That it was a sad and miserable thing that it should so continue, and that it would never be well untill all things were

[1] *Walwins Wiles*, p. 12.   [2] *Just Defence*, p. 24.

common; and it being replyed, will that be ever? Answered, we must endeavour it: It being said, That this would destroy all Government; answered, That then there would be lesse need of Government, for then there would be no theeves, no covetous persons, no deceiving and abusing of one another, and so no need of Government, &c. but if in such a case they have a form and rule of government to determine cases, as may fall out, yet there will be no need of Judges, &c. but if any difference fall out, or any criminall fact be committed, take a Cobler from his Seat, or a Butcher from his shop, or any other Tradesman that is an honest and just man, and let him hear the case, and determine the same, and then betake himself to his work again.[1]

The arguments here are so apt, and the tone of actual speech so well caught that it is very hard to think this passage is pure invention. Nor does Walwyn anywhere deny having used these or similar words. On the contrary, he ignores this particular point apart from the general reference to the *Agreement* already noted. His son-in-law Humphrey Brooke, who must have heard a good deal of his conversation, offers only a qualified refutation:

'Gainst such as these, what means more effectual than scandals? and what scandals more odious then Atheism and Communitie? By the first, all that are religious are incens'd, by the last, all that are rich. And though the whole progresse of Mr Walwyns life and conversation doth clearly evidence the false imputation both of one and the other; yet having happily scattered in familiar discourses, some words, that by the extremity of wresting and mis-application, for want of observation of the coherence, by taking a piece only, or part of his speech; all which, such as came purposely to betray, must needs be supposed to be very much inclin'd unto; 'tis no wonder, if so many years watching and way-laying him, some words be not gathered, which in a perverted sense may look that way.[2]

Finally, on Ireland, Walwyn was supposed to have said:

That the sending over Forces into Ireland is for nothing else but to make way by the blood of the Army to enlarge their territories of power and Tyranny, That it is an unlawful War, a cruel and bloody work to go to destroy the Irish Natives for their Con-

[1] *Walwins Wiles*, pp. 13–14.   [2] *Charity of Church-men*, pp. 2–3.

sciences, (though they have kill'd many thousand Protestants for their Consciences) and to drive them from their proper natural and native Rights.[1]

and that,

> the cause of the Irish Natives in seeking their just freedoms, immunities, and liberties, was the very same with our cause here, in indeavouring our own rescue and freedom from the power of oppressors.[2]

It is certainly remarkable, and must surely be significant, that neither Walwyn in his *Just Defence*, nor Brooke in *The Charity of Church-men*, ever mention Ireland, and this is the only specific accusation to which no reply is made. The only possible inference, I think, is that these passages do in substance represent Walwyn's opinions. It is interesting, in view of the importance of the subject, to compare other Leveller statements on Ireland. At about the same time as the *Just Defence* Thomas Prince published *The Silken Independents Snare Broken*—written in the Tower while he was in close everyday contact with Walwyn. This is also a reply to attacks in *Walwins Wiles*. Prince writes:

> In your Epistle you likewise say *That the sending of Forces to Ireland* &c. These are your words, and pray keep them to your selves for me; for where have I expressed so much? . . . .
>
> If *England* were settled, as afore mentioned, the goodnesse of the Government would invite the Irish, with a desire unto it; there would then be some hopes (sending over faithful men, those who would make conscience of their waies, such as would keep their engagements) that the Irish would soon be reduced; as being willing to change their condition of bondage for freedom, and willingly render the chief Authors and agents in that inhumane butchery up to justice, whereby much innocent blood might be saved.
>
> Also care ought to be taken, that if when the Irish are overcome, that none of those imployed, do turn the gaining thereof to their own domination; for what are we better for all the victories gained these 8 years? Are not the People more burthened than ever? Wise and honest men will acknowledge it.

[1] *Walwins Wiles*, p. A3.   [2] *Ibid.*, p. 21.

And for keeping out of Rebels, I am not only against any that shall invade the Land from abroad; but I am against all that any waies invade our liberties within the Nation.[1]

A few months earlier, about April 5th, Ireland was also discussed in *The English Souldiers Standard to Repaire to, for Wisdome and Understanding.* The plan to invade Ireland, it declares, aims at destroying England's liberties. Therefore:

Whatever they may tell you, or however they may flatter you, there is no less danger lies at the bottom of this business for Ireland, and therefore it behoves every one of you to lay it to heart: and before you resolve upon a new Engagement, first see a new Representative of the Army established, by free Election of every Regiment; and refer yourselves to their Counsel and advice in all things, to be disposed of as they shall see cause; and neither admit of disbandings, nor of new listings, nor of any undertaking for *Ireland*, or of any other service, but as that Councell shall advise.

For consider, as things now stand, to what end you should hazard your lives against the Irish: have you not been fighting these seven years in *England* for Rights and Liberties, that you are yet deluded of? And that too, when as none can hinder you but your own Officers, under whom you have fought? and will you go on still to kil, slay and murther men, to make them as absolute Lords and Masters over Ireland as you have made them over *England*? or is it your ambition to reduce the Irish to the happinesse of Tythes upon trebble damages, to Excise, Customs and Monopolies in Trade? or to fill their prisons with poor disabled prisoners, to fill their land with swarms of beggers; to enrich their Parliament-men, and impoverish their people; to take down Monarchical Tyranny, and set up an Aristocratical Tyranny; or to over-spread that Nation as this yet is, with such Wasps and Hornets as our Lawyers and their Confederates? Or if you intend not this, or would be sorry to see no better effects of your undertakings, it certainly concerns you in the first place, and before you go, to see those evils reformed here; that when occasion shall justly invite you thither, you may carry a good platform in your hands, such a one as possibly they may never fight against: And it would

[1] Prince, *op. cit.*, pp. 6–7.

be much more to be wished, that you might overcome them by just and equall offers, then by strength and force.[1]

A clear political line can be seen in these two statements. The invasion of Ireland may be necessary in the future to prevent it being used as a Royalist base. But any invasion would be morally wrong and dangerous to English liberties unless democratic institutions are first created in the Army and throughout the nation. After England's affairs have been settled on the basis of the *Agreement of the People*, it should be possible to go to Ireland not as conquerors but as friends, offering them the same advantages as have been secured at home. Such a programme stands in sharp contrast to that of the Grandees and the City Companies, who saw Ireland only as a field for plunder and profit-making and as a means of disposing of an inconveniently intractable Army. It is of the greatest significance that the first English democrats were also the first to oppose on principle a war of colonial conquest.

Walwyn not only replied, on the whole most effectively, to the charges made against him. He also made a damaging counter-attack on the moral standards of men who, calling themselves Christians, had pretended friendship, accepted his hospitality, and were all the time seeking evidence with which to destroy him, and who were so cowardly that they dared not bring forward their accusations till he was helpless in prison:

> I should even expire with wonder, at his impudence, and at his uncharitablenesse, that he and his friends, people of a Church, that call themselves Saints, and a people of God, should harbour this wretched slander six years amongst them, and be bringing it forth this time, and that time, but finde no time their season but when I was violently taken out of my bed, and house, and made prisoner: if this be their way of visiting of prisoners, would not it make men think they had forgot the Scriptures; nay, might they not go to the heathens to learn some Charity.[2]

Having pursued his enemies down all the avenues of slander which they had opened, he ends with a contemptuous dismissal:

> And so I have done with you, and all your Wiles; and henceforth,

---

[1] *Op. cit.*, pp. 9–10. H. N. Brailsford, *The Levellers and the English Revolution*, p. 498, attributes this pamphlet to Walwyn. If so, and this was known or suspected at the time, the stress laid on Ireland in *Walwins Wiles* can be better understood.

[2] *Just Defence*, p. 10.

he that is filthy, let him be filthy still; and he that is ignorant, let him be ignorant still; he that is so fouly partiall in his Conscience, as after this my Just Defence, to believe your slanders of me, let him remaine so still; and he that through a perverse ignorance, shall henceforth doubt my integrity, let him remaine ignorant still: I would gladly be free from this Restraint, because I fear it will prove prejudiciall to many more besides my self, if not already; and I trust God will open some just way; however, I have peace within, because in all that hath befallen me; my will is not to harme any man, nor to dishonour God; affliction being still to me, a better choice then sin.[1]

In a very real sense these were Walwyn's final words. While he and his companions remained in prison, defending themselves against these attacks, the defeat of the Army mutiny at Burford on May 14th, and the defeat and death of William Thompson a few days later effectively ended the Leveller movement as a serious political force. Their influence and popularity still remained great. When, after a treason trial, Lilburne was acquitted by a London jury on October 26th, there were scenes of unrestrained popular rejoicing. These demonstrations, we are told, "made the Judges for fear, turn pale, and hang down their heads; but the Prisoner stood silent at the Barre, rather more sad in his countenance than he was before".[2] This acquittal, which was followed by the release of all four prisoners, was indeed a victory, but the Party was already defeated beyond hope of recovery. Lilburne continued to fight till he was mentally and physically broken by imprisonment and frustration, but he fought on as an individual whose ruling instinct was to fight. Overton slipped back into the shadowy underworld of intrigue and back-street printing from which the Leveller movement had called him.

Walwyn's circumstances and character were entirely different. At 49 he was already accustomed to a settled family life. His political activities had never brought him prominently into public notice, nor do they seem to have prevented, though they must at times have interfered with, his business as a silk merchant. Nor was his temperament that of a fighter for a lost cause. There is little in any of his writings to suggest that he *enjoyed* conflict, as Lilburne and Overton so obviously did. If he wrote or organised it was from a sense of public duty and to

[1] *Just Defence*, p. 34.
[2] *The Triall of Lieut. Collonell John Lilburne*. Theodorus Verax [Clement Walker], p. 151.

secure some end which he believed both desirable and attainable. In the new situation after 1649 there is no reason to suppose that his ideas changed, but equally none to suppose that he continued to campaign actively for them. Perhaps he continued to hope that their time would come again.

He is believed to have taken the Engagement, which pledged all citizens to be "true and faithful to the Commonwealth of England as it is now established without a King or House of Lords". This no doubt he could conscientiously do with perhaps some such mental reservation as that with which he had previously taken the Covenant. And he evidently continued a quiet interest in public affairs. In December 1650 he published a pamphlet *Juries Justified*, a reply to another by Henry Robinson suggesting that they might be dispensed with.

Though there were no direct references to his Levelling past, it is clear from *Juries Justified* that his underlying attitude had not changed. Walwyn opened by explaining why he was breaking silence:

> Though a silence hath seized me, equal to his that was born and continued dumb, till his father was in danger of being murthered; yet retaining still a sincere and vigourous affection to my Native Countrey, and seeing this mans Knife offering at the throat of our preservours (such I esteem our Juries) for *Englands*, and for this its fundamental essential liberty, I could not hold my peace; but must tell *Mr Robinson*, he deals most injuriously with his Countrey, whereof he must either speedily repent or be made ashamed.[1]

He objects most strongly to Robinson's implication that the jury system is unsatisfactory because the people of England are too ignorant or too stupid to make it work. To the objection that "there is not a competent number of understanding and fit men in all the lesser divisions of a County", he replies that there are plenty in every Hundred and even in every Parish.[2] Defeat had not destroyed that confidence in the integrity and ability of ordinary people which had always been at the root of his political thought:

> Understanding is indeed very good, but as I take it, there is not so great a want thereof in *England*, as there is of conscience, a faculty that puts one to the doing of what is approved to be ones duty.[3]

And, rather later,

[1] *Juries Justified*, p. 1.   [2] *Ibid.*, p. 2.   [3] *Ibid.*, pp. 3–4.

Nor is right and wrong so difficult to be discovered in Causes
and Controversies, but that an ordinary capacity (careful to keep
a good Conscience, and that is tender of an oath) shall soon per-
ceive the true state thereof.[1]

A tribute to Henry Marten, "a true Englishman . . . always manifest-
ing a most zealous affection to his Countries liberties", emphasises the
importance of this aspect of the jury, as representing the whole people,
with an anecdote of how Marten:

upon the bench at *Redding*, where it being his lot to give the
charge to the Grand-Jury, in the first place, he wisht them to be
rightly informed of their own places and authority, affirming it
to be judicial, when as their own (meaning the Justices) was but
ministerial; and therefore desired them not to stand bare any
longer, but to put on their hats, as became them, and not to under-
value their Countrey, which virtually they were.[2]

The jury could also be a defence of the ordinary citizen against
tyranny, and Walwyn concluded with what must be an oblique
reference to the jury which, by acquitting Lilburne in 1649, had saved
him also from destruction:

And do this man what he can, the many good mens lives and
estates, that have been preserved by Juries, will never be forgotten while *England* is *England*; and wherein I deem myself
so much concerned, as in gratitude I justly owe my Countrey
this service; [i.e. to correct Henry Robinson] but have done it
gently, as judging gentle *Correction* to be the best; and the rather,
because the Objector is of my acquaintance.[3]

In 1652 Walwyn spoke in defence of free trade, by which he meant
primarily freedom from the restraints imposed by monopolist companies and corporations, a long-standing concern to the Levellers[4].
His last public appearance is among a list of notabilities which Harrington suggested in 1659 as a committee to consider his proposals for a
new constitution. The list is of too varied a character to mean much

---

[1] *Juries Justified*, p. 9.   [2] *Ibid.*, p. 3.   [3] *Ibid.*, p. 13.
[4] Margaret James, *Social Problems and Policy During the Puritan Revolution*, pp. 155–7.

more than that he was still regarded as a person of some consequence, and, by Harrington at least, as a man of integrity.[1]

At some time, and for reasons we do not know, Walwyn abandoned his business as a merchant to become a medical practitioner. Though without professional qualifications, his serene rationalism and his humanity must have served him well in this new calling, and these qualities are very apparent in a little book *Physick for Families: Or The New, Safe and Powerful way of Physick, upon constant proof Established,* which was published in 1681, apparently just after his death, since his will was proved on January 14th of that year.[2]

Physick for Families lists thirty-three medicines prepared by Walwyn, with the disorders for which they are appropriate. Since no indication is given of their composition, it is impossible to form any idea of their value, but the general principles laid down are admirably enlightened, and suggest that, at the worst, Walwyn's patients would have suffered less at his hands than they did at those of the orthodox doctors of the time. On the principle that "it is irrational that anything should be given to the sick which is not safe and good for the healthfull",[3] Walwyn condemned all the violent and painful methods commonly used:

And therefore, though I am far from wishing so much evil to Practicers with *Opium* that every one of them should be obliged to take the same quantity, which at any time they prescribe (which is one of the Rules I always bind my self to in whatsoever I advise) yet I do heartily wish that the whole old method of Physick aforementioned, in all the particulars of Glisters, Bleedings, Purgings, Vomitings, Sweatings by Minerals, Issues, Cuppings, Blisterings &c. were all so well and thoroughly Opiated, and laid a sleep for ever, that they might never more rise again in Reputation with Physicians.[4]

For him the study of medicine properly began with the study of man himself:

---

[1] Maurice Ashley (*The Greatness of Oliver Cromwell*, p. 273), speaks of an arrest of Walwyn in 1653. He gives no authority for his statement and I have not found any evidence to support it.

[2] The identity of Walwyn the Leveller with Walwyn the physician is convincingly established by W. Schenk (*The Concern for Social Justice in the Puritan Revolution*, p. 59n). Even without this, I think that the ideas in *Physick for Families* are so characteristic as to leave little room for doubt.

[3] *Physick for Families*, p. 36.   [4] *Ibid.*, pp. 40–1.

I conceived it undeniably requisite, that all provisions and preparations desined for help of Mankind ought in special manner, both
in purity, efficacy and pregnancy to hold due and just proportion
to the peculiarity of Humane Temperature and Constitution, and
that all administration of the gross, impure, improper, unbenign
nature, must needs produce cross and perverse effects.[1]

Working on this basis he found "new aids both to Diet and Medicine"
which were effective "solely from their powerful friendliness to
Humane Nature".

For the rest, he advocated kindness, a relaxed and cheerful attitude
and avoidance of all excesses in diet and living:

Be sure to excuse the sick from over great and busie talkers, offerers
of casual, trifling Medicines, sad, sighing and dejected visitants;
to withhold all unkindness; gently persuading from all rash
adventures upon wine, unusual doubtful diet, hot waters, eager-
ness for drink, and too much thoughtfulness; but by friendliness,
keep them in all quietness and hopefullness, without any the
least shew of fearing their dissolution.[2]

As a frontispiece to the volume is the only known portrait of
Walwyn. He is shown at the age of eighty, but still with every appearance of mental and physical vigour. The face is strong and dignified,
but not without hints of humour and sympathy—very much in
keeping, indeed, with what we know of him from his writings.

While, as has been said, we do not know the reason why Walwyn
abandoned trade for medicine, there is no reason why we should assume
that it was from economic necessity rather than deliberate choice.
His relationship with Humphrey Brooke, his son-in-law and devoted
supporter and a distinguished physician, would have made the change
easier. And there is evidence of a long-standing medical interest not
only in *A Parable, or Consultation of Physitians upon Master Edwards*
but in medical analogies and images scattered among his other writings.
More than this, his whole approach to politics suggests that he saw
himself primarily in the role of healer. Even so bitter an opponent as
Edwards is addressed as a poor, sick soul to be rescued from his own
self-inflicted disorders. And Walwyn presents himself as the Compassionate Samaritan, whose first office for the man fallen by the wayside
was to bind up his wounds and pour in soothing oil.

[1] *Physick*, p. 3.   [2] *Ibid.*, p. 17.

So it is not impossible that, when the time of open political activity came to an end, he found a merely commercial life more and more distasteful and saw in medicine a continuation of his healing task in a literal instead of a figurative form. This would be in keeping with the extremely orderly and consistent course of his development. Every stage in his thinking was a reasoned and in a sense predictable extension of what had gone before. Liberty to preach and worship without restraint led logically to an equal liberty to write, print, present petitions to Parliament and to agitate for democratic reforms. The conviction that all men could be saved by accepting the freely offered grace of God was not different in kind from the conviction that all men could enjoy the rights of citizenship by accepting the privileges offered in *An Agreement of the People*.[1]

There is a further sense in which this change of occupation would be especially consistent for Walwyn. All his life he had opposed exclusive professionalism—the claim of university-reared ministers with their elaborate equipment of Latin, Greek, Hebrew and theological jargon, to a monopoly in the word of God, the claim of professional lawyers or politicians to monopolise public office. He was the champion of the reasoning and disinterested layman, both in religion and politics, who brought to them the adequate gifts with which he believed all men were, at least potentially, endowed by God and nature. What was more natural than that, in the course of time, he should come to invade another closely preserved area of professional privilege?

In this, too, he would be, in a sense, fighting a battle for democracy. Earlier he had insisted that it was the congregation and not the minister who must come first, that Parliament must be the servant and instrument of the people who elected it. The simple principle laid down in *Physick for Families* (however it may have worked out in practice) was that medicine must begin with the needs of the sick and not with the traditional systems of doctors. In the interest of the patient he was prepared to challenge and set aside old custom and precedent, just as he had done in religion and politics.

It is this readiness to set aside the past which gives Walwyn, and, indeed, the Levellers as a whole, their peculiar importance. Overton had declared, "whatever our Fore-fathers were; or whatever they did or suffered, or were enforced to yeeld unto; we are men of the present age, and ought to be free".[2] They did no doubt appeal to the past at

[1] Some apparent limitations are discussed in *Leveller Democracy* elsewhere in this volume.
[2] *Remonstrance of Many Thousand Citizens*, p. 5.

times, like Winstanley with his anti-Normanism which some of them shared, but, also like Winstanley, they knew how to combine the appeal to history with its repudiation. And in this repudiation Walwyn seems to have played a specially important part, as is shown by his denigration of *Magna Carta*, "that mess of pottage", in which Lilburne and Overton appear to have followed him. They were, indeed, ready to defend the rights which they thought were guaranteed in *Magna Carta*, but the recognition of their limitations led to the replacement of *Magna Carta* by the *Agreement*, a new charter of popular liberties more appropriate to the men of the present age.

Standing upon the past but appealing beyond precedent to the future, Walwyn was far from being, as he has sometimes been represented, a man of essentially medieval outlook. Rather he was an exponent of secular humanism, of reason and nature, equally opposed to the hierarchical conceptions of feudal society and the devil-take-the-hindmost ethic of growing capitalism. In distinction from both he demanded a just, if still imperfect, society, not handed down from above but built up from below, "by reducing the Common-wealth to so good a pass that every man by care and easie labour, might have wherewithal to maintain himself and his Family in some comfortable manner".[1]

A NOTE ON TEXTS

Though there is no complete edition of Walwyn's writings, many of the most important have been reprinted during this century. *Tracts on Liberty in the Puritan Revolution*, ed. by W. Haller, contains, in Vol. I, *The Power of Love* and, in Vol. II, *The Compassionate Samaritaine, A Helpe to the right understanding of a Discourse, Englands Lamentable Slaverie, A Whisper in the Eare of Mr. Thomas Edwards* and *A Prediction of Mr. Edwards his Conversion. The Bloody Project, The Vanitie of the Present Churches, A Manifestation, Walwyns Just Defence* and an excerpt from *The Foundation of Slaunder* are included in *The Leveller Tracts*, ed. by W. Haller and H. Davies, which also contains *Walwins Wiles* and *The Charity of Church-men*. Don M. Wolfe printed *A Still and Soft Voice* as an appendix to *Milton in the Puritan Revolution*. The *Petitions* of March 1647 and September 1648 may be compared in his *Leveller Manifestoes*. Two pamphlets sometimes, but I think with insufficient reason, attributed to Walwyn are *No Papist nor Presbyterian* and *Tyranipocrit*. The first appears in *Leveller Manifestoes* and excerpts from the second in *British Pamphleteers*, Vol. I, ed. by George Orwell and Reginald Reynolds.

[1] *Charity of Church-men*, p. 8.

7

arti - Macpherson

Leveller Democracy—Fact or Myth?

I. THE POINT AT ISSUE[1]

One of the important historical advances made in the last thirty or forty years has been a new understanding of the part played by the Levellers in the English Revolution. Earlier historians had relegated them to a very secondary position. Gardiner, in his *History of the Great Civil War*, while devoting considerable space to their activities, as was inevitable in a work planned on such a generous scale, treats them as rather a disturbing factor, cutting across the main stream of development. Trevelyan, in *England Under the Stuarts*, dismissed them in the most cursory manner.

Today, a number of detailed studies, and, more useful still, of volumes in which their most outstanding writings have been made easily accessible, so that for the first time they can speak for themselves, make it possible to come to a juster estimate. We now see them as important in two ways. First, as having played a central part in the political struggle at its most critical stage, and second, as having made an important contribution to English political thinking.

For some time the generally accepted view had been that the Levellers were the first English democrats, forerunners of the advanced radicalism of the age of the French Revolution and of the Chartists. It was thought, in particular, that in principle they stood for a policy of universal manhood suffrage. More recently this view has been challenged by Professor C. B. Macpherson in a remarkable book, *The Political Theory of Possessive Individualism* (Oxford, 1962). His arguments have been accepted by many seventeenth-century scholars, including Christopher Hill, who summarises them as follows:

[1] *Abbreviations:*
Wolfe—*Leveller Manifestoes of the Puritan Revolution*, ed. Don M. Wolfe, 1944.
Woodhouse—*Puritanism and Liberty*, ed. A. S. P. Woodhouse, 1938.
Haller and Davies—*The Leveller Tracts, 1647–1653*, ed. William Haller and Godfrey Davies, 1944.

By reading the texts more carefully, Professor Macpherson is able to demonstrate that in all their programmatic statements the Levellers excluded paupers and servants from the franchise; and that even in their more rhetorical flourishes they would restrict the vote to "freeborn Englishmen", those who had not lost their birthright. In a very interesting appendix Professor Macpherson argues that whilst the Leveller franchise proposals would have doubled the number of voters in 1648, the adoption of manhood suffrage would have multiplied it by $5\frac{1}{2}$ times. That is to say, the Levellers proposed to enfranchise rather more than 10 per cent of the unenfranchised adult males. One could argue with the details of the calculations by which Professor Macpherson reaches this conclusion: but the tendency is difficult to deny. Terrifying though they seemed to their opponents in the seventeenth century, the Levellers were not democrats in the modern sense. Their electorate would have been composed of heads of households, men economically independent.[1]

This view now seems well on the way to becoming a new orthodoxy.

Let us first be clear as to what is at issue. It is a fact that in all their later programmatic statements the Levellers *did* make substantial exceptions about those to whom the franchise could be granted. This, I think, has never been seriously disputed and I am certainly not disputing it here. What has to be considered, then, is the extent of these exceptions, the reasons for which they were made and their bearing upon the underlying political philosophy of the Levellers. It is with the greatest diffidence that one ventures to dissent from the views of such authorities as Macpherson and Hill, to whom we all owe a debt which entitles their conclusions to the greatest respect. All the same, I do not think that the last word has been said on this question. I certainly make no claim to have said it here, but hope that it may be possible to take the discussion a few small steps further.

II. THE DOCUMENTS IN THE CASE

Let us begin by considering the main programme statements in which the Leveller attitude to the franchise is set out. These are the four versions of *An Agreement of the People, The Case of the Army Truly*

[1] *Past and Present*, April 1963, pp. 87–8.

Stated and the *Petition* of January 1648. All these are printed in full in Wolfe's *Leveller Manifestoes*.

The first of these statements, chronologically, is *The Case of the Army*, dated October 15th, 1647. Signed by the Agents of five regiments, it has all the marks of a policy statement drafted by the Leveller leadership collectively. A large part deals with special army problems, but it ends with a number of political points. Number 4 demands:

> that a law paramount be made, enacting it, to be unalterable by Parliaments that the people shall of course meet without any warrants or writs once in every two years upon an appointed day in their respective Countyes, for the election of their representors in Parliament, and that all the freeborn at the age of 21 yeares and upwards, be the electors, excepting those that have or shall deprive themselves of that their freedome, either for some years, or wholly by delinquency. . . .[1]

A few lines later it declares that "all power is originally and essentially in the whole body of the people of this Nation".

Clearly, there are phrases here whose meaning is debatable. Who are "the people", or "the whole body of the people of this Nation"? What is meant by "freeborn"? Who are those who "have or shall deprive themselves" of their freedom? No doubt this excludes delinquents, i.e. Royalists, but Professor Macpherson argues that it also excludes those who have deprived themselves of freedom by accepting wages or alms, but I can see little justification for this. It is on the face of it improbable that a document of this sort, having specified delinquency as a reason for disfranchisement, would have included these other grounds in so unspecific and ambiguous a way.

The first *Agreement* appeared on November 3rd, 1647. It is addressed to "all the free Commons of England" and the relevant clause reads:

> That the People of England being at this day very unequally distributed by Counties, Cities and Burroughs, for the election of their Deputies in Parliament, ought to be more indifferently proportioned, according to the number of the Inhabitants: the

[1] Wolfe, p. 212. Woodhouse, p. 433, gives the concluding words as "deprived themselves of that their freedom, either for some years or wholly, by delinquency". If this reading is accepted it would clearly mean that delinquency, and not the other grounds, is meant.

circumstances whereof, for number, place, and manner, are to be set down before the end of this present Parliament.[1]

Here, again different interpretations are possible, but it should be noted that there are no references to any exceptions and the phrase "according to the number of the Inhabitants" certainly suggests manhood suffrage, since if any such wholesale exceptions as Professor Macpherson suggests are implicitly assumed, some such phrase as "according to the number of the electors" would surely have been more appropriate. Passages later in the *Agreement* speak of "an equall just Government" and "equal Government for a free people", both of which may reasonably be taken to imply manhood suffrage.

The first document in which specific exceptions other than delinquency are made is the *Petition* of January 1648. This appeared after the Putney Debates and other developments of which it will be necessary to say more presently. The passage dealing with the franchise runs:

> That therefore, that Birth-right of all Englishmen, be forthwith restored to all which are not, or shal not be legally disfranchised for some criminal cause, or are not under 21 years of age, or servants, or beggars;[2]

It should be noted that the franchise is declared to be "the birth-right of all Englishmen", and is to be restored "forthwith" to all not specifically excepted. This can certainly be interpreted as meaning that it is regarded as a natural right and that these exceptions are temporary.

They are repeated in a more specific and detailed form in the second and the third (or "Officers") *Agreement*, appearing on December 15th, 1648, and January 15th, 1649. Both these documents represent a compromise, following discussions between the Levellers, the Army leaders and representatives of the Independents. They are in fact the Leveller and the Grandees' versions of what was agreed at these meetings and differ in some important respects. The Levellers repudiated the "Officers" version, but the clauses dealing with the franchise are identical except that the latter omits the phrase "such as have subscribed this Agreement" and the lines from "and such as shall not subscribe" to the end of the passage quoted. This omission has a certain importance in view of the Levellers' intention that the *Agreement*

---

[1] Wolfe, p. 226.   [2] Wolfe, p. 267.

should be a national covenant tendered to the whole people for approval, but it is not really relevant to our particular argument. The clause reads:

> That the Electors in every Division, shall be Natives or Denizons of *England*, such as have subscribed to this Agreement; not persons receiving Alms, but such as are assessed ordinarily towards the relief of the poor; not servants to, or receiving wages from any particular person. And in all Elections (except for the Universities) they shall be men of one and twenty yeers old, or upwards, and Housekeepers, dwelling within the Division, for which the Election is: Provided, That until the end of seven yeers next ensuing the time herein limited; for the end of this present Parliament, no person shall be admitted to, or have any hand or voyce in such Elections, who have adhered to, or assisted the King against the Parliament in any of these Wars or Insurrections; or who shall make or joyn in, or abet any forcible opposition against this Agreement; and that such as shall not subscribe it before the time limited, for the end of this Parliament, shall not have Vote in the next Election; neither, if they subscribe afterwards, shall they have any voice in the Elections next succeeding their subscription, unless their subscription were six months before the same.[1]

The fourth, and final, version of the *Agreement* was issued by the Levellers on May 1st, 1649, after the Grandees had gone back on the understanding reached at the discussions just mentioned, and while the Leveller leaders were imprisoned in the Tower. Here the exceptions to the franchise reappear in a somewhat modified form:

> That the Supreme Authority of *England* and the Territories therewith incorporate, shall be and reside henceforward in a Representative of the people consisting of four hundred persons, but no more; in the choice of whom (according to naturall right) all men of the age of one and twenty yeers (not being servants, or receiving alms, or having served the late King in Arms or voluntary Contributions) shall have their voices; and be capable of being elected to that Supreme Trust, those who served the King being disabled for ten years onely.[2]

It will be noted that here the stipulation that electors should be rate-payers and householders has disappeared. This may be taken as the

---

[1] Wolfe, p. 297. "Officers" *Agreement*, Wolfe, p. 342.   [2] Wolfe, p. 402.

final form in which the Levellers embodied their demands upon this question. Indeed, from this point the whole movement declined so rapidly that no further programme documents were issued.

What is essential to remember is that all these documents were not merely abstract statements of political theory—they were party programmes, weapons in an active political campaign and modified from time to time in accordance with the changing situation and the practical needs of the struggle. It is therefore necessary to look at them not only from the standpoint of political theory, as Professor Macpherson seems too inclined to do, but in relation to the actual events then taking place. This is what I shall try to do in the next three sections. In passing I may remark that Hill's distinction between programmatic statements and rhetorical flourishes does not seem to me entirely justified. No doubt the former have a greater authority, but it is also true that men are more likely to reveal their real beliefs in the heat and passion of debate than in more formal statements where they are being statesmanlike and diplomatic and where questions of tactics and expediency have to be carefully considered.

III. THE PUTNEY DEBATES

The first version of the *Agreement* was less a fully considered political programme than a draft drawn up as a basis for discussion. It was this draft which was under consideration at the debates of the Army Council which opened at Putney church on October 28th, 1647. *The Case of the Army* was then also under consideration. At this time the Army Council included delegates or Agents elected by the rank and file of the regiments and of representatives of the junior officers as well as the higher officers. This was the time when Leveller influence in the Army was at its height and when political demands for a more democratic England were occupying the minds of the soldiers almost as much as their own military grievances.

It was at Putney that the question of the franchise first came into prominence. Up to this time it was only one among many Leveller concerns—annual Parliaments, the subordination of the representatives to the electors, religious toleration, civil liberties and a variety of social and political issues had hitherto been equally or perhaps even more prominent in their propaganda. Now the question of exactly who was entitled to elect the sovereign parliament was seen to be of special importance.

In the debate that took place Ireton was the main speaker for the Grandees, supported by Colonel Rich and others. Cromwell in the chair tried to preserve some appearance of impartiality but was always ready to come to Ireton's help at difficult moments. On the other side were two civilian Levellers, John Wildman and Maximilian Petty. Among the soldiers the outstanding spokesman was Colonel Thomas Rainborough, with Edward Sexby and other rank-and-file Agents.

After the clause quoted above had been read, Ireton opened the attack:

It is said, they are to be distributed according to the number of the inhabitants: "The people of England," &c. And this doth make me to think that the meaning is, that every man that is an inhabitant is to be equally considered, and to have an equal voice in the election of those representers, the persons that are for the general Representative; and if that be the meaning, then I have something to say against it.[1]

To this Petty replied:

We judge that all inhabitants that have not lost their birthright should have an equal vote in elections.

Clearly here is a note of ambiguity, almost of weakness. Perhaps sensing this, Rainborough springs in immediately:

I desired that those that had engaged in it might be included. For really I think that the poorest he that is in England hath a life to live, as the greatest he; and therefore truly, sir, I think it's clear, that every man that is to live under a government ought first by his own consent to put himself under that government; and I do think that the poorest man in England is not at all bound in a strict sense to that government that he hath not had a voice to put himself under; and I am confident that, when I have heard the reasons against it, something will be said to answer those reasons, insomuch that I should doubt whether he was an Englishman or no, that should doubt of these things.[2]

A little later he says, "I do hear nothing at all that can convince me, why any man that is born in England ought not to have his voice in the election of burgesses."[3] And Clarke puts the claim firmly on the basis of natural rights:

[1] Woodhouse, p. 52.   [2] Woodhouse, p. 53.   [3] Woodhouse, p. 55.

The grand question of all is, whether or no it be the property of every individual person in the kingdom to have a voice in elections; and the ground on which it is claimed is the Law of Nature, which, for my part, I think to be the law which is the ground of all constitutions.[1]

In view of all this it seems to me that Professor Macpherson goes somewhat beyond the evidence when he writes:

But the only consistent construction of the debate as a whole suggests that the Levellers (and their opponents) assumed that servants and alms-takers, as well as criminals and delinquents, had lost their birthright.[2]

On the contrary, it seems to suggest that on both sides the debate at least opens on the understanding that what they were talking about was manhood suffrage. If not, it is difficult to see what all the heat and passion was about, especially in view of statements by Ireton and Rich. Ireton is prepared to allow some extension of the suffrage:

The objection does not lie in that, the making of the representation more equal, but in the introducing of men into an equality of interest in this government, who have no property in this king-dom, or who have no local permanent interest in it. For if I had said that I would not wish at all that we should have any enlargement of the bounds of those that are to be electors, then you might have excepted against it. But what I said was that I would not go to enlarge it beyond all bounds, so that upon the same ground you may admit of so many men from foreign states as would outvote you.[3]

If all that the Levellers were proposing was a franchise that would add another 10 per cent to the 10 per cent who were already electors, it seems strange both that Ireton should have objected so strongly to their proposals, and that, when he had declared himself in favour of some extension, no one took him at his word and said, in effect, "Very well, we are agreed on some extension—now let us sit down to dis-cuss just what extension we can all accept." Instead, the debate went on as if nothing important had been said, and almost at once Rich remarked:

If the master and servant shall be equal electors, then clearly those

[1] Woodhouse, p. 75.   [2] *Possessive Individualism*, p. 122.   [3] Woodhouse, p. 62.

that have no interest in the kingdom will make it their interest to choose those that have no interest.[1]

A strange remark if everyone on both sides was tacitly agreed that servants were excluded anyhow!

Nevertheless I think we can discern a certain difference between soldier and civilian Levellers, and it is striking how constantly, when Petty or Wildman intervene, the discussion loses its force and is diverted into technicalities and side issues. It was perhaps unfortunate that at these crucial debates the Leveller leadership was represented only by Petty, a quite minor figure, and the politically dubious Wildman. If Lilburne, then in prison, had been able to be present, it is tempting to wonder if the debates might not have taken a different course.

At any rate it was Petty who, in response to a question from Cromwell, first formulated the definite exclusion of servants and takers of alms. For this he gave a quite definite reason which needs to be noted:

> I conceive why we should exclude apprentices, or servants, or those that take alms, is because they depend upon the will of other men and should be afraid to displease them. For servants and apprentices, they are included in their masters, and so for those that receive alms from door to door.[2]

What he seems to be saying is not that the franchise is not a right to which all are entitled by Natural Law, but rather that in existing circumstances there are some for whom the exercise of this right is not possible, a point to which we shall return. This was no doubt true. At a time when voting was open and public it would be virtually impossible for servants to vote in a way displeasing to their masters, and to give them the vote, however formally democratic, would have meant in practice to place large blocks of votes in the hands of the very rich, blocks by which elections might well be turned. In the particular circumstances of the time, when Royalist nobles and gentry were disfranchised for delinquency, it would have meant restoring a large measure of political power to the most hostile elements. Yet Petty's statement seems to have come remarkably pat for a spontaneous reply to a question, and it may be permissible to wonder if there may not have been a measure of collusion here.

His statement seems to have brought this part of the debate to an end (which in itself is surely an indication that the point had not previously been understood) and the Council passed on to discuss other matters. Some days later a resolution on this basis was agreed. The minutes of this part of the debate have not survived, but the text of the resolution is given in *A Letter from Several Agitators to their Regiments*:

> We sent some of them to debate in love the matters and manner of the Agreement. And the first article thereof, being long debated, it was concluded by vote in the affirmative: *viz.*, *That all soldiers and others, if they be not servants or beggars, ought to have voices in electing those which shall represent them in Parliament, although they have not forty shillings per annum in freehold land.* And there were but three voices against this your native freedom.[1]

The text, once more, is slightly ambiguous, but in the context of what was said during the debates it must mean that all soldiers, regardless of social status, and all others except servants and beggars, should be electors. The disfranchisement of delinquents was not specifically mentioned because it was never an issue at Putney.

IV. CORKBUSH FIELD AND AFTER

This victory was followed up with a resolution, proposed by Rainborough, for a general Rendezvous of the Army. At this it was intended that the *Agreement* should be put before the Army for endorsement as a first step towards its nation-wide implementation. Cromwell and Ireton, who, no doubt, were among the "voices against", had other ideas and were soon able to launch an effective counter-stroke. There followed a period in which the situation was changing almost from day to day, and a short time-table of events may therefore be helpful.

1647. November 4th The Army Council passed the franchise resolution.

5th Resolution for a general Rendezvous of the Army.

9th The Agents ordered to return to their regiments.

It is revealed that three Rendezvous are to be held.

Lilburne released from prison by order of Parliament.

[1] Woodhouse, p. 452.

11th   The King escaped from Hampton Court.
15th   First Rendezvous held at Corkbush Field,
       Ware.
       Abortive mutiny crushed.

December 15th   Army Council meets at Windsor. Recon-
       ciliation between Grandees and Army
       Levellers.

30th   *Putney Projects* published.

1648. January   3rd   Cromwell moves vote of No Addresses to
       King in House of Commons.

May   Second Civil War.

This was, perhaps, the decisive period of the Leveller challenge.
Instead of a single Rendezvous, at which their programme should be
adopted by a united Army, the Grandees now arranged to hold three
sectional meetings at which authority and discipline would be asserted.
To the first of these, at Corkbush Field, two regiments, Harrison's
horse and Robert Lilburne's foot,[1] appeared, contrary to orders,
without most of their officers and wearing copies of the *Agreement*
in their hats. Even more significant, perhaps, Rainborough came, without his regiment, together with Colonel Eyres, Major Scott and other
officers. In his report to the House of Lords Fairfax wrote that,

> Colonel Rainborough with some others, tendered this enclosed
> Petition, together with the *People's Agreement* annexed thereunto.
> And (by what hands I yet know not fully) very many copies of the
> same Agreement were dispersed among the soldiers, thereby to
> engage them.[2]

Lilburne, just out of prison, had come down to Ware and was waiting upon events, and it seems clear that the Levellers were expecting a
decision and were hoping to carry the Army against Fairfax and Cromwell. If any officer could have done this, that officer was Rainborough.
But the circumstances could hardly have been more unfavourable.
The King's escape from Hampton Court only four days earlier raised
the threat of renewed war, in which he might find new allies even
inside Parliament itself. At such a moment the prestige of Fairfax and

---

[1] Robert Lilburne, John's brother, had previously been a Leveller supporter, but by
now had moved over towards the Grandees.

[2] Maseres, *Select Tracts*, I, p. xlii. The Petition declared that the Army had fought for
its native rights and had waited long to secure them. Therefore they must remain in arms
to secure their freedom. It asked Fairfax to continue to lead them to these ends.

Cromwell, generals with an unbroken succession of victories behind them, was immensely strengthened. Whatever the political differences, Cromwell had earned genuine respect for his conduct in the field, while Fairfax, though in truth just as hostile to Leveller aspirations, had always managed to avoid political commitment and so represented a fund of unused goodwill on which the Grandees could draw.

In any case, the soldiers were pulled in two ways. As citizens their political sympathies were with the Levellers. But as members of a victorious and well disciplined army their sense of military obligation was always powerful. In certain circumstances, off duty or in discussion, their political convictions might prevail: on the parade ground, under command, they were likely to act rather as soldiers. So it turned out at Ware, and the stirrings of mutiny were soon crushed. Rainborough was also a soldier with a magnificent military record and no more immune than the rest to such influences. As a high-ranking officer he could hardly initiate a mutiny, though he might have taken command if one had developed. At Ware he certainly came to the very verge of mutiny, but was unable to take the final step. As things turned out he must have seen that any hope of carrying the Army for the *Agreement* against its leaders had now vanished—the most that could now be hoped for was to divide it. And as a soldier he would have seen that to divide the Army in the existing circumstances would have been fatal. It would have led with certainty to a Royalist victory and the end of all he had been fighting for. Therefore new tactics were unavoidable.

He was not alone in this realisation. In spite of their victory Cromwell and Ireton must also have seen the danger of their position. Discipline had been restored, but the Army had not changed its political convictions overnight. Its loyalty had still to be kept, especially as the developing alliance between Royalists and many Presbyterians, backed by the Scots, made a renewal of war almost certain. They, too, could see that they needed the support of the Levellers, inside and outside the Army, even if this involved distasteful political concessions.

The result was another meeting of the Army Council at Windsor from December 15th, the last which the Agents of the regiments attended, at which a reconciliation was reached. Rainborough and others apologised for acts of indiscipline and promised that they would not be repeated. There is nothing to suggest that they repudiated any of their political aims. On the other side, officers and others under arrest were set free and restored to their commands and a general amnesty given for all past acts. On the political side the Grandees undertook that there should be no more attempts at agreement with the King—a Leveller demand which Ireton had strongly resisted at Putney. This was shown to be a genuine change of policy when Cromwell on January 3rd moved and carried a motion in the House of Commons that no further Addresses should be made to Charles. The unity of the Army was restored, but on the basis of an important shift to the left by the Grandees.

V. THE FATE OF THE AGREEMENT

The publication of Wildman's *Putney Projects* on December 30th, with its all-out attack on the Grandees, suggests that the civilian leaders were slower to accept the new tactics than their colleagues in the Army. After the defeat at Ware they concentrated their attention increasingly on winning mass support in and around London. Strong party organisation, with branches and a dues-paying membership, was built up. A weekly paper, *The Moderate*, was published and a stream of petitions with thousands of signatures were drawn up and presented. In this position of strength, as spring came on, with the likelihood of war increasing, they seem to have gradually accepted the new situation. By May, when the second Civil War broke out, they were ranged alongside the Army leaders, whatever political differences still existed. On August 3rd Lilburne wrote to Cromwell, setting out to give battle to the Scottish Army:

> . . . to demonstrate unto you that I am no staggerer from my first principles that I engaged my life upon, nor from you, if you are what you ought to be, and what you are strongly reported to be; although, if I prosecuted or desired revenge for an hard and almost sterving imprisonment, I could have had of late the choice of twenty opportunities to have payd you to the purpose; but I scorn it, especially when you are low; and this assure your self, that if ever my hand be upon you, it shall be when you are in your full glory, if then you shall decline from the righteous wayes of Truth and Justice: Which, if you will fixedly and impartially prosecute, I am
> Yours, to the last drop of my heart bloud,
> (for all your late severe hand towards me)
> JOHN LILBURNE[1]

[1] Haller and Davies, p. 414.

"Which letter &c." he adds, "as I have been told by the Bearer[1] was not a little welcome."

When the war was over, Cromwell's need of Leveller support was if anything greater, committed as he was to the trial and execution of the King and the abolition of the monarchy in the face of a hostile majority in the House of Commons. Here a difference appears between the Army Levellers, who supported the prosecution, and the civilians. Lilburne, while not opposed in principle to trying Charles, objected to the form taken by the specially appointed Court (on which he refused an invitation to serve) and wished in any case for the trial to be postponed till after a new constitution had been established on the basis of the *Agreement*. Otherwise, he argued, monarchy would only be replaced by a military dictatorship still more odious. It was necessary for the Grandees to secure at least the tacit and temporary support of the Levellers.

In November, after some acrimonious bargaining, a committee was set up representing the Army leadership, the Parliamentary Independents, the Independent churches and the Levellers. The result was the second and third versions of the *Agreement*, which, as has been said, represent rival views of what was agreed. They were thus compromise documents, not arrived at without considerable difficulty. Lilburne wrote afterwards:

> . . . all parties chosen of all sides constantly meet at White-hall after the Army came to town, saving the Parliament men failed, only Master Martin was most commonly there, and a long and tedious tug we had with Commissary Generall Ireton only, yea sometimes whole nights together, Principally about Liberty of Conscience and the Parliaments punishing where no law provides, and very angry and Lordly in his debates many times he was; but to some kind of an expedient in the first, for peace sake we condescended in to please him, and so came amongst the major part of the 16 Commissioners, according to our originall Agreement, to an absolute and finall conclusion; and thinking it had all been done as to any more debate upon it, and that it should without any more adoe be promoted for subscriptions, first at the Councill of Warre, and so in the Regiments, and so all over the Nation; but alas poor fools we were meerly cheated and cozened . . . and that which we Commissioners feared at the first, viz. that no tye,

[1] Edward Sexby, a leading Agent at Putney who was later to write *Killing No Murder*.

promises nor ingagements were strong enough for the grand
Juglers and Leaders of the Army, was now made clearly manifest.[1]

When the discussions were ended, Lilburne writes:

> having an exact copy of what the greatest part of the foresaid
> sixteen had agreed upon, I onely mended a clause in the first
> Reserve about Religion, to the sense of us all but Ireton and put
> an Epistle to it, of the 15 of December 1648, and printed it of my
> own accord, and the next day it came abroad.[2]

This was the second Agreement, and the clause on the franchise
embodies the greatest concessions which both the Levellers and their
opponents were ever prepared to make. The latter abandoned their
insistence that it be confined to freeholders in the counties and freemen
of corporations in the boroughs. The Levellers, in addition to the
earlier exception of servants and takers of alms, were now prepared to
restrict it also to those who were ratepayers and householders. This is
in line with what I have been arguing, that, while in favour in principle
of manhood suffrage, they were ready to recognise the practical
problems involved and were willing to make tactical compromises if
these would lead to the acceptance of their programme as a whole. It
must be remembered that while the suffrage question had been central
in the Putney debates, it was, in relation to the whole long-term
Leveller campaign, only one of a number of issues and perhaps not the
most important. If they could secure agreement for a broadly elected
Parliament, regularly meeting, subordinated to the electors, with
firmly limited power to infringe civil and religious liberties, the precise
extent of the franchise was of lesser immediate importance.

They quickly found, however, that the Grandees had no intention of
honouring their undertakings to implement the *Agreement*. Instead, the
rather weakened "Officers'"*Agreement* was merely laid formally before
the House of Commons, which did not even trouble to debate it. On
the same day that the third *Agreement* was published, January 20th,
1649, the trial of the King opened. By the time it was clear that no
steps would be taken to make it effective he had been executed. With
a purged House of Commons the Council of State was firmly in control
and the Grandees felt strong enough to do without Leveller support.
On March 28th, Lilburne, Walwyn, Overton and Prince were arrested
and taken to the Tower. It was from the Tower, and over their joint

---

[1] Haller and Davies, pp. 422–3.   [2] Haller and Davies, p. 423.

signatures, that the fourth and last version of the *Agreement* was issued.

This is in many respects the clearest and most radical formulation of the Leveller programme, and, so far as the franchise is concerned, may fairly be taken as the final expression of what they considered practicable under existing circumstances. The stipulation that electors shall be ratepayers and householders has now disappeared. Servants, takers of alms and Royalists are excluded. The latter are barred from being elected to Parliament for ten years only, and it seems a reasonable deduction that the same time limit applied to the electors also, though this is not specifically stated. The *Agreement* is declared as being "Tendered as a Peace Offering to this distressed Nation", and one may infer that the Levellers, who were always optimistic about human nature, expected that the reason and justice of their proposals would, in a comparatively short time, win the assent of the great majority of the people.

Their hopes were never put to the test. The publication of the *Agreement* was followed quickly by the Army mutiny that ended at Burford on May 14th. The movement steadily declined from this point and soon ceased to be a serious factor in English political life.

VI. FIGURES AND INTERPRETATIONS

Professor Macpherson includes in his book an elaborate statistical appendix. Briefly, it may be summarised as estimating that of an adult male population of 1,170,400, some 212,100 already enjoyed the franchise at this time. Under the wider franchise specifically demanded by the Levellers, excluding servants and alms-takers, but including soldiers who would otherwise have been disfranchised, 204,600 new voters would have been added. Of these, he estimates, 22,100 would have been soldiers. This seems an extremely low figure in view of the large numbers who served in the many Parliamentary armies and garrisons at various times and in various theatres of the war. He appears to arrive at it by assuming that only those serving at the time of the debates were to be reckoned—an assumption for which I can see no evidence at all. This, however, is a minor matter, since even if the figure were doubled or trebled it would not really change the general pattern. It is this whole quantitative approach which is open to considerable criticism.

In dealing with seventeenth-century England we are not using statistics in any modern sense, we are talking about estimates—it would not

be unfair to say about guesses. Professor Macpherson bases his figures
on the analysis of English population and class distribution made by
Gregory King in 1688, assuming, reasonably enough, a rise in population of 10 per cent over the intervening forty years. King's figures have
been widely accepted by historians as intelligent guesses. They may
possibly be quite accurate, but they are based on nothing more than
suppositions. Even granting, however, that they were accurate for
1688, it does not follow, as Professor Macpherson assumes, that they
were accurate for 1648. On the contrary, this was a time of very rapid
economic change, when individual petty-production was declining
and wage-labour increasing. On King's figures as interpreted by
Professor Macpherson two thirds of the population are to be classified
as servants or paupers against only one third independent producers—
including not only farmers and artisans but all other classes—professional people, gentry, traders and others. It may be questioned if such a
picture is really true of England in 1688, let alone 1648. My guess,
which may be no worse if no better than anyone else's, is that it greatly
overestimates the number of wage-earners at both dates.

Further, Professor Macpherson interprets King's already rather
schematic figures in an extremely schematic way, more appropriate
to England of the nineteenth century than of the seventeenth. At this
time, when the class of wage-earners is only evolving, it is surely nonsense to draw a hard and fast line between wage-earners and individual
producers. All sorts of intermediate categories existed, into which a
very large proportion of the population undoubtedly fell. Under the
putting-out system many shades and graduations existed between the
servant proper and the fully independent artisan. In the extractive and
other industries it was common, and remained so well into the nineteenth century, for groups of workers to enter into collective contracts.
Perhaps more important still numerically were the hosts of cottagers,
with common rights, patches of land or part-time crafts, who eked
out a living with sporadic wage earnings. In bad times such people
might also come to the parish for poor relief. Are all these to be regarded
as "servants" or "paupers", and, more to our purpose, would the
Levellers have so regarded them? I think not.

Professor Macpherson himself argues that the Levellers regarded
servants and paupers as self-excluded from citizen rights because they
had lost their property in their own persons, because they "depend
upon the will of other men" as Petty put it. These large intermediate
groups cannot properly be looked upon in this way. No doubt many

of them were poor, but the Levellers consistently argued that poverty could not be a reason for disfranchisement, and historically these groups have generally been noted for an independence of outlook and a readiness to defend their rights. They could be far less dependent than many farmers and small tradesmen under the thumb of landlords or customers.

This leads us to a consideration of some of the terms used in the argument. Professor Macpherson treats the word "servant" in the widest possible way as synonymous with "wage-earner":

> The term servant in seventeenth-century England meant anyone who worked for an employer for wages, whether the wages were by piece-rates or time-rates, and whether hired by the day or week or by the year.[1]

No doubt it could be and often was used in this sense, but it could have a less extended meaning, as is indeed suggested by the phrase used in the second and third *Agreements*, "servants to a particular person". This suggests that what may have been intended was the personal servant, the apprentice, or the man living in his master's house, as many did at this date, and need not be taken as excluding all wage-earners. It can hardly, on any interpretation, have covered all the intermediate groups already referred to.

There is evidence, too, to suggest that servants were not a permanently separate section of the community, but that this was a condition through which a large part of the population passed at a certain stage of their lives. The typical servant was a young, unmarried person living in the household of his master. On marriage he set up a household of his own and would then be classed as a labourer, craftsman, cottager or husbandman. At Ealing in 1599, 60 per cent of those between 15 and 19 years were servants. At Clayworth, out of 67 persons who were servants in 1676, only one was still in service there in 1688; at Cogenhoe, of 31 persons listed as servants in 1618, only one was still in service in 1628. While the evidence is insufficient to be conclusive, it certainly suggests that most servants could expect to become householders and would then, on the basis of the Leveller proposals, qualify for the franchise unless barred on other grounds. Evidence about the total number of servants is also scanty, but Mr. Laslett estimates it as between 10 and 15 per cent of the population and gives figures ranging between

[1] *Op. cit.*, p. 282.

25 per cent in Ealing and 5·7 per cent in Stoke-on-Trent. Even if this should prove an underestimate it certainly presents a very different picture from Professor Macpherson's blanket disfranchisement of the majority of the population. And it must be remembered that a very large proportion of servants were minors who would not be voting in any case.[1]

"Takers of alms" is hardly less ambiguous, and this is underlined by the use at times of the word "beggars", for example in *The Case of the Army*, the Putney resolution and in John Harris' pamphlet *The Grand Design* of December 1647. A beggar is quite different from the artisan or cottager who is forced in emergency to seek parish relief, and they again from those who are habitually dependent on such relief or on the charity of the rich. It could fairly be argued, I suggest, that "takers of alms" might refer to the first and third of these categories but not to the second.

Once more, we find an ambiguity of language which may even have been intentional. The words used may have had different implications for the Levellers and for their opponents, and, if the time had ever come for the matter to be put to the test, could have become a battleground. In such a case their meaning would have been determined by the actual relations of political forces, local and national, under which the electoral rolls were drawn up. It is by no means impossible that the Levellers, who were very shrewd tacticians, were aware of these ambiguities and hoped to be able to profit from them.

There is a further sense in which all these quantitative estimates are somewhat irrelevant. What we are concerned with, after all, is not what the actual results of the Levellers' proposals might have been, but with their policy and intentions. Even granting, as I see no reason to do, that the effect of their proposals would have been to leave two-thirds of the male population still disfranchised, it does not follow that this is what they intended. They seem to have thought of England as still a country of small-scale, independent producers in which wage-labour was exceptional apart from personal service. As A. L. Merson writes:

The Levellers had no figures like King's. They are more likely to

[1] The details of this paragraph are taken from Peter Laslett, *The World we have Lost* (1965) and Peter Laslett and John Harrison, Clayworth and Cogenhoe, in *Historical Essays Presented to David Ogg* (1963). While many of Laslett's conclusions seem questionable, what he has to say about the position of servants in seventeenth-century society may be provisionally accepted.

have been thinking in terms of a social order that was passing away than of one still incompletely developed; in terms of 1608 rather than of 1688. They are likely, too, to have been thinking in terms of town communities, in which the struggle for democracy had a long history and in which the proportion of proletarian, may have been smaller than in the countryside at this times except perhaps in London—a big exception in this context. Their programme, finally, contained demands which would have maintained and perhaps increased the preponderance of petty production and the opportunities for apprentices and servants to become masters.

It still seems easier to make sense of the Levellers' ideas on the traditional assumption that they were thinking in terms of a largely pre-capitalist society of small producers.[1]

If this is so, they could have regarded the exclusion of servants and alms-takers as a minor as well as a tactical exception. And here, too, the general perspective becomes relevant. They stated repeatedly and with obvious sincerity that they were defenders of the rights of property. But it is clear that primarily they were thinking of the small property of the common man, which they saw, and rightly, as threatened by the rich, the nobility, the monopolists and corporations, rather than by the unpropertied masses. The small producer was for them the norm, and a society in which rich men could have scores of servants while thousands depended upon alms was abnormal and even monstrous.

Their franchise proposals were not meant to be taken in isolation but as part of a programme of democratic reform which would transform England. In the society they envisaged the ordinary man would be secure in his small property, pauperism would disappear or at least be greatly diminished and the old process by which the apprentice, after a short period as a journeyman, might expect to become a master, would be strengthened. In such a society exceptions to the general principle that every man who lived under a government ought to have a voice in choosing that government would largely, though not, of course, entirely, take on a temporary character and become increasingly infrequent. The people of England would, by degrees, recover their lost birth-right. This may have been a utopian dream, but that is something they could not have known.

<hr/>

[1] *Marxism Today*, October 1963, p. 315.

VII. THE BIRTHRIGHT

"I am resolved to give my birthright to none",[1] declared Sexby at Putney, echoing, perhaps, words Overton had written a year earlier:

I'le not sell my birthright for a messe of pottage, for Justice is my naturall right, my heirdome, my inheritance by lineall descent from the loins of Adam, and so to all the sons of men as their proper right without respect of person *not by favour of Lords &c.*

What is this but an utter disfranchisement of the people, and a meer vasselage of this Nation, as if the Nation could have nothing by right, but all by favour, this cannot hold with the rule of *Mine and Thine*, one to have all, and another nothing: one's a gentleman, th' other a beggar; so that the birthrights, freedoms and properties of this Nation are thereby made these great Mens Alms . . . as if we ought them by Villein Service, and held all the rights and properties we have, but by Tenure in Villeinage, and so were their slaves for ever.[2]

In this passage we touch the heart of Leveller political thinking, particularly in relation to the franchise. In the passages which we have been considering, from the various versions of the *Agreement*, and other programme documents, it is possible, according to how we choose to read them, to find one or other of two sharply opposed political ideas. One is that the right to a voice in government is a *privilege*, attached to certain forms of property ownership, which it may be proper to extend to some who do not yet enjoy it. The other is that it is a natural right, and so proper to all, even though it may not be possible for all to enjoy it under existing conditions.

In their immediate results these two views may be similar. In their underlying philosophy they are totally opposed. The first represents the Whig political outlook, the second that of radical democracy. All the evidence seems to me to show that it was the second and not the first view that was held by the Levellers. This interpretation is in keeping with the wording of the franchise clause in the final version of the *Agreement*. The two preceding versions had been the outcome of discussion and compromise, and here the clause is purely descriptive. The electors shall be "natives", qualified in a certain way. In this version

---

[1] Woodhouse, p. 69.
[2] *A Defiance against All Arbitrary Usurpation* (September 1646), pp. 6–7

the Levellers were able to speak in their own language, and so it is declared that "according to naturall right" the choice of a Representative should be in all men of the age of one and twenty years and upwards. Only after this statement of general principle are the exceptions listed.

Overton stated the principle in its most general terms in *An Arrow against All Tyrants* (October 1646):

> For by naturall birth, all men are equally and alike borne to like propriety, liberty and freedome, and as we are delivered of God by the hand of nature into this world, every one with a naturall, innate freedome and propriety (as it were writ in the table of every mans heart, never to be obliterated) even so are we to live, every one equally and alike to enjoy his Birth-right and privilege; even all whereof God by nature hath made him free.[1]

Lilburne applies this general principle to the franchise in several of his early pamphlets. *In the Charters of London* (December 1646) he writes:

> The only and sole legislative law-making power is originally inherent in the people and derivatively in their commissions chosen by themselves by common consent and no other. In which the poorest that lives hath as true a right to give a vote, as well as the richest and greatest.[2]

And five months later he expands this, in *Rash Oaths Unwarrantable*, and gives it a theoretical justification. Parliaments should be elected regularly,

> so that all the people (without confusion and tumult) may meet together in their several divisions and every free man of *England*, as well poore as rich, whose life estate &c. is to be taken away by law, may have a Vote in chusing those that are to make the law, it being a maxim in nature, that no man can justly be bound without his own consent.[3]

All these passages, admittedly, come from early Leveller writings, when the principles and programme of the party were still developing. They are none the less relevant for that, since they show the roots from

---

[1] Cited from Frank, *The Levellers*, p. 96 and Haller, *Liberty and Reformation in the Puritan Revolution*, p. 281.
[2] Cited from H. N. Brailsford, *The Levellers in the English Revolution*, p. 117.
[3] Cited from Frank, *op. cit.*, p. 123 and Haller, *op. cit.*, p. 303.

which their later practice sprung. Later, as the struggle developed and they made a serious bid for political power, the tactics of the Levellers underwent frequent changes in accordance with the circumstances. Yet through all these changes a constant thread can be traced, and I can see nothing to indicate that the basic principles which lay behind their political activities were ever abandoned or seriously modified.

All the Leveller programme documents in which the right to the franchise is restricted have been quoted above. It may be worth noting that the only such recorded statement by any individual is that of Maximilian Petty, also quoted. Petty may or may not be representative of Leveller thought; we do not know enough about him to venture any guess about what might be in his mind. But about Rainborough and Lilburne, Overton and Walwyn, we do know a good deal more. I find it impossible to believe, with the whole evidence of their lives and writings before me, that when they spoke of the rights of "the people", or "the free-born commons of England" or "the poorest that lives", these men intended in principle the tacit exclusion of any part of the English nation, whatever exceptions might in practice be demanded by existing circumstances.

Index